The Practice of Wholeness

Spiritual Transformation in Everyday Life

Lorena Monda

Golden Flower Publications

Golden Flower Publications
P.O. Box 781
Placitas, NM 87043

Cover Design and Text Illustrations by George Amaya and Randy Cordova.
Back Cover Photo by Lisa Elena Monda.

The Practice of Wholeness: Spiritual Transformation in Everyday Life /by Lorena Monda.
ISBN 0-9678137-0-0
Library of Congress Card Number: 00-102626

May this work help to alleviate suffering
and inspire reverence for all beings.

This book is dedicated with love to my parents,
Gerald Monda and Catherine Ciccone Monda.

Acknowledgments

This work is a synthesis of what I have learned from many sources. In this light I would like to honor my teachers:

Spirit, which gave me this book in outline form fifteen years ago and then offered the experiences which filled the pages.

My home, the Earth, which teaches me about life and the rhythms of transformation.

My spiritual teacher, Thich Nhat Hanh, who teaches me about the joy of practice and reminds me of the miracle of the present moment.

Lisa Elena Monda, my daughter, who daily teaches me about humanness and makes me practice what I preach.

My partner, John Scott, who shows me the depth and breadth of love.

My family members: Jerry, Cathy, Lisa, George, David, Tracey, Steven, Kristi, Douglas, Christy, Adeline and Andy Monda, Marion and Frank Ciccone, Frank Ciccone, Jr., Jerry and Gail Miller. The children: Austin, Samantha, Michael Joseph, Harrison, Haley, Michael, Anna, Conner, Emily, Nicholas, and Daniel.

My teachers: Karla Schwartz, Phyllis Berman, Alan Lowenthal, Kate Larson, John Davidson, Stuart Watts, Stuart Mauro, Ted Kapchuk, Sara Quanyin West, J. Michael Moore, Phil Del Prince, Debra Hay, Gabrielle Roth, Bill Stott, Dee Pye, Yvonne Agazarian.

My students and clients, to whom I owe enormous gratitude for their courage to put my words into practice and their willingness to share with me their deepest selves. It is they who show me how the process of transformation really works.

David Lauterstein and John Conway of The Lauterstein-Conway Massage School, whose faith in me encouraged me to develop some of this material and allowed me free rein to teach it. The students of the third semester classes, who went with me wherever I took them, and whose willingness and insight helped me do my best work.

Judy Reeves and the Texas Council on Family Violence, who made this material available to a wider audience.

Joy Cunningham, Gretchen Paulig, and Julia Kate for making a home for me away from home in the years I spent teaching this work in Austin. And Karen Umminger and Sara Strandtman for doing likewise.

The Crybabies, my original Unfolding of Emotion buddies.

My spiritual family, The Order of Interbeing.

My dear, young friend, Darcie Silver, whose violent death took me through the depths of my despair into life beyond "the wall."

And these wonderful people who are ever with me, friends and allies across space and time: Marietta Soldevilla, Alfonso Catasus, Jackie Arahill, Laura Crocker, Beth Boucek, Liz Ronald, Mark McClintock, Larry McCraw, Cathy Cauley, Jim Clower, Sid Morrison, Marie Murray, Mickey Houlihan, David Willing, Joe Lay, Bill Steward, John Dahlrose, Donna Ray, Derek Wilson, Jace Edelberg, Beverly Bakken, Kelly Murphy, Lynsay Tunnell, Tarika Prem, Steve Bratman, Farishta, Gretchen Wachs, Mary Saunders, Whit Reeves, Gail Rice, Heloise Gold, Judy Blocklinger, Bill Pugsley, Diane Carr, Darla Johnson, Ruth Powers, Gene and Rhonda Cooke, Susan Morgan, Zanna Briski, Lisa Soileau, Steven White, Sally Crocker, Lori Ann Gardner, Kimberly Patterson, Morgan Holford, Caer Reider, Diane Polasky, Tonya Edmond, Wissie Slator, Denise Coady, Laura Robbins.

Special thanks to the people who helped make this book a reality: Sandy Ingerman, an angel in human form, who magically appeared and gently convinced me to stop talking about it and write already. My friends and colleagues who read the manuscript in its early and later versions: Gaynl Keefe, Cecilia Conley, Lisa Holland, Rich Armington, Norma Kwestel, Paulette Christopher. Phyllis Berman, my college mentor, who came out of the past, armed with poetry, to encourage me to continue when I was stuck. Dianne Lorang and Winnie Devlin for inspired editing. Arnie Kotler and Therese Fitzgerald for being inspiring people. John Scott at Golden Flower for saying, "Yes." And most especially, Laura Cooley, my soul sister, who "got it" from the beginning and never, ever gives up on me.

For your love, wisdom, and inspiration, I bow to you in gratitude.

Contents

Introduction xv
How to Use this Book: Basic Tools xix

Part One
The Elements of Wholeness

Chapter 1 The Wisdom of the Body 1
Chapter 2 The Unfolding of Emotion 31
Chapter 3 The Realm of Mind 65
Chapter 4 The Expansive Spirit 107

Part Two
The Elements of Transformation

Chapter 5 The Door to Transformation 123
Chapter 6 Getting Stuck 141
Chapter 7 Integration and Alignment 169
Chapter 8 The Mystery: Entering the Unknown 189

Part Three
The Practice of Wholeness

Chapter 9 The Cycle of Transformation 221
Chapter 10 Life Beyond the Wall 239
Chapter 11 Connection 251
Chapter 12 Practicing Wholeness 279

Resources 283

Once the whole is divided, the parts need names.
There are already enough names.
One must know when to stop.
Knowing when to stop averts trouble.
Tao in the world is like a river
flowing home to the sea.

Lao Tsu
Tao Te Ching
XXXII

Introduction

I am a realist. The contents of this book came from my life experience—as a healer and a patient, a teacher and a student, a mother and a daughter, a lover and a friend, a skeptic and a spiritual aspirant—and from the experiences of my fellow human beings.

I think you will find the ideas in this book self-evident. A friend of mine suggested I call it *A Beginner's Guide to Being Human*. I want the ideas in this book to evoke in you the sense that "I already know this," so that you can go beyond ideas into actual practice. There are many books filled with important ideas that, in reality, change very little about our lives. It is practice that is at the heart of transformation.

Years ago, while practicing Western psychotherapy and Oriental Medicine, I noticed that only a small minority of clients in personal growth processes actually made deep, core transformations that they integrated into their daily lives. Most people come away from therapy, personal growth workshops, lectures, books, spiritual retreats, and healing sessions filled with inspiration and insight, but they lose the "high" after a few days or weeks. So, I began to ask, "What do people who make core changes in their lives do that other people don't?" Observing hundreds of clients and students, I came to realize that insight is not enough. Insight gets us in the door of transformation, but what truly fuels the transformation process is practice. In Eastern cultures, the recognition of practice as the path to mastery is well ingrained. In our culture, we expect mastery after one or two weekend workshops.

As I watched the transformation process in students, clients, and myself, I noticed that core transformation happens when we can meet and accept all parts of ourselves, face things as they are, and weather the uncertainty inherent in change. What we are practicing, in essence, is mindfully being with and learning to tolerate the various parts of ourselves—our bodies, emotions, thoughts, attitudes and beliefs, longings and aspirations—and learning to accept the unknown. This kind of practice unfolds over time and entails coming to peace with our humanness, as life, as it is, unfolds before us. This practice yields a transformative process that is ultimately spiritual—inclusive and expansive—integrating all aspects of ourselves and connecting us to a greater whole.

We live in exciting and terrifying times. So much is available. We are exposed to a wide range of experiences, some beautiful and some horrible. We have explored our individuality and separateness to the nth degree, yet even with therapy and spiritual seeking, we often feel overwhelmed and incomplete. How can we satisfy the many parts of ourselves? Our internal fragmentation finds expression in the daily battles within ourselves—our head versus our heart versus our body versus our spiritual aspirations—and in how we act out these struggles in our lives and our relationships.

Externally, the fragmentation of society by gender, age, sexual preference, race, class, special interest—and the numerous other ways we divide ourselves into "us" and "them"—leaves us wondering how we can live together in peace and harmony. And our separation as humans from animals, plants, and minerals unearths a more basic question: If we keep on like this, can our species even continue to exist?

In order to answer these questions, we must find ways to embrace our fragmentation, not just through unifying principles, but through unifying practices—practices that bring us together as individuals, couples, families, communities, cultures, planet, and universe. These I call *The Practice of Wholeness*.

Wholeness is the BIG picture, the matrix of our being. Many spiritual teachings point to it. It is the way modern physicists describe the universe. Miraculous and mysterious, wholeness takes us beyond duality into the fullest expression of being. It is not enough to be on a spiritual path toward it. Wholeness is available right here and now. To find it, we must practice being whole.

We can invoke wholeness, learn to recognize, tolerate, practice, cultivate, and sustain it. We can give it expression and let it move into the world through our words, actions, work, art, and the example of our daily lives.

The time to start is now. Some of the tools for practicing wholeness are in this book. The rest are inside of you and in the world around us. I invite you to join me in the practice of realizing our deepest desire—to be whole.

How to Use this Book: Basic Tools

The book in your hands is meant to be used as a workbook, to encourage and guide you in carrying out the practices which cultivate spiritual transformation and a deep sense of wholeness. To facilitate this, it is helpful to bring a few tools of your own.

Curiosity

Curiosity—about being human, despair, transformation, wholeness—is what brought this book into being. This curiosity is not so much about why, but more about how and what. What are elements common to our humanness? How do we feel when we are stuck? What is despair? What are the elements of transformation? How does wholeness feel? What kinds of practices lead to a sense of wholeness?

Curiosity leads us away from our judging mind (How does our judging mind work?), and into our natural, open mind—our true mind. Curiosity is a playful, open part of ourselves which, when turned toward ourselves and our world, can yield much insight and wisdom.

When applying the ideas in this book to yourself or to the world around you, use your curiosity freely. It will make the process much more enjoyable.

Mindfulness

Mindfulness is the capacity to bring our consciousness to what is going on inside of us and around us in the present moment. When we are mindful, we are aware. For example, in this present moment we are aware that we are reading a book. But we can turn our mindfulness toward specific things—our breath, our body, our thoughts, our feelings, our aspirations—which are also present with us as we read. We can turn our mindfulness toward the things around us. Mindfulness is a tool that allows us to be present—as a neutral witness—for whatever our awareness is turned toward. This neutral witness enables us to look and listen deeply. It allows us to be present for what is, without having to necessarily do anything about it. It allows us to engage our curiosity and to learn about ourselves and our world without getting caught in our fears or judgments. If we feel fear or judgment, we simply turn our mindfulness and curiosity toward it. Mindfulness calms us, creates space inside of us, and allows the wonders of our true selves to unfold before us.

Willingness to Practice

The most important tool that we can bring to this book is our willingness to practice the ideas presented. Practice involves taking action. It is through practice that we replace our old habits with new habits. Spiritual practice entails taking the kinds of actions that help us cultivate our true self. We know that we can have spiritual beliefs and ideas, but the true test of our spirituality is in the way we live our daily lives.

Sometimes we think spiritual practice has to look a certain way. It is easy to get caught in a form. But almost anything can be used in service of spiritual practice. Each chapter contains practice exercises which aid us in coming into our wholeness. These exercises put us in touch with the various parts of ourselves and with the elements of transformation that lead to wholeness.

The practice exercises can be used in a number of ways. They are meant to give the practitioner direct experience with the concepts discussed. How you use them is up to you. You can do them in order or pick ones that appeal to you. You can do them as written or improvise them to suit your particular circumstances or needs. After you get familiar with the idea of practice, you can make up your own exercises to help you integrate what you are learning into "felt experience." The main thing is not to rely only on insight, but to use spiritual practice to cultivate responses, actions, and habits that align with your spiritual aspirations.

You may find it helpful to have a journal (a large unlined notebook or newsprint pad) dedicated to your practices, and some colored pencils, crayons, or markers.

Mindful Curiosity Practice—"Checking In"

Here is an exercise to help you practice using your mindfulness and curiosity. I often use it when I teach to familiarize students with mindfulness and the elements of wholeness. You can have someone read this practice to you slowly, or if you are doing it by yourself you can read it slowly into a tape recorder, pausing to allow yourself time to follow the instructions. Then play the tape back to yourself. Or you can simply read a few sentences at a time, taking time to stop and follow the instructions.

Find a comfortable position—sitting with your back straight but not rigid, or lying down. If you are sitting in a chair, place both feet on the floor and your hands comfortably in your lap. Turn your attention toward yourself. This means to direct your awareness inward, away from outside distractions. Your eyes can be open or closed as you do this, whatever makes it easier for you to direct your attention inward. Sometimes it helps to follow your breathing for a few breaths. Breathe in and out through your nose, and follow your breath with your attention until you feel that your attention is inside rather than outside of you.

In this exercise, you are going to direct your attention toward various parts of yourself. These parts are the elements of wholeness. Try to let the part of you that is paying attention be a neutral witness. It helps if you invoke your curiosity for this exercise. Pretend you are someone you have just met and want to get to know better. If you find yourself making judgments about what you are witnessing, just notice it. You can simply say, "Here is the part of me that makes judgments." If you become uncomfortable at any point, allow yourself to notice the discomfort. Another thing that helps is to dedicate this exercise to your wholeness. Invoke your spirit by asking it to show you what is important for you to experience right now at this stage of your practice.

Take your time. The more time you take, the more you will experience.

Begin by turning your attention toward your body. When you do this, where is your attention drawn? Are you drawn to a particular area of your body? To discomfort? To places that feel pleasurable? You do not need to do anything to change what you notice. Just notice... How does your body feel? Is it easy or difficult to notice what is going on in your body? Are there places in your body that are absent from your awareness? What are they? What is your relationship to your body right now? Is it friendly or unfriendly? If your body could talk, what would it be saying to you right now? Take some time to listen to your body.

Now, turn your attention to your emotions. What emotions do you bring to this moment? Is it easy or difficult to access your emotions? Are the emotions about something happening in the present moment or something in the past or future? Again, you do not have to do anything to change these emotions. Just notice... Where in your body do these emotions live? What is your relationship to your emotions? What are your present emotions saying to you?

Next, turn your attention toward what is going on in your mind at this moment. This can include thoughts, attitudes, images, judgments, and memories. Notice what is going on in your mind. What thoughts are you thinking? What attitudes do you bring to this moment? Again, just notice. Is it easy or hard for you to witness what is going on in your mind? What is your relationship to your mind?

Finally, bring your awareness to whatever it is that you call your spirit. Is it easy or hard to do this? Where does your spirit live in you? How does this part of you feel right now? What hopes and aspirations does your spirit have for you by reading this book? Do you let yourself feel your hopes and dreams? What is your relationship to your spirit? Let your spirit give you a message—what is it saying to you?

When you feel ready, thank yourself for showing yourself to you. Then slowly come back into the room. Take a few moments to write down or make a mental note of what was important for you from this exercise.

When people do this exercise, they have many different responses. For some, it feels quite familiar; for others, difficult. In either case, don't judge what happens to you. Practice trust in yourself by turning your attention inward and allowing your spirit to speak to you. This is called checking in—and it can be done regularly. When you get used to it, you can do it fairly quickly. It is helpful to begin every exercise in this book with such a check in.

Part I
The Elements of Wholeness

Humanness is the simultaneous experience
of body, emotions, mind, and spirit.

Chapter 1
The Wisdom of the Body

Everything that happens to us while we are alive happens through our bodies. We sense the world around us, feel our feelings, think our thoughts, and experience ourselves through our bodies. We may be used to thinking of our bodies as the lowest form of ourselves, separate from our minds or spirits; there is much in our culture that promotes this belief. When we are sick, we sometimes treat the sick part of ourselves as if it were separate from the whole of us, like part of a machine. We have doctors that work with our ears, doctors for our backs, doctors for the digestive system, and still others for what goes on in our minds. These doctors usually do not talk to each other about us. They may not understand that the ringing in our ears can be related to our back pain, chronic diarrhea, or anxiety.

In Western Medicine, we have terms like *psychosomatic*, which refers to the interaction between the psyche and the body, and *psychogenic*, which refers to disease processes that originate in the mind. Recently in the West, we have begun to study in earnest the relationship between the body and the mind. Much new research is dedicated to discovering the mind's influence on the body and the body's influence on the mind.

In other systems of medicine, Oriental Medicine for example, the body and mind have never been seen as separate. It is understood that the mind plays a part in physical illness, just as physical symptoms affect the mind. *All* illnesses have physiological, emotional, mental, and spiritual components, just as all human experience is a simultaneous experience of body, emotions, mind, and spirit. The person is viewed as whole, not separate in any way from his or her body, feelings, thoughts, or spiritual nature. Our bodies are seen as the foundation of our humanness, the matrix for emotions, mind, and spirit. Our bodies are an expression of our whole selves in dynamic motion and change, a source of intelligence and information about what we need in order to live our lives as whole beings.

Body Image

When we hear the term "body image" we generally think about the way we look in our bodies and how we feel about that. In my experience, body image includes not only how we feel about the way we look, but how we view our bodies as a whole—the general relationship that we have to our physicality, to our body's structure, its functions, and its needs.

The relationship you have with your body determines the degree to which you can happily be in your body. This relationship also affects your ability to feel yourself physically and your ability to get useful information from your physical sensations—information which can help you feel healthy and whole.

Body image is defined by our culture, family life, and personal experience. Our culture plays a great image-making role in regard to our physical norms. Information about how our bodies should look, what health is, standards for physical beauty, how we should age, what we should wear, what our sexuality should be like, what each gender should look like, which body functions and illnesses are okay and which are embarrassing, and many other aspects of our physicality are evident to us through images in popular culture. The waif-like fashion models, the Miss and Mr. America pageants, the increasing popularity of liposuction and cosmetic surgery, the latest fad diets, the monopoly of Western Medicine, the issue of reproductive rights, the sex education debate, the sexual images from magazines, movies and TV, the lifestyles of the rich and famous—the unconscious messages we receive from these things in our culture all affect how we relate to our bodies. We are so inundated with these messages that we often don't question our cultural norms.

On a more intimate level, our body image is also created by our family life and personal experiences. It is within our families that we learn how to pay attention to and take care of our physical bodies. Our caretakers, overtly and by example, give us information about our physical bodies: bodily functions, touch, sexuality, pleasure, self-care, beauty, diet, grooming, illness, health, growth, development, reproduction, and aging. In some families the functions, needs, and development of the body are seen as natural; in others they are seen as shameful; and in others they are simply ignored. When you are a child, how your bodily needs are handled, how you are treated when you are sick, how your vitality and sexuality are dealt with by your caretakers, deeply affect your relationship with your body.

Events in our personal experiences outside of our families also affect our relationship with our bodies. Experiences in the schoolyard, in puberty, and with early sexual encounters affect our body image as adults. Physical trauma—physical and sexual abuse, rape, accidents, invasive medical procedures, chronic pain and illness—can especially affect us, as trauma can cause us to abandon the "felt sense" of our bodies. Even after the overt physical effects of trauma are healed, the emotional, mental, and spiritual effects can cause us to fear really feeling ourselves. We may lose trust in our bodies, feel extremely vulnerable and out of control, afraid to feel ourselves because we may relive the traumatic thing that happened to us. If the non-physical pain of trauma remains unhealed, we may be left frozen out of our bodies, unable to trust our own felt sense of life.

Body Messages

Bodily experience includes such things as sensation, energy flow, structure, physiological function, movement, gesture, and posture. Rather than being separate from the rest of ourselves, the body is a wealth of information about the physiological, psychological, emotional, and spiritual elements of our being. Through our bodies we translate these elements of being into felt experience.

In our culture we learn to pay attention to the most obvious aspects of our bodies—our looks, physical strength, and overt physical symptoms. We train our bodies to perform, to do our bidding, to look good. We are less skilled at attending to the seemingly subtler messages that our bodies give us about our unconscious beliefs, feelings, and spiritual needs. When we learn to pay attention to these messages from the body, we have the experience of being able to see deeply into ourselves and into others. Students who are learning to understand the language of the body are astonished at how much of themselves that they thought was hidden is available to the perceptions of others.

People who are adept at translating the language of the body are able to see our health, our attitudes and beliefs, our feelings and longings, and our coping strategies and psychological protections. Our bodies do not lie. We take our experiences and translate them into posture, gesture, and quality of energy. Kim's longing for contact is revealed in her habitual gesture of placing her hand to her heart. Jeff's chronic anger is seen in the set of his jaw. Marsha's tendency to withdraw from life is manifested in her cold hands and feet. Peter's dishonesty is observed as a flash in his eyes. Our minds can hide us from ourselves, but our bodies know and express what is really going on.

The body communicates to us a felt sense of our happiness and satisfaction through sensations of pleasure, a feeling of being in our bodies, strong and flowing energy, a sense of health, a feeling of openness, a full range of motion and expressiveness. When we are unsatisfied or out of balance, we let ourselves know this through tension, inflexibility, blocked energy, loss of awareness of our physical body, constrictions, lack of vitality, reduced immune function, and various symptoms of illness.

Physical symptoms are signals to us from the whole of our being. Our bodies are exquisitely sensitive and respond to our internal and external worlds. Externally, changes in weather, geography, the physical environment, and the emotional and energetic climates around us register on our physical, emotional, and energetic systems. Our bodies also respond to what is going on inside of us: our emotions, thoughts, beliefs, attitudes, spiritual aspirations, and longings.

We may be used to thinking of symptoms as bothersome events that interrupt our lives and must be dealt with when they can no longer be ignored, but symptoms are really messages to ourselves about what is going on with us. If we learn to pay attention to these signals, we gain much information about what we need to be healthy, content, and whole.

Illness

Illness is part of the human experience. According to Oriental Medicine, illness is caused by several types of factors:

—External factors such as severe, prolonged, or unseasonable climatic and environmental conditions that tax the body's ability to defend against invasion by pathogens.

—Internal factors such as mental attitudes or emotions that are prolonged, severe, or repressed.

—Lifestyle factors such as diet, exercise, sex, work, and rest.

—Factors such as heredity and trauma.

Oriental Medicine puts a premium on the regulation of the body toward balance and harmony, and to listening to the signals that communicate imbalance in the early stages so rebalancing the body is not too difficult. Signs such as skin coloration, sound of the voice, strength and quality of the pulse, color and condition of the tongue, body odors, words the patient uses, where and when the symptoms occur, and dreams the patient has all communicate the type of imbalance. Treatment may include lifestyle changes such as eating or not eating particular foods, physical or meditative exercises, and recommendations about breathing, sleep, sexual activity, and work.

In our culture we are not taught to pay close attention to our bodies. As a result, we often miss the early stages of illness and do not pay attention to the body's signals until we are quite sick. I spend a lot of time in my work teaching people how to recognize these early physical symptoms so they can prevent illness in themselves and their children. My daughter, Lisa, was prone to lingering coughs when she was small. By watching her over time, I learned that her coughs were precipitated by a number of signals: she would act unusually irritable, get dark circles under her eyes, and want to be held more. Usually these preliminary symptoms started if she had been overstimulated, hadn't had enough sleep, or had been eating too much "party food." Once I learned to catch the warning signs, I could care for her before she got a cough. As a result, she has learned to listen to her body's signals and is rarely sick.

Anita, a patient of mine, suffered from extreme migraine headaches that she got almost every two weeks for ten years. The first time she came to me, she was in the second day of a headache that she expected to last for three days. Even though the things I did helped alleviate her headache, I was not satisfied. I wanted her to learn how to prevent the headaches, so I asked her if she could recognize when one of her headaches was starting. She said it was only just before a headache, when she would have visual disturbances, that she would know one was coming. I asked her to pay attention to all aspects of herself right before a headache and to keep a record of everything she could recall from all parts of her life the day before and the day of the headache. Anita learned to recognize a group of physical and emotional signs that often occurred the day before a headache. She began to come to me for treatment when she recognized these signs and would avoid the headache altogether.

Eventually, she was able to recognize the signs signaling a headache *five days before* the headache. Once she could do this, she was able to prevent her headaches through dietary changes and relaxation and meditation exercises, and no longer needed my services.

Symptoms are the body's way of getting us to pay attention. If we are not used to listening to ourselves, the symptoms must get stronger in order to be felt. When the symptoms get severe enough, we usually do start paying attention. What do our symptoms tell us? That can vary. Sometimes the information is as simple as get more rest, change your diet, get some exercise. Sometimes the symptoms reveal parts of our psyche that need attention or healing. Sometimes our symptoms are the results of repressed emotions or unfulfilled spiritual longings. Many people who have unhealed psychological trauma in their personal histories begin their odyssey of healing when physical symptoms become serious enough to need their attention.

As I was beginning to write this chapter on the body, I received a call from a cousin from whom I had not heard in years. She had been having chronic back pain that had put her in bed for several weeks. While lying around, she decided to do some research into alternative medicine, since her doctor hadn't done much for her. Up to this point she thought that alternative medicine was quackery, although she admitted that she did not know very much about it. In the course of her reading, she decided to see a chiropractor and was impressed with the dramatic improvement that resulted. Now she was curious about Tai Chi, a Chinese movement meditation. Thus, her back pain had led her to some new resources.

As many of my patients can attest, sometimes our symptoms lead us to dramatic changes in our lifestyles. Because Oriental Medicine is so unfamiliar to them, most Westerners only come to it when conventional allopathic medicine has failed. Oriental Medicine teaches us to be sensitive to our bodies; in fact, it makes us more sensitive.

While learning to listen to their bodies' signals, my patients have been led to heal past trauma, take up spiritual practices, pursue buried interests, practice art, find new work, discover and respect their physical and psychological boundaries, change unsatisfying relationships, learn how to communicate feelings, volunteer to help others, follow their dreams, and bring passion, or commitment, or love, or limits into their lives.

Many times, the symptoms go away once the message has been received. When they don't go away, in cases of intractable illness, the work becomes learning how to be whole within those symptoms. Recently, I worked with a man who has AIDS. Before his diagnosis several years ago, he had been an inspired and accomplished musician. When he came to see me, he was depressed and his sister was worried that he was dying. I asked him what in his life inspired him now and he said nothing did. He felt he couldn't play his music because he did not have the energy. His life was spent observing his symptoms change and waiting to be too sick to take care of himself. Besides treating him, I gave him the spiritual exercise of finding something inspiring in every day. I also asked him to play a little bit of music every day, within the limits of his energy. Eventually, as he practiced this, he discovered that he did have the energy to play his music, and as he allowed his daily inspirations to feed his creativity, he became less focused on his symptoms and generally felt better. Although he sometimes still had feelings of anger, sadness, and despair because he still had AIDS, the quality of his being with himself changed. He was not just waiting to die; he was living the life he had as fully as he could.

Symptoms can be our teachers. They can tell us what we need, disclose our mistakes, and show us our limitations. But the purpose of paying attention to our bodies' signals is not to cause us to blame ourselves for what happens to us. Currently, there is a popular notion that we cause our own disease, that disease comes from our thoughts, negative affirmations, or from some spiritual lesson we need to learn. This is an incomplete and somewhat dangerous view. For a critically sick person—already vulnerable—far from being helpful, such a view feels cold, analytical, and judgmental.

People with severe illness commonly report feeling guilty. They sense that other people look at them as if they had brought their illness upon themselves. Often people with a major disease fall prey to other people's theories of why they are sick. Rather than contributing to the healing process, these theories may undermine the resilience of the sick person who may already be wondering "Why me?" while needing to use all available energy to deal with the consequences of their illness.

A friend of mine had an accident that resulted in a knee injury. As she hobbled around on crutches, everywhere she went, friends and strangers alike looked knowingly at her knee, quoting various sources about the real "meaning" of knee injuries ("Knee injuries have to do with fear." "What is it that you are being inflexible about?") and asking her what it was that she was supposed to learn from this. Finally, sick of all the analysis, she said, "Sure, I've tried to understand what this injury means for me, and in the end, what I learned was this: accidents happen, and I can deal with them!"

It is important to realize that while all illness has psychological and spiritual components, these components are not necessarily the cause of the illness. Many factors contribute to illness including some beyond our immediate control such as heredity and many aspects of our environment. Because we cannot have power over all conditions, we cannot control everything that happens to us. The danger in the notion that we cause our disease is that it implies if we can do everything right, if we can know everything there is to know about ourselves or our bodies, if we can control enough of the variables or think the right thoughts, we will never get sick. It is understandable that we should want to try to comprehend, control, and find singular causes for frightening illnesses, but illness is an unavoidable part of life: Often we do all we can, and we still get sick.

Several years ago, I had an ectopic pregnancy that resulted in emergency surgery and the loss of a much-wanted child. At first, I was angry at myself for letting something like this happen to me; I thought I should know better. But as I looked back, in all honesty, there was nothing that I could have done differently to avoid what happened.

Although it was difficult, and certainly something that I would not have chosen for myself, going through the experience itself offered much in the way of spiritual richness. Because I am sensitive to anesthesia, it took me several months to recover from its effects. Whenever I started to speed up to my normal pace of life, I lost a sense of myself and felt dizzy. This forced me to slow down and, from this slower pace, I noticed things that I normally didn't: my feelings, for example, and my body's signals. When I was tired, I had to rest. If people were overwhelming me, I had to ask them to stop. I had to learn to say "no" and to cut back on a schedule that was busier than I wanted it to be. I also noticed the world around me in more detail: my beautiful house, the trees outside my bedroom window, my daughter, my partner, my friends. They seemed more precious to me than ever.

Beyond providing clues to our physiological or medical needs, the messages we receive from our bodies and from our symptoms are uniquely personal. Other people can provide information about our bodies, but the best way to learn the language of your particular body is to communicate with it directly, to listen to the messages within, to see what they have to tell you and where they lead you—to find your own meanings and trust your felt sense of self.

The strength and wisdom that come from illness emerge when we are caring and compassionate with ourselves and with others who are ill. It is the wisdom that life offers us—the whole of life, with its beauty and its suffering.

Caring for Our Bodies

Caring for our bodies gives us the most basic form of nourishment we need to live our lives. Our fundamental attitudes toward self-care are learned in childhood as outlined in Chapter 3, *The Realm of Mind*. Since we experience spiritual growth and wholeness through our bodies, good care of our bodies forms a basis of support for our spiritual growth. Poor care of ourselves is a continuum that can range from benign neglect to overt abuse. On the neglectful end of the spectrum are behaviors like forgetting to eat when we are hungry, not getting enough rest, and ignoring our need for exercise. Abuse can range from destructive habits like smoking, eating unhealthy foods, and body building with anabolic steroids, to actual self-mutilation.

Your body communicates to you what it needs with a series of signals. Your ability to pay attention to these signals is a matter of your habits and what you have been taught. Your relationship to caring for your body is based in some part on how you were cared for and how you were taught to care for yourself. Sometimes we must undo years of habitually ignoring the body's signals to learn to pay attention to our physical needs.

Lynn, a focused, hard-driven, and successful administrator,

lived on soft drinks, vitamins, and candy bars for energy, with an occasional meal on the go. Though she was often exhausted and irritable, she pushed herself from deadline to deadline. She rewarded her accomplishments with expensive clothing and jewelry but, other than that, she had little time for herself, and her single-mindedness about work left her little time for friends. She viewed spending time taking care of herself as interfering with her professional goals.

Later, her goals changed and she wanted to have a child. After several miscarriages, Lynn was forced to take a look at how she cared for her body. The doctors were unable to find anything structurally wrong with Lynn's reproductive system. From another perspective, however, Lynn was a mess. Tense, undernourished, and exhausted, her body had barely enough energy to support her own life much less that of a developing fetus.

Lynn's assignment was to learn how to take better care of her body. As she practiced slowing down, resting when she needed to, and making sure she ate well—she realized how she had been mistreating herself. She began to understand that her habits were not life-supporting and were actually consuming her energy at an unnatural pace. With an emphasis on self-care, Lynn felt much better, had more energy, was more efficient at work—and she gained skill in nurturing, which would be invaluable as a parent. Because she really wanted a child, Lynn used the same focus and determination that had been so successful in her work toward taking care of herself. Two years after changing to more life-supporting habits, she gave birth to a healthy child.

Lynn realized that she had lived her life from an attitude of neglect toward her own needs and was determined to let her child teach her about normal human needs. Although she reports that she is sometimes shocked by how much care and attention we humans need, she is happily attending to her child and herself, and generally feeling her life is more balanced.

What Our Bodies Need

Basically, besides shelter and clothing, our physical needs include air, food and water, rest, movement, and contact. Although we know this, giving ourselves what we need is another matter altogether. Many of us have learned to neglect our physical needs until they become difficult to ignore. As we saw in the section on body image, we bring many kinds of beliefs and habits to the act of giving ourselves what we need. When our bodies get what they need, we have a better chance at being healthy and happy. We have energy that we can use to attend to the other parts of ourselves: our emotions, our minds, and our spirits. Indeed, as we become more sensitive to the other parts of ourselves, it becomes more important to pay attention to our physical needs. If we expect to be emotionally balanced, mentally clear, and spiritually expanded, we must cultivate a body that can support that kind of energy.

If we pay attention to our bodies, we notice that when we have the right information about our options, our bodies can tell us what we need. Contrary to some beliefs, attending to our physical needs is essential to our spiritual development and wholeness.

Air

Breathing is the most basic act of life. Besides supplying us with the oxygen that our cells need to live and eliminating the carbon dioxide that the body produces as waste, breathing is the basic and essential rhythm of taking in and letting go, found in all parts of our life.

Although breathing occurs automatically, we can use it as a source of nourishment. Deep, full breathing brings energy to all parts of our body. We can remember every day to stop and take a few deep breaths. We can send our breath to areas of our body that feel tight, tense, or weak—breathing in new energy and exhaling our tensions and stress. As a way to clear our minds, we can spend a few minutes following our breathing, paying attention to it. We can do this at stoplights and in long lines instead of feeling tense and worrying about being late. Even though this will not make the traffic move faster, we will feel refreshed rather than stressed. Using breath as nourishment can be like taking a mini-vacation—some simple time for ourselves. As I write, I feel less tired and tense at the end of a long session if I remember to stop now and then and take a few mindful breaths.

We can learn a great deal by giving attention to our breathing. *Are your breaths full or are they restricted? Do they feel as if they go to all parts of your body or are they just in your lungs?* When we are chronically anxious, sad, or angry, changing our breathing pattern can change the way we feel.

A client, Ben, had a feeling of anxiety most of the time. Even when the things in his life were going well, he felt as if he were waiting for something bad to happen. Along with examining the beliefs that contributed to his anxiety, we noticed that most of the time, Ben's breathing was shallow and slightly rapid. While the feeling of anxiety contributed to this breathing pattern, the breathing pattern also contributed to the anxiety. Ben began to practice slowing and deepening his breathing. Although this was hard at first, he noticed that he felt calmer as a result. As his body got used to the idea that he could calm himself with his breathing, he felt more empowered. Although he could not control everything that could possibly happen to him, he could provide himself some serenity and nourishment by slowing and deepening his breathing. When he no longer had an "anxiety" breathing pattern, he no longer felt constantly anxious.

Food and Water

Besides air, there are no more essential sources of nourishment for our physical bodies than food and water. While this is a simple fact, our relationship with this form of nourishment can be very complicated. We only have to look around us to be inundated with complex, often contradictory messages about food. Our confusion about our relationship with food and with feeding ourselves shows up in various forms in our lives. Many people suffer from eating disorders which range from chronic, uncontrolled over-eating to extreme under-eating. Our eating habits also reflect our attitudes about providing ourselves with nourishment. *Do you live on junk food, eat on the run, or wolf your food down without tasting it? Is food where you find your emotional comfort? Does it divert you from getting your other needs met directly? Is it a form of punishment? Are you comfortable with it? Afraid of it?*

Oriental Medicine views what we eat as a basic building block of our health. Beyond calories and vitamins, what we eat has a particular energy that interacts with our own energy. Some foods can exacerbate the psychological and emotional states we are trying to heal. Oily foods, for example, can create a feeling of heaviness that will be calming for some people. For other people, however, eating oily foods will contribute to feelings of frustration and being "stuck." If we eat a big meal of heavy food before an important meeting, we may feel sleepy and less able to think clearly. Our energy has gone toward digesting the food and is less available for other things. Sweets may offer comfort or a burst of energy to some, but they may leave others feeling tired, irritated, or depressed. Some people do well on a diet of raw foods, while others are actually weakened by such a diet. Some people are able to live healthily without eating meat, while others feel healthier with small amounts of animal protein. The point is not to praise some foods as cure-alls ("Everyone should eat raw foods.") and condemn others ("Eating meat is bad."). We are all different. Beyond our nutritional needs, our energetic needs are different. The point is to pay attention to the effect what we eat has on us.

How we eat is as important as what we eat. If we sit down and eat a meal in anger, it will be less nourishing to us than the same meal eaten when we are calm—even though the nutritional content of the food is the same. Our state of mind while eating, our pace, and the way we chew our food all affect our digestion and the amount of nourishment available to us from our food.

Because my own relationship with food is not always smooth, I started a group called Mindful Lunch, inspired by an eating meditation that I did with my spiritual teacher, Thich Nhat Hanh. While staying at Plum Village, Nhat Hanh's monastery in France, we spent the day in many forms of mindfulness: walking, sitting meditation, doing daily chores, and eating. I discovered that eating in mindfulness was the most difficult for me, so when I returned home I started a "Mindful Lunch" group. Every Thursday, a few of us gathered with our lunches and sat for 45 minutes eating slowly and mindfully without talking. This was an opportunity to slow down and just eat. Though we did not talk to each other, we stayed mindful that we were eating as a community and acknowledged each other's presence. The practice was powerful and brought to light numerous aspects of our relationships with food.

We became aware of the presence of our food on our plate—its appearance, its color, and its texture. We noticed how beautiful it was, how it was alive, how it had come from the earth to support our being alive. We became aware of how much we had in quantity and variety, and of people for whom a small portion of what was on our plates would seem like a feast. We became conscious of everything it took to get our food from the earth to our plates, all the elements involved—the sun, rain, soil, farmers, pickers, truckers, and grocers, and our own efforts in preparing the food.

Members of the group realized that Mindful Lunch did not begin for them at noon on Thursday, but in the grocery store when they selected the food to bring and in the kitchen when they prepared the food. We became more aware of the act of preparing our food and became more mindful as we did so. We noticed what it felt like to actually be eating. Slowing down and paying attention while eating made some of us aware of how uncomfortable we were while eating—with letting others see us eat, with taking the time to slowly taste and chew our food. When uncomfortable, we practiced paying attention to our breathing and allowed ourselves to be present.

One of the group members, a chronic overeater, noticed if he practiced slowing down and really being with himself while eating, he needed less food to feel satisfied. Another member realized that the panic she felt while eating was related to stressful, unhappy times with her family at the dinner table. Usually she avoided eating or ate very rapidly to keep herself from feeling this panic. As she returned weekly to the Mindful Lunch, she learned another response to eating—one of quiet, mindful eating with others practicing the same thing—which left her feeling happy and peaceful. Another member was able to learn how to taste his food and feel the effect it had on his body. Over time, he was able to make choices about what he was eating that were more supportive of how he wanted to feel.

In the course of our practice, eating became a sacred act. By eating what is good for us, by eating it in a way that is conscious and supportive, we are affirming life. And we are not alone. The earth, the heavens, the farmer, and our loved ones with us at the table are all supporting us in our affirmation of being alive.

Rest

In Oriental Medicine, we have the understanding that there are some illnesses that will not get better unless we have rest. We can get all the treatment we want, take medicine, and change our diet, but unless we rest it will be like pouring our efforts into a black hole. Webster's dictionary has several definitions for the word "rest": "1) peace, ease, and refreshment as produced by sleep, 2) refreshing ease or inactivity after work or exertion, 3) a period or occasion of inactivity, as during work or on a journey, 4) relief from anything distressing, annoying, tiring, etc., peace of mind, mental and emotional calm; tranquility."

It is important to get a sense of the need you have for rest and whether or not you let yourself and others know of this need.

When do you rest? Is it only when you are asleep? Is it on that big vacation in the future? Is it the catnap you wish you could take after lunch? Do you allow yourself to have rest in your daily life? How do you feel about resting? Do you feel unproductive? Lazy? Deserving? Do you long for rest, but not allow yourself to have it?

Take some time to stop reading this book and just rest. Notice what comes up for you as you do so.

Rest provides us with tranquility, refreshment, stillness, and a feeling of spaciousness. It takes us from the world of doing back into the world of being. Our relationship with rest tells us a lot about how we feel about just being. Are we safe? Are we enough? Rest gives us the space in our busy lives to feel ourselves, to hear ourselves, to let new information come in, to let ourselves notice things we may otherwise miss. It allows us to be truly in our bodies with our feelings and our thoughts. It allows our spirits to take hold of our lives and steer us toward what we need. It gives us the energy to cope with the things that we must face. Knowing how to rest has a lot to do with knowing how to stop, with knowing when enough is enough, with faith in our own timing and in things unfolding in due course.

When I was a child, I loved to sit and just "watch the light change." The light in Miami where I grew up changed often with the tropical sky and I could sit and watch the subtle changes in color for a long time. It seemed such a perfect contrast to the kinetic bustle of life in my family. My mother would come upon me at these moments and say, "What are you doing wasting time sitting there doing nothing?" Because there was always so much to be done in my large family, I learned that it was not okay to be "doing nothing." I developed a pattern of long days full of work that lasted until I had my own child in my late twenties. Periodically, I would let myself rest when my body became sick enough to make me, and to this day I sometimes have the feeling that rest must wait until everything else is done.

When I tell clients who are exhausted that they need to rest, they typically tell me that they don't have time, they will lose momentum if they rest now, they will rest on their two-week vacation. My experience is that people who do not know how to rest cannot rest on their two-week vacations. Rest, like food and air, is something that we need every day. For these clients, their practice is learning how to bring a little rest into each day, even if it is just five minutes. To have five minutes that just belong to us, that have no demands attached to them, where we are free to not do anything, is a luxury for most of us.

People often feel that they are resting when they are watching TV, reading, playing golf, or spending time at a hobby. But if our activities are not performed with a sense of ease, tranquility, and spaciousness, we are simply filling our time with something else to do, not resting. It might be more restful to stare out the window, meander through the garden, close our eyes and listen to the rain fall while taking a few deep, mindful breaths.

We must also learn to cultivate a sense of restfulness as we perform our daily activities. This is a difficult thing if we think that rest makes us lazy, inefficient, and less productive. Some of us think that to seem productive, competent, and important, our tasks must look difficult, stressful, hurried, or taxing. It is my experience that people who learn how to practice restfulness in their daily activities are often more productive, efficient, and creative than people who are always in overdrive. Practicing restfulness makes us healthier physically and happier emotionally, and allows us to live without the sense that time is our enemy.

Learning how to rest takes practice, but we cannot wait for lulls in our busy schedules in order to find peace. If we wait for rather than practice restfulness, peace will never come because we will not know how to tolerate it.

Movement

Just as we need rest, our bodies also need movement.

Movement keeps our energy flowing; it keeps us from feeling stuck. Movement is a natural state of life: All life is in motion. When we move, we allow our energy to better circulate—not just our physical energy but the energies of our psyches and spirits as well. Movement teaches us about doing and about our relationship to space. Through movement, our bodies communicate information to us about our internal states and our relationship to the world around us. Movement is a form of expression. It can be a forum for our creativity, a source of ritual, a dynamic manifestation of our deepest selves.

Everyone knows about the benefits of physical exercise like walking, jogging, aerobics, or calisthenics: we feel better, have more energy, burn calories. But not all of us find it easy to exercise in these ways. Because I did not enjoy working out, I had to discover a different relationship to exercise. About ten years ago, I began to schedule what I called a movement practice session each day. I began to explore movement—beginning with just listening to my body and noticing what it wanted to do. The sessions took the form of a "daily dance." Sometimes the movements my body wanted were slow and luxurious, other times they were vigorous and powerful or light and playful. Sometimes I danced a theme, an attitude, an emotion, an idea. Some days my dance seemed holy, a sacred prayer of gratitude and connectedness to myself and the world. Other days my dance was entirely uninspired, distracted, bored. My daily dance told me about myself—about what my body wanted, about how I felt physically, emotionally, mentally, and spiritually. It allowed me to discover myself through my body. It allowed me to expand the way I expressed myself, to open up areas that felt blocked or numb, to strengthen parts that felt weak, to acknowledge the parts of myself that wanted to fly.

My daily dance also put me in touch with the wide variety of movement practice available in the world: sports, dance, Tai Chi, Chi Kung, Authentic Movement, Yoga, stretching,

Continuum Movement, and martial arts. These practices may have different goals, but they all allow our bodies to express themselves through doing.

When I was first learning to meditate, I found sitting meditation difficult. My body wanted to move or shift, and sitting still was most distracting. One day in a park, I was watching a group of people who were learning Tai Chi, a slow, moving meditation and martial art. Seeing that I was fascinated, the teacher asked if I would like to join the class. After learning a few movements, I realized that this was my ticket to meditation. With my body moving, I could quiet my mind and achieve the calm equanimity of meditation that was such a struggle for me when I was sitting still. Over the years, my practice of Tai Chi has calmed and strengthened my body, and also allowed for sitting meditation to be much less of a struggle.

One of my movement teachers, Gabrielle Roth (see *Resources*), teaches five basic rhythms to be used as a spiritual practice. These rhythms—flowing, staccato, chaos, lyrical, and stillness—represent basic ways of moving through the world. Each are associated with a particular emotion, energy, purpose, and life phase. Generally, each of us is more familiar and comfortable with one or two rhythms, but at different times in our lives, other rhythms will manifest themselves. By practicing the rhythms, we expand our range of responsiveness to life. In Gabrielle's work, the rhythms are a sacred dance practiced at three levels of relationship: with self, with another, and with the group. This practice allows us to expand our range of movement, to know ourselves and others better, to heal wounds to our wholeness, and to offer our wholeness to ourselves, to others, and to our planet.

The best movement practices allow us to be mindful of our bodies as we move. They allow us to progress in ways that honor both our individual bodily needs and our inherent body wisdom, rather than overriding our body's intelligence. The best movement forms teach us to cultivate a relationship with our bodies—so that instead of doing something obsessive and debilitating to our bodies, we are one with our bodies. These forms allow us to go toward wholeness—grounding and expansion, form and energy. They help us bring all of ourselves with us—because movement practice, while seeming to be "just for our bodies," can also be a spiritual practice.

Contact

Our bodies need contact. Studies with infants indicate the importance of physical contact in their development. The quality of this early contact affects our nervous systems and teaches us about our boundaries—where we begin and end. Early contact also teaches us about our relationship to the world outside ourselves—is it soothing, harsh, nourishing, available, distant? When we are infants, we need what I call *Primary Contact*. Primary Contact communicates a basic message: *You are here, I am with you. You are welcome and safe. You do not have to do anything for me; just be.* This kind of contact grounds us in our bodies and allows us to feel ourselves. It creates space for us. It soothes us and makes us feel welcome, in relationship with the world around us.

Because our experiences with contact as children are so wide-ranging—from neglectful to healthy to violating—and because cultural norms about contact are so varied, our needs for contact as adults are also wide-ranging. For this reason, I talk about *contact* instead of *touch*. While contact may include touch ("touch" is the root of the word "contact"), contact is not limited to physical touch. Some people who have been physically abused or neglected find physical touch to be a painful experience, even though they may block out their awareness of this pain. For some people, satisfying contact can be in the form of being seen or truly heard, acknowledged, greeted, given eye contact, or just the physical presence of another nearby.

Because contact is a basic physical need, it is important to know your relationship to it. *Are you satisfied with the kind and amount of contact in your life? Do you feel the contact that you receive? What kind of contact is nourishing to you? Where did you get your ideas about contact? Do these attitudes reflect what you truly want or what you were taught you could have? How do you contact others? What is reflected in this contact?*

Our relationship to contact includes being in contact with ourselves and with the world around us, and allowing others to be in contact with themselves and with us. By mindfully attending to our relationship with contact, we learn about our boundaries, limitations, needs, personal histories, longings, and satisfactions. We also learn about others—how they are like us but they are not us, and how they have similar or different boundaries, needs, personal histories, longings, and satisfactions. We become aware of whether we honor these things in ourselves and others in a mindful way—or whether we neglect them, violate them, act them out, deny them, or indulge them.

Contact can heal as well as teach us. Through contact we can establish our sense of self, undo old patterns, expand our range of responsiveness, learn new relationships, and touch all aspects of ourselves. Many forms of healing through physical contact (bodywork) are available: massage, energy work, laying on of hands, polarity, acupressure, and shiatsu among them. I often recommend some kind of bodywork for my psychotherapy clients, especially those who have suffered physical abuse or neglect. When a bodywork practitioner is sensitive to these experiences, bodywork can help bring unhealed parts of ourselves to consciousness, and help us gain a felt sense of the insights gained in psychotherapy.

The mindful practice of contact gives us respect for our physical boundaries and limitations and for the physical boundaries and limitations of others. Mindful practice is useful both for simple contact and complex contact like sex. Mindful contact allows us to bring our whole selves with us—our bodies, emotions, minds, and spirits—into the present moment, and into relationship with others and the world around us.

Mindful Body

Mindful Body entails learning to trust yourself in your body, to allow your body to create a space for all parts of yourself. Your body is an expression of yourself—not merely your lowly form, but the matrix for all of your experiences in this lifetime. The practice of Mindful Body expands your awareness of your body: its signals, symptoms, messages, needs, and inherent wisdom. It helps you to develop a relationship to your physical boundaries and limitations that is positive and respectful.

Mindful Body involves being in actual relationship with your body, noticing what that relationship is, and learning to communicate with your body. It involves giving yourself what you need, nourishing yourself, and doing the things that support your healing, all of which allows you to expand your physical sensitivity, your felt sense of experience, and your range of expression and movement. Practicing Mindful Body allows you to embrace your human form, and to feel deeply and truly alive.

Practicing Mindful Body

Check In

Practice checking in with your body, every day or several times a day. Take a few moments to stop and return your awareness to your body. How does your body feel? Where are you holding tension? What parts of your body feel good? What parts of your body want your attention? What kind of attention does your body want? What message is your body giving you?

Honor

Spend a day in honor of your body. Check in with your body throughout the day. Adorn your body. Wear beautiful clothes, eat only nourishing foods, allow nourishing contact.

Relationship

On a large piece of paper, draw a picture of your relationship to your body.

Ask yourself: What is my relationship to my body? Where did I learn this relationship? In your journal, allow yourself several pages of free writing* to answer these questions.

Think of a time when you were sick or injured as a child. How were you treated by your caretakers? Write about this experience. How do you treat yourself now when you are sick or injured?

Rules

List at least ten rules that you learned in your family about:

your body
sexuality
aging
taking care of your body
injury or illness

These rules can be things you heard overtly ("The body is sinful.") or things you learned by observing how other people dealt with their bodies (sexuality, aging, self-care, injury or illness) or how they dealt with you with regard to your body (sexuality, aging, self-care, injury or illness). Mark an "E" for explicit rules and an "I" for rules learned more implicitly by observation.

---

*Free writing practice is uninterrupted and uncensored writing for a certain length of time or a certain number of pages. Just let the words flow. Do not worry about style, grammar, spelling, or making sense.

Keep this list in a place where you can add to it as you discover more rules.

Giving Your Body a Voice
You can do this alone or with a friend. Find a quiet place. Check in with your body, allow yourself to feel your body, and allow your body to have a voice. Begin with the sentence: "I am *(your name's)* body." Listen inside for what your body has to say and actually allow the voice of your body to speak aloud. Let your body speak about you in the third person. Your body can talk about the relationship it has with you, what it wants from you, and so on. Give your body time to have its say.

If you would like a record of what your body has to say, you can speak into a tape recorder. Notice your reaction to what your body has to say.

Allow your body to write you a letter. Write back.

Have a dialogue with your body. You can do this aloud or on paper.

Give a voice to one of your symptoms, or to your illness.

Have a dialogue with your illness. Ask your illness for help.

Expanding Your Relationship
In your journal, write about the kind of relationship you would like to have with your body.

Caring for Your Body
In your journal, ask yourself:

> How do I nourish my body?
> What is my relationship to food?
> How do I rest? What stops me from resting?

Make a contract to do at least one nourishing thing for your body every day for a month. Do that thing.

Air

Spend some time just sitting and following your breath. You do not have to change your breathing; just allow your mind to follow your breath. To help focus your mind, as you breathe in, you can say to yourself, "Breathing in, I know I am breathing in." As you breathe out, you can say to yourself, "Breathing out, I know I am breathing out." Do this for fifteen or twenty minutes.

When agitated, hurried, or upset, stop for just a few seconds and allow yourself to follow your breath for a couple of cycles.

Food

Have a mindful meal. From the beginning of the meal to the end, practice paying attention to the food on the plate before you, eating slowly and chewing thoroughly. Practice seeing and tasting the food you are eating. Connect your food with the earth that produced it and the many hands that brought it to you.

Spend the first ten minutes of each of your meals eating mindfully.

Prepare yourself a delicious, healthy meal. Set a beautiful table. Arrange the food attractively on your plate. Sit down and eat unhurriedly, letting yourself feel nourished by your food.

Movement

Spend some time dancing, allowing your body to lead the dance. Lead the dance from different body parts:

your head
your shoulders
your arms

your hands
your spine
your hips
your knees
your feet
your heart
your bones
your blood

Lead from your whole body.
Notice how these different parts change the dance.

Let your body try out different movements:

expansion
contraction
smooth
spastic
slow
fast

Exaggerate your movements—get really big.
Hold back your movements—get really small.
Use a lot of space in the room.
Use only a little space.

Let your body try out different attitudes.

Contact

Find a place on your body that wants contact. Place your hand on that place or have a friend place his or her hand there. Let that part of your body talk to you about what kind of contact it would like. Give yourself that kind of contact or have your friend do this. Have it be exactly how you want it—the exact pressure and pace, what body part makes the contact (fingertips, palm, etc.). Listen for what this contact says to your body. Allow yourself to take in the contact and its nourishing messages.

Spirit
Draw a picture of how your spirit expresses itself through your body.

Altar
Make an altar to your body to honor it as if it were sacred. Find things from nature or the world around you, or make something to express your relationship to your body. Visit your altar daily; spend some time with it in contemplation. Allow the altar to change as your relationship to your body changes by adding or taking away offerings.

Creativity
Invent a practice that helps you cultivate a better relationship with your body. Spend time doing this practice regularly.

Experiencing Wholeness in Your Body
Turn your attention to your body. Bring your consciousness to the bottom of your feet; feel them connected to the ground. As you hold the bottom of your feet in your consciousness, bring your consciousness to the top of your head. As you hold both the bottom of your feet and the top of your head in your consciousness, bring your consciousness to the front of your body. Now add the back of your body. Add the sides. Hold the bottom of your feet, the top of your head, the front, back, and sides of your body in your consciousness at the same time. Notice what this is like and how different it is from how you usually hold your body in your consciousness. Practice sitting, standing, walking, moving, and lying down in this consciousness of your whole body. Practice keeping this consciousness as you interact with others and go about your day.

Chapter 2
The Unfolding of Emotion

I hate you, Mommy! I hate you!" Here was my beloved two-and-a-half-year-old daughter, fists clenched, screaming and stomping in a fit of rage, her first official "temper tantrum" in progress.

Hearing those words for the first time stopped my breath. I felt a knot in my stomach and was filled with a variety of emotions (guilt, anger, fear, and sadness), questions (What have I done to make my child hate me? How do I handle this?), and memories (of my own "hateful" fits as an adolescent and of a friend's four-year-old who, for the first several months of our friendship, greeted me with "I hate you, Raina!"). This was potent stuff. As I allowed my feelings and thoughts to settle, I realized I was curious: What was this about? What would happen if I explored it further?

I took a breath, sat down next to my raging daughter, and asked, "You hate your mommy, Lisa?"

"Yes!"

"Who else do you hate?"

Lisa named almost everyone we knew, even the kitty.

Then I asked, "Lisa, who do you love?"

She looked at me with confidence and declared, "I love *Lisa* and I love a *monster*!" Then her anger gone, she giggled.

We began playing a game in which she was a monster attacking me. I took my turn as the monster, then we both became "fierce monsters" or "bad witches" or "wild tigers." We played this game for weeks, with Lisa making up the rules and incorporating child and adult friends in various ways. Sometimes she used her real anger, growling, "I'm angry!" Sometimes she conjured up anger to fit the game.

It was an illumination for me when I realized that Lisa was *practicing emotion*, just as she had practiced crawling, walking, and making her first sounds. She was exploring the parameters of anger, how it feels and how it is expressed, and I began to see my role in this exploration more clearly.

In the years since this discovery, I have watched my child explore and practice other emotions: grief at the death of a loved one, excitement about daily activities, sadness in goodbyes, fear of the unknown, disappointment in unfulfilled friendships and unsatisfied desires, courage, glee, and joy in being alive. With each of these, she seemed to feel a bodily sensation of some type, put her experience into words, and explore a range of emotional expression.

I have learned that my role is not to judge Lisa's feelings, or make light of them, or protect her from painful emotions, or intrude upon or take control of her emotional expression. Rather, as her parent, it is my job to guide her: to help her recognize emotions in bodily sensations, name those emotions, and mindfully express them in ways appropriate to the situation.

Emotional experience is natural, as is the impulse to express it. Emotional experience begins in the body—in physical sensation, perception, and thought—and moves outward into the world. This natural flow is mediated by individual temperament, and by verbal and nonverbal teachings from family and culture. The ability to uniquely express our emotions, just like the ability to uniquely express our physical or intellectual capacities, develops with nurturing and practice.

As adults, we may be called upon to remember, or perhaps learn consciously for the first time, the many aspects of emotion. For example, we are accustomed to thinking of emotions as discrete experiences. The word "anger" usually conjures up concrete images that are distinct from those associated with joy, grief, or fear. We wonder how children can instantaneously convert from howling to giggling. We have forgotten or have never learned, that emotion is not static: It is energetic—fluid and dynamic.

We may also have opinions about which emotions are "good" and which are "bad," which ones can be revealed and which are best kept hidden. We have cut ourselves off from the primary experience of emotion within our bodies, which ultimately has separated us from ourselves. When we look for better ways to deal with and control "negative" emotions, we seldom remember that all emotions (love, hate, joy, sorrow, fear, courage, hope, despair, desire, aversion, or anger) are natural and can serve a positive, constructive purpose. We rarely permit ourselves to feel okay about being angry, or sad, or afraid. In fact, we feel insulted if someone tells us that we are "emotional."

We have forgotten or have never learned, that the experience of emotion within our bodies is distinctly different from the expression of emotion out in the world. We also forget that each emotion has many different qualities or names, each manifested internally and through a wide range of external expression.

Our emotions are the second set of elements that make up our wholeness. Our relationship to our emotions is most important, and knowing about this relationship is an essential part of the practice of wholeness.

In the following sections we will explore our relationships to the emotions of fear, anger, joy, sadness, and compassion. We will discover how these emotions are experienced in our bodies, what mental constructs arise around them, and how we express them. Rather than trying to eliminate or transcend our emotions, we will work toward cultivating a rich, expansive, and compassionate relationship with them. We will practice experiencing them and using them as allies for both spiritual development and wholeness. So come to these sections prepared to feel.

Why We Feel the Way We Do

Our relationship to our emotions is mediated by several factors: our temperament, our family, our culture, and our personal experience.

Temperament

Temperament defines our basic responses to our internal and external world. Some of us are quick to respond and easily aroused into action while others are slower, preferring to "wait and see." A clear example of the differences in temperament can be seen in the case of the two babies who are sitting in the same room. One baby gets cold and begins screaming. The other baby, also cold, goes to sleep. Like these two babies, each of us has different emotional thresholds. These thresholds rely as much on our nervous systems and individuality as they do on what we have learned.

Family Learning

From infancy until about seven years old, we experience the world primarily through our bodies and our emotions. During this time we are intently learning about ourselves and the world. Our parents tell us the names of things, including the words for what we are feeling. From our families, directly and indirectly, we learn the rules about our emotions: if, when, and how we may experience and express them.

Fear is a reflection of our vulnerability, anger a reflection of our power, joy a reflection of our expansiveness, sadness a reflection of what is important to us, and compassion a reflection of our sensitivity toward ourselves and others. We learn from the way our family members treat these parts of our wholeness. Our parents' emotional attitudes, strengths, and limitations are passed on to us verbally and by example.

Culture

While the basic emotions of fear, anger, sadness, joy, and compassion exist cross-culturally, the way these emotions are experienced, the meanings these emotions carry, and how these emotions are expressed differ from culture to culture. These "rules" are learned through our family and beyond—through the media (movies, books, TV, song lyrics, billboards, and so on), in school, in our religious institutions, and through our interactions with other families.

Personal Experience

Our emotional repertoire is refined by our own personal experience—in school, on the playground, in relationships, in therapy, and throughout our lives. We learn that we can show some feelings to some people and not to others. Some of our interactions allow for deeper internal experience and external expression of emotions, while others stifle our feelings.

The Functions of the Emotions

Our emotions are functional; they are essential elements of humanness. We are not used to thinking of emotions like this, especially the perceived negative emotions like fear, anger, and sadness. We tend to shy away from them, believing they are not good for us, a necessary evil that we should control or, for the spiritually minded, transcend. As I tell my students and patients over and over again: "So sorry, but fear, anger, and sadness are not going to go away. We can't get rid of them. We need to get to know them, so that we can develop a good relationship to them and learn how to use them in the service of our spiritual unfolding. I repeat, they are not going away."

When we cut ourselves off from a relationship with our emotions, we end up blocked, numb, uninspired, or acting out in ways that are ineffectual or destructive. Emotions are a form of energy that can be utilized in the service of wholeness.

Fear*

Fear awakens us; it makes us alert; it heightens our senses. In the present, fear can signal a real and present danger and prepare us for action. Fear also tells us when we are at the edge of the unknown. When we extend ourselves beyond the familiar, we enter a new realm. This is the "void," a place of raw energy before things are manifested. It is the brink of the future with all of its limitless possibilities. It is a place of transition where, when people ask us what are we going to do next, we are embarrassed to admit, "I don't know." We tend to feel very uncomfortable here.

Fear of the unknown can take three forms:

Fear of the unknown based on past experience

We often construct a future in our minds based on what has happened to us already. An unfortunate consequence of this kind of fear is that we will actually recreate reality based upon our past scripts. We do this by ignoring all the crossroads in our

*In Oriental Medicine, the unknown or void is known as the *Water Phase*. It is associated with its appropriate emotion, fear. The "emptiness" of the Water Phase is often filled with our projections. This is echoed in the work of Yvonne Agazarian, the originator of Systems Centered Therapy, who talks about the normal fear (and excitement) associated with "sitting on the edge of the unknown" as opposed to the fear experienced in negative future predictions or constructed realities. Much of the material that follows is based upon these two sources. Another great resource for exploring emotions is the work of Gabrielle Roth (see *Resources*).

journey that offer to take us in other directions. We overlook all the ways in which our present situation is different from previous ones, and focus only on the similarities.

Fear of the unknown based upon future predictions

This fear is related to the first kind, but it is also a separate process. Sometimes, we have no prior experience with a particular "unknown," yet we predict the outcome, for better or worse. When I decided to write this book, I became aware of a number of future predictions that I was making. On the negative side were predictions such as: "I'll never be able to do it" and "It will never be published." These negative future predictions kept me in a state of frozen inactivity for many years. Oddly enough, the positive predictions ("It will be successful." "My life will be changed by it." "I will affect the lives of others.") scared me, too.

These predictions take the energy away from the present and project it into the emptiness of the unknown. We scurry to fill the void because we are afraid of emptiness. It is scary not to know. Eventually, I had to stop making predictions and sit down in front of the computer to write. Resisting the urge to fill the void leads us to the third kind of fear of the unknown.

Fear of the unknown based on the practice of "sitting on the edge of the unknown" in present time

Like all aspects of living in the present moment, sitting on the edge of the unknown takes practice. Because fear heightens our senses, when we let ourselves be with it, we notice many things. We notice that this kind of fear feels very much like excitement. From this heightened state of awareness, we are linked to our unconscious, to our intentions, and to new connections. We notice a kind of magic in the world, a synchronicity. By not trying to do anything to fill up the void, we become a recipient of dreams, inspiration, insight, wisdom, and gifts—tangible and intangible. Doors that we never noticed before suddenly open. Tolerating this kind of fear and working with its energy connects us with our curiosity, our expansiveness, and our courage.

Fear of the unknown is the guardian of the gate to our creativity—a walk through the jungle, a new frontier. Embracing it unlocks the gate so that we can explore beyond the wall of what is safe, secure, and familiar—and delve into the realm of possibilities.

Anger

Anger provides us with energy that, if used correctly, can mobilize our plans and decisions into actions. If we allow ourselves to feel our irritations, we experience a sense of readiness, a willingness to do something. Anger is the emotion wherein we assert our sense of self, our boundaries, our wants and rights. It is also a signal that our boundaries have been crossed, challenged, or violated—a basic statement of "No!" It may be associated with an interference in the free-flowing movement of energy toward manifestation or expression. Anger is also considered one of the so-called negative emotions, often strongly defended against, or acted out.

Anger that is defended against

When we defend against our anger it shows. On the physical level we can experience tension, muscle and joint pain and stiffness, headaches, cramps, nausea, a sensation of something stuck in our throat, or fatigue. Behaviorally we will blame, complain, nag, indulge in obsessive fantasies, feel stuck, become stubborn, resentful, bitter, passive-aggressive, selfish, negative, or moody, or turn our anger inward as depression, self-blame, self-criticism, or guilt. We usually defend against our anger because we learned that there was something bad about having it.

Anger that is acted out

This kind of anger physically manifests in jitters, tics,

tremors, anxiety attacks, diarrhea, or retching. Behaviorally, we feel restless, manic, have tantrums, rages, scream, become controlling, belligerent, hostile, violent, or engage in other dramatic, destructive behavior. We act out our anger because we have not been taught how to use this energy constructively.

Present time anger

Like fear, anger may concern the past or our projected expectations of the future. Or it can be about something that is happening right now in present time.

Anger is a mobilization of energy that allows us to assert ourselves in the face of impediments to our progress, or violations of our boundaries or sense of self. We can use this energy to take ourselves from the formlessness of the unknown into manifesting our plans, decisions, and intentions. With our anger intact and available, we can cultivate a strong sense of ourselves, our needs, our boundaries, and our rights; and by extension, as we mature, the needs, boundaries, and rights of others. Anger is where our fierceness, our sense of what is right, and our benevolence live. The capacity for anger enables us to have the strength and energy for the curiosity, spontaneity, and surprise which make up the experience of joy.

Joy

Joy is one of the most difficult emotions to contain. By nature it is expansive; it wants to go out into the world. The purpose of joy is to connect us with spirit, with the creative, and with the world around us. Although in our culture we often think of joy as excited exhilaration (jumping for joy), it can also appear as quiet radiance, pleasure, clarity, inspiration, devotion, unblocked creativity, the ability to manifest plans and dreams, and peace. Joy is the feeling of alignment, of everything working. It is the movement of the spirit, the feeling of the true self sensing, knowing, and expressing itself in relation to the world.

Giving our joy away

While it is natural to want to share our joy with others, we must also be able to hold it in our bodies. I call this learning to tolerate joy. Although joy is considered a positive, much-sought-after emotion, we often give this energy away before we even have time to acknowledge and feel it ourselves.

A client of mine, Debra, was a perfect example of how we do this. She was an extremely creative actress involved with scores of successful projects, who cared for others and talked non-stop. When we worked together, her joy was strong and easily accessible. After each session, she leapt up from the treatment table ready to take on the world. Her energy, however, got scattered in many directions at once. She took on too many projects, gave away all of her free time, talked to everyone she met about a great idea or experience, and became distracted by all the possibilities. Unable to contain her joy in her body, she couldn't feel how happy she was. When she tried, the physical sensation felt too strong, too powerful, and in the end, confusing.

As she learned to contain joy within her body, she became more clear, more focused, and more effective in her work. She realized there was as much happiness in quiet moments as in big productions. She acknowledged her joy and let herself feel her happiness. It then moved from her into the world—not in manic, talkative energy, but as a powerful radiance that was wordlessly experienced by those around her.

We also give our joy away to the envy, jealousy, and unhappiness of others. How many of us have had the experience of telling someone an absolutely fabulous piece of news only to have them say blandly, "Oh, that's nice," or begin telling us about the unfortunate things in their lives? This deflates us. We feel we cannot have our joy without the participation of others, because joy is about connection. How can we be happy when there is so much suffering in the world? As we learn to contain and cultivate our sense of joy, we also learn that it can be an infinite source of energy for the alleviation of suffering, and a source of compassion for others.

Sadness

Life includes both expansion and limitation. Sadness is the energy that puts us in touch with and helps us understand limitation. Sadness arises with loss or endings. It helps us to let go. Grieving is not an event, but a process which needs time and space. Sadness has its own wisdom; it puts us in touch with both the big picture and with life's subtleties.

Our sadness allows us to know what is important, to understand our connections, hopes, and longings. When we are in touch with our sadness, we become more aware of our sensitivity, our softness, and our ability to be attached—the part of us that cares. It is a mistake to think that sadness excludes joy or happiness. It is possible to feel our sadness fully and still be happy. Our joy can be expansive enough to contain our capacity to grieve.

Defending against sadness

As with the other perceived negative emotions, we tend to defend ourselves against feeling our sadness. Doing this, according to Oriental Medicine, can cause these physical patterns: respiratory diseases, fatigue, digestive problems, or skin ailments. On a behavioral level, we end up feeling melancholy, despondent, or hopeless. We might be unable to feel connected with anyone or anything. Or we might hold on to something which no longer exists, using denial to avoid the fact that things must change or end, or that life does not always feel wonderful.

Sometimes we think that our sadness is too much for us to handle, that by giving in to it we will be overcome by grief. But defending against sadness robs us of experiencing our strength and flexibility. We lose sight of our capacity to face and accept all of life’s facets. Unacknowledged sadness can trap us in the past; it can cut us off from our sensitivity and the wisdom that comes from living.

When Mark, a graphic artist, allowed himself to really feel his long-repressed sadness over the loss of his father as an adolescent, he connected with a part of himself left behind at his father's death: the perceptive, artistic part that he had to give up in order to be strong for his mother and younger siblings. As he rediscovered his sadness, he began to paint beautiful, sensitive watercolors. This was something he had longed to do all of his life but never did because it was not "practical." Although the process was painful, Mark discovered that, contrary to what he had learned in his family, he was strong enough to feel his grief. As he allowed his sadness to teach him, he found an inner wisdom, peace, and capacity for creativity that he never knew he had.

Our felt sadness sensitizes us to the subtleties and beauty of the present moment. It helps us live more fully and teaches us to appreciate what we have. It can also orient us toward what we long for, and propel us into the unknown.

Compassion

Compassion comes from the Latin *compati* which means "to suffer with." The dictionary tells us that compassion is "sorrow for the sufferings or trouble of another or others, accompanied by an urge to help." Like joy, compassion connects us to others. Our capacity to feel compassion is directly related to our capacity to deeply feel our feelings of fear, anger, joy, and sadness. As we develop stamina for these feelings in ourselves, as we learn more about how to experience them without denial or acting out, we deepen our capacity to witness, tolerate, and participate in the feelings of others, without harm. We develop detachment, not from others, but from the past's realities and the future's projected outcomes. We become capable of being with whatever is happening in the present moment.

We come to understand that all our feelings are a part of our wholeness, and we are better able to deeply be with our feelings and those of others, without allowing our judgments to stop us. As a result, we are able to use the energy of our feelings to experience the many aspects of ourselves: our aspirations, power, creativity, connectedness, and longings. We are able to extend ourselves to others. We more easily understand their feelings and sufferings and are less likely to take personally what they are experiencing. We are able to act from our innate desire to alleviate the suffering of others.

Compassion is the energy of our wholeness. It is expansive and inclusive. It can tolerate all the parts of ourselves and of others unconditionally. Deep compassion is a sign that we have made peace with our humanness and with life as it is.

Mixed Feelings

Mixed feelings are a normal part of the emotional experience. Most major events in our lives are accompanied by more than one emotion. How many of us have felt joy, fear, and even some sadness at the thought of becoming parents? In working with parents-to-be, I have found that most of them worry about their mixed feelings; they feel guilty because they are not overcome by pure joy. I tell them it is good they are aware of their fear, because being a parent is a scary thing, certainly a big entry into the unknown. Sometimes these new parents are sad about a way of life that is ending for them. It is important for them to acknowledge this ending.

For some reason, we feel that it is wrong to have mixed feelings about things. We think that our feelings should be unwavering, pure. But they aren't. Feelings are energy. They are dynamic; they move, change, and vary depending upon the meanings and thoughts we give to them. Mixed feelings are natural, speaking to us of the depth and richness of life.

Mixed feelings may also mask an unpleasant feeling with one that is less uncomfortable. *Do you cover up your anger with your sadness, or vice versa? Your vulnerability with your anger? Your joy with your fear?* We will explore more about what we do with our feelings in the section on expression below.

In some instances, we use mixed feelings to avoid taking action. For example, most of us have mixed feelings about making major commitments. Randy came to me to work on his ambivalence about committed relationships. He said he wanted to have a long-term relationship; he was sad he didn't have one, but according to him, there were no committed women "out there." Though unaware of his own mixed feelings about commitment, his actions demonstrated his ambivalence, which drove his potential partners crazy. As we uncovered his mixed feelings, Randy was astonished to find that he used them to avoid the experience of a real, day-to-day relationship, while he was waiting for the one, perfect woman who would inspire a singular, pure "YES!" in him. He had met a number of women who initially seemed perfect, but eventually mixed feelings developed and his wavering ruined the relationships.

We worked directly with his mixed feelings, allowing him to acknowledge them, recognize their importance, and present them in an honest way to his lovers. He discovered that his ambivalence stemmed from many ideas he had about how he was supposed to be in relationships and what relationships were supposed to look like. As Randy got more comfortable with his mixed feelings, he began to see that he could live with them. His relationships then became more honest, real, and satisfying.

The Components of Emotion

The experience of emotion goes through several stages. Emotion begins in the body as physical sensation. Then a mental component is added which helps to translate the experience into some kind of meaning. Finally, we express the emotion in some way.

Bodily Sensations

Emotional experience originates as a set of physical sensations. These are what we feel in our bodies when we are experiencing a certain emotion. In my classes and groups, I ask my students to list what goes on in their bodies when they feel anger (fear, sadness, joy, or compassion). The following is a fairly typical list for anger:

heart pounds or beats faster
face gets tight
eyes squint
teeth and jaw clench
neck gets stiff
breathing gets stronger
stomach knots up
knees get weak
body gets shaky
arms feel strong
body gets hot
see red
feel more power
voice trembles or breaks
feel more focused
body gets tense all over
get spacey, dizzy, or flustered

Some of these sensations are shared by many; others are more specific to individuals.

A lot of us don't know what we are feeling. We have learned to ignore our bodies and are unaware of what our bodies are expressing until we have severe or chronic symptoms. We don't know that we are angry, scared, or sad until we are acting out in extreme or destructive ways. Awareness of the particular sensations we experience with emotions helps us identify what and how we are feeling. The physical sensations we feel with our emotions are signals that something is going on: we are on the edge of the unknown or in danger, someone is transgressing our boundaries, we are ready to connect with the world, or we're losing something important to us.

These signals are functional; if attended to they offer us information about how we are doing and what we might need. I urge you to practice checking in with your body to notice what your body is doing in situations where you are feeling sad, scared, angry, joyful, and compassionate.

Mental Component

The mental component to emotion includes the name we give to our bodily sensations, and the thoughts, attitudes, and beliefs we have about our emotions. While the physical component occurs naturally, the mental component is learned. Our parents tell us a particular configuration of sensations and behaviors is "anger," or "being defiant," or "being bad," and that another set of sensations and behaviors is "fear," or "acting like a scaredy cat," or "making a big fuss over nothing." We are taught that another set of sensations and behaviors is "sadness," or "being a baby," or "being a sissy," and that yet another set of sensations and behaviors is "compassion," or "kindness," or "being too sensitive." Thus, we learn basic attitudes about our feelings.

Students in my classes came up with these attitudes about anger when completing the sentence, "Anger is ____________":

bad
unhealthy
what you feel when you don't get what you want
energy
powerful
hurtful
a healthy emotion

a motivator
all encompassing
a way to be seen
a way to control others
a pressure reliever
unchristian
violent
natural

Our attitudes about our emotions affect how we feel, whether we acknowledge our feelings, and how we express them. If we believe that fear is a sign of weakness and it is best not to show weakness lest others take advantage of us, then we are not free to feel our fear. By cutting ourselves off from this elemental emotion, we cut ourselves off from learning about trust and creating a world for ourselves where our vulnerability can exist without harm. We miss opportunities to bring people into our lives who can see our vulnerability and give us their kindness, comfort, and protection.

Our attitudes about our emotions also affect how we feel when other people have or express their feelings. If we believe all anger is our fault, we will take the anger of others personally. If we believe sadness is a private matter best not expressed, we will have no tools to comfort a friend who is grieving. If we believe we should conquer fear, we may bully our children, friends, or clients away from their fear, and deprive them of the understanding and wisdom that comes from knowing this emotion.

We also learn rules for each emotion: which emotions are okay to feel and express, how each emotion can be expressed, and how we are to act toward other people's expressed feelings. As children, we learn these rules from things we are told directly by our caretakers ("Big boys don't cry." "Don't be a bleeding heart." "Anger is not lady-like." "Just ignore your brother when he acts like that.") and from observing how people act when they are experiencing their emotions. ("Dad is violent when he is angry, so anger is bad.") Children are observant. They don't know much about the world, so they gather information from every source.

Here are some of the rules and messages about anger that my groups have come up with:

Anger is okay for men but not for women (or vice versa).
Don't be angry.
Don't make a scene.
If you get angry, someone will hurt you.
There's something wrong with you.
Don't answer back to authority figures.
Only the person with the power can get angry.
Your anger is silly.
Anger doesn't get you anywhere.
You look ugly (stupid, foolish) when angry.
You're being bad (defiant, stubborn, unchristian, unreasonable).
If you ignore it, it will go away.
Angry people hurt others.
Being angry is the same as being cruel (violent, hateful).
Don't take it out on people or things.
If someone is angry with you, you deserve it.
Keep it in the family.
If someone is angry, it's your job to calm them.
Mask your anger with a smile.
Deny, lie about, or hide your anger.

There are many rules and messages for each emotion. Most of them reflect our caretakers' abilities to experience that specific emotion, to understand its function, and to express the emotion in some way. Some families are better with some emotions than others; other families stifle all emotional experience. In my own family, we could handle any emotion as long at is was not being experienced in the moment! We could talk about how angry, sad, scared, or happy we were in the past or would be in the future, but we did not know how to be with each other as we were actually experiencing these feelings.

As we become conscious of the specific rules we learned about emotions, we can free ourselves from those messages which don't allow us to experience or express what we feel. Then we are more empowered to feel our feelings, to learn from them, and to develop a range of emotional expression appropriate to situations and effective in helping us get what we truly need.

Other aspects of the mental component of emotion are time and meaning. As mentioned in the previous section, our emotions can be about something that is happening in the present time, something that happened in the past, or the way we imagine something will be in the future. Many of us react to present events while carrying unresolved, unexpressed, or unacknowledged feelings about the past or future.

The meanings we give to the events in our lives also affect our emotions. We will explore in greater detail the role of meaning in the next chapter, *The Realm of Mind*.

Expression

The word "emotion" comes from the Latin *emovere* which means "to move out." Emotion is energy which begins in the body and wants to move out into the world. We learn how to express our emotions by watching other people express theirs, and by expressing ours and experiencing the consequences. Many years ago, I met a woman from Japan who spoke beautiful English. When I asked her where she had learned to speak so well she replied, "I learned the basics in school in Japan. But when I came to this country, I realized that I did not have fluency in the emotional aspects of the language, which are so different from my native tongue. These I got from watching American soap operas!" Like my Japanese friend, we learn emotional expression from the dramas of everyday life.

We learn much about the expression of anger, for example, when we are in our "terrible twos." One of the reasons parents think the "twos" are "terrible" is that the child is beginning to act out his or her will. Children at this age enjoy saying "NO!" and "MINE!" In fact, they are practicing saying these things as they begin to discover their newly found independence and separateness from the merged state of infancy. They can walk, they can express themselves, they have intention and direction, and at this age, they really begin to assert it. A two-year-old child will say "NO!" to everything, even things she wants. She does this in order to experience her power.

Two-year-olds talk about fierceness, about being stronger, bigger, faster. One of my daughter's favorite games at this age was "Let's fight." In this game, she would push against me as hard as she could just to feel her own strength. Defy the two-year-old and you see anger in a raw and powerful form. A parent's response to this strong expression of self is the basis of the child's learning about personal power and anger. Obviously, the two-year-old needs a balance between the opportunity to feel his power without being overwhelmed or crushed, and the need to learn healthy and appropriate ways to express this power. It is up to our families to provide this lesson.

Sometimes in our families, our caretakers teach us to express ourselves in healthy and effective ways. Some parents teach their children to be direct with their anger, to cry when sad or write poems about their sadness, or to talk about or draw pictures of their fears. It is my experience, however, that most emotional expression is learned indirectly, and somewhat haphazardly. Most families do not think about teaching their children how to have their emotions. This leaves our range of emotional expression limited to familiar, usually unconscious reactions.

Indeed, many times we do not know that we are expressing an emotion, and some of our behavior denies us a direct experience of our feelings. Here are some of the things people in my groups say they do when I ask them how they express their anger:

Slam doors.
Cry.
Use foul language.
Yell.
Throw things; break things.
Clean house.
Shop.
Move furniture.
Say "I'm angry."
Eat.
Pace.
Smoke, drink, do drugs.
Have sex.
Take it out on loved ones.
Act "pissy."
Dance.
Argue.
Obsess about the details.
Turn the music up.
Get critical.
Isolate myself from others.
Write angry letters.
Smile.
Use the silent treatment.
Be sarcastic.
Exaggerate.
Use humor.
Distract myself.
Get competitive.
Play sports, run, lift weights.
Say "I'm fine."

Confront.
Play the piano.
Have revenge fantasies.
Try to calm down.
Blame.
Get sad.
Sulk.
Get passive-aggressive.
Sabotage things.
Make mistakes.
Practice mindful breathing.

There are many things that we can do with our emotions. But when we are doing these things, are we aware we are expressing something? *Is your shopping spree an expression of your sadness? Are your distractions expressions of your joy? Is your compulsive organizing an expression of your fear? Is your impatience an expression of your anger? Do you hide your feelings behind humor or smiles? Might there be better, more effective ways to express your feelings?*

Generally, when we first begin expressing something, our expression is raw, unrefined, perhaps a bit explosive. This is true both of children and of adults who have repressed their emotional expression. We hold on to our outrage, then it explodes in harsh words. We stifle our grief, then sob at a minor hurt. We smother our joy, then exhaust ourselves with mania. We suppress our fear, and become bigoted, hateful, or suspicious.

As we consciously practice our emotional expression, it becomes easier, smoother, and more refined. Words become less blaming, more expressive of what we need. Joy becomes less manic, more peaceful, less needful of others' approval. Grief becomes less painful, softer, more gentle. Anger becomes less adulterated by past hurts and more guided by mindful words and actions.

As we mature in the unfolding of our emotions, we can even begin to create from them, a process that transforms the simple expression of emotion into something beyond the personal. Over the years, for example, I have learned to channel my outrage about child abuse into writing articles, giving talks, and teaching classes. The introduction to this section, in fact, was written from such anger and sadness. We can draw, paint, dance, or make movies. We can write poetry, plays, our personal histories, and letters to Congress with the energy of our emotions.

The first step is becoming mindful of what you do with your emotions—your fear, anger, joy, sadness, compassion. *How do you act with these feelings; how do you act out?* From there you can begin to look at your emotional expression. *Are the ways you express emotion effective; do they communicate your feelings? Do they get you what you want and need? Are there new ways of expression that might be more effective?* You can look at the kinds of expressions you use. *Are they all indirect? Confrontational? Dramatic? Timid? How can you expand your range of emotional expression?*

A second level of awareness about emotional expression has to do with what we do when other people are expressing their emotions. When I ask my groups to tell me what they do when someone else is angry, here are some of the things they come up with:

Get defensive.
Tune it out.
Get scared.
Get more alert.
Blame myself, feel that something is wrong with me.
Get concerned.
Get angry.
Make jokes, try to lighten things up.
Try to distract the other person.
Listen.
Encourage.
Assess and judge.

Criticize.
Get in the middle of it.
Try to calm things down.
Leave.
Placate the other person.
Get hurt feelings.
Diffuse the other person.
Apologize.
Flow with it.

Becoming conscious of what we do automatically when someone else is feeling or expressing an emotion can be an eye-opener. Our responses to emotions in others are typically automatic and unconscious. These responses don't always make sense. How many times have we been around someone who was angry and we assumed we were going to get hurt? Or been with someone who is sad, and automatically assumed they needed cheering up? Or been envious of a loved one's happiness?

A client, Martha, lost a child shortly after childbirth and was amazed by the lengths to which well-meaning people went to try to cheer her up. She discovered there was no "cheering up" from such a deep loss. Over time, she felt as if she had to hide her grief from her friends, who went so far as to tell her how long her grieving period should last. Martha wanted to experience her grief process—not by cheering herself up, but by allowing herself to be with the grief, by letting herself feel it, by letting it inform her.

Because she did this, she was able to face death and to glean depth and wisdom from her experience with it. Because her grief slowed her down, Martha was able to appreciate with stunning clarity the beauty and joy in ordinary daily life: a flower, the kindness of a stranger, the light falling on her writing desk. She was able to see her two living children more deeply, and to cultivate a relationship in her heart with the child who died. All this would have been denied her if she had moved away from her grief too quickly.

Like our responses to our own emotions, our responses to the emotions of others are learned overtly and by watching how emotions are handled by others. Bringing our awareness to what we do with the emotions of others is a powerful tool that can dramatically alter our relationships. Seeing that the emotional expressions of others are theirs—not about us—we free ourselves to experiment with being with other people in their feelings. This enables us to be compassionate. We can acknowledge the effect we have on others, change the things about ourselves that hurt others, and allow others to feel, express, and learn from their own emotions.

Expanding Our Emotional Range

Expanding Our Capacity to Feel

As we get used to the idea that our emotions are not going away—that they are an important part of our lives—we can begin to apply our curiosity to how our emotions express themselves in our bodies. The basic practice is to learn to tolerate the sensation of emotion in our physical bodies, and to recognize the emotions that go with particular physical sensations.

Some emotions feel pleasant and mild. Others elicit stronger sensations. Imbalance is created by strong emotions that are long-standing and don't allow other experience in, emotions that are stifled and blocked, and emotions that are acted out in destructive ways. It helps to remember that emotions are just energy. They are normal; when acknowledged and mindfully expressed, they are a healthy force in our lives.

To explore our capacity to tolerate the physical sensations of our emotions, we must learn to simply be with them, to hold a space for them within our physical bodies before we act on them or stifle them. For some people, this begins with allowing themselves the opportunity to feel, and bringing mindfulness and curiosity to what they feel. For others, it involves holding on to their feelings before they express them so they can express them mindfully.

Many times we act out our emotions before we even know what we are feeling. We shout at a loved one and then say to ourselves, "Oh, I guess I was angry." We seek out experiences that help us discharge our emotions, like beating on pillows, yelling, or behaving over-dramatically. However, these responses may not help us understand our emotions, expand our capacity to be with them, or get us what we need. On the other end of the spectrum, we stifle the experience of emotion so that the body absorbs the feeling before it enters our consciousness. Our reward takes the form of tension, stress, and other physical symptoms.

When we avoid feeling what we think are negative feelings, we fail to develop the capacity to hold our emotions in our bodies. As a result, we don't feel the positive ones either. As our capacity to feel fear, anger, and sadness deepens, so does our capacity for joy and compassion.

As you become more curious about your emotions, you can also become more aware of their subtleties and a wide range of emotional possibilities. *Which emotions are you good at? Which ones do you avoid? Do you spend a lot of time in anger, for example, and neglect feeling your fear and sadness? Do you use sadness to cover up anger? Do you have joy in your life? Do you let yourself really feel joy in your body? How does your body respond to the various emotions? How do you express your fear (anger, sadness, joy, and compassion)? What stops you from you allowing yourself to feel certain emotions?*

We somehow believe that if we feel our emotions, we will die, explode, be crushed, hurt, or overwhelmed by them. *But we won't.* Emotions are simply energy; we all are capable of holding this energy within our bodies. When we learn to experience emotional energy within our bodies, to bring our consciousness and curiosity to it, we begin to experience ourselves in new ways. Allowing ourselves to feel permits us to practice bringing resources—comfort, clarity, calmness, right action—to our difficult feelings, and to more fully experience our more enjoyable feelings. As we learn how to have a good relationship with our emotions, we feel free. We are no longer at the mercy of our feelings. We become able to transform the energy of our emotions into something that works for us in our lives.

Expanding How We Think About Feelings

The first step to expanding how we think about feelings is to bring mindful awareness to the thoughts, attitudes, beliefs, and images we have about our emotions. We can explore our attitudes about emotions in general and about specific emotions. For example, we can notice whether we think it is okay to cry, but not to get angry, or to show anger, but not fear. We can discover whether we think it is okay to talk about emotions after the feelings have passed, but not to show them when we are actually feeling them. We may discover that certain feelings access memories of events in our childhood that were painful or pleasant. We may believe that people who cry easily are weak, or that everyone should cry, or that anger should be transcended, or that we should vent our anger by pounding on pillows. We can observe our beliefs about the consequences of feeling our feelings.

We can also explore the meanings we give to the emotions of others. We may learn, for example, that when other people are angry, we feel it is our fault; when someone is sad, we feel we have to cheer him up; or when someone is joyful, we feel the lack of joy in our own lives.

As we become mindful of the mental aspects of our emotions, we can consciously add new messages. We can add the idea that emotions are an intrinsic part of our humanness: They can teach us, they are worth learning how to feel and express, and within their energy is richness, wisdom, and strength. We can allow our emotions to guide us to new meanings. To our emotional self we can bring our curiosity, our openness, and our compassion.

Expanding Our Range of Expression

When pounding pillows and using "batakas" (padded bats used for venting anger) were in vogue in therapeutic circles, I didn't get much out of this form of expression, even though other people apparently did. It was only later, as I was practicing understanding my emotions more fully, that I realized this was not a form of expression that added to my wholeness. Coming from a family where the expression of anger was very demonstrative, sometimes violent, I had no difficulty ranting and raving. I did not particularly want this tendency to escalate. What was missing from my repertoire was the ability to clearly and articulately communicate to others what my anger wanted: "I want you to stop hurting me; I want to be considered; I want my boundaries respected."

Rather than "getting my anger out," it was more helpful for me to learn how to clearly communicate the reason for my anger. To do this, I had to move away from the feeling of power that acting out my anger gave me, and more toward my underlying vulnerability.

For others, expanding the range of physical expression is useful. I have taught clients how to yell "NO!" and "MINE!" and how to feel their anger in their bodies and literally push back with it. Some clients have to learn to use their anger to gather strength in arms and legs that feel weak and useless. Others have to learn how to avoid physically taking in the emotional energy of others by pushing outward at the points affected in their bodies. Even pounding pillows can be useful, if it is done with mindfulness and not just with discharge as its goal.

For some, crying is an important addition to their emotional repertoire; for others, it could be learning to express sadness in tender words or gentle touch.

There is no one particular way that is right for expressing a particular emotion. The range of emotional expression is limitless. We have choices in how we express ourselves. The point is that emotional expression need not be reactive or unconscious. Expression can be direct—with words, motions, or body language—or it can be channeled into art, poetry, dance, impassioned letters, articulate lectures, or acts of compassion.

The practice is to explore how we already express each emotion, and then to see what is missing in our expression and what can be added to our repertoire. If you notice that you talk too much about feelings, practice simply letting them be in your body. If you notice that you feel them in your body too much, practice drawing pictures, or giving your feelings a voice. If you stifle your emotions with tension and stress, practice inviting your mindfulness in and letting yourself experience the emotion that lives in the tension. Watch how someone you admire expresses herself. Add something from her repertoire to yours.

When I am teaching, students ask me for examples of healthy emotional expression and say, "You expressed that so eloquently. How did you do it?" Practice. Learn the words. Steal them from others. Add them to your repertoire. Know that, at first, new lessons feel awkward or unfamiliar: *They are supposed to.* Practice is the heart of transformation.

Practices for the Unfolding of Emotion

Check In

Practice checking in with your emotions every day or several times a day. Take a few moments to stop and return your awareness to your emotions in the present moment. What are you feeling? Where does that emotion live in your body? What kinds of thoughts go with that emotion? What does the emotion want? What kind of nourishment can you give yourself around this emotion?

Honor

Spend a week in honor of your fear (anger, sadness, joy, or compassion). Do some exercises for that emotion each day.

Definitions

Fill in the blanks with examples from your life:

Fear is____.

Anger is_______________________________________.

Sadness is______________________________________.

Joy is____.

Compassion is___________________________________.

Feelings

List at least ten things that make you fearful (angry, sad, joyful, or compassionate).

Dancing Your Emotions

Do a fear (anger, sadness, joy, or compassion) dance. Spend time with it. Do not think about your movements or worry about how they look. Allow them to come from your body, letting your body tell you what it knows about this emotion.

The Shapes of Your Emotions

Move your body into postures that represent the shapes of your fear (anger, sadness, joy, or compassion). Take your time. Each emotion has many shapes. If you are working with fear, for example, find a posture (shape), hold it, and then move into another posture, hold it, and move on. Do your fear dance, from posture to posture, for about fifteen minutes. These shapes can tell you a lot. Allow your body to tell its story.

Bodily Sensations

Make a list of the bodily sensations that you feel when you feel fear (anger, sadness, joy, or compassion). Keep your list on the wall and add to it as you experience new sensations.

Rules

List at least ten rules that you learned from your family, culture, and life experiences about fear (anger, sadness, joy, or compassion). These rules can be things you heard overtly ("Don't be a scaredy cat."). Or they can be things you learned by observing how other people dealt with their fear (anger, sadness, joy, or compassion) or dealt with you when you were feeling your fear (anger, sadness, joy, or compassion). Mark an "E" for explicit rules and an "I" for rules learned more implicitly (by observation). Keep this list in a place where you can add to it as you discover more rules.

Emotional Expression

List at least ten things you do with your fear (anger, sadness, joy, or compassion). As you observe yourself through the day, add to the list. Note your particular kinds of expressions. What kinds would you like to add to your list? Which would you prefer to express less often? Practice expanding the range of your expression; practice stopping yourself from expressions that do not serve you.

Emotional Expression in Others

List at least ten things you do when other people are expressing or feeling fear (anger, sadness, joy, or compassion). Add to the list as you observe your interactions with others. Note the things in your responses you would like to change.

Giving Your Emotions a Voice

You can do this alone or with a friend. Find a quiet place. Allow yourself to feel your fear (anger, sadness, joy, or compassion). Give that emotion a voice. Begin with the sentence: "I am *(your name's)* fear (anger, sadness, joy, or compassion)." Listen for what your fear (anger, sadness, joy, or compassion) has to say, and actually allow its voice to speak aloud. Let your emotion speak about you in the third person. Your emotion can talk about the relationship it has with you, the purpose it serves in your life, what it wants from you, and so on. Give it time to have its say.

If you are alone, you can speak into a tape recorder if you would like a record of what your emotion has to say.

Allow your fear (anger, sadness, joy, or compassion) to write you a letter. Write back.

Have a dialogue with your fear (anger, sadness, joy, or compassion).

Relationship

Draw a picture of your relationship with your fear (anger, sadness, joy, or compassion).

Expanding Your Relationship

Write about the kind of relationship you would like to have with your fear (anger, sadness, joy, or compassion).

Make a new relationship contract that begins like this:
When I am afraid (angry, sad, joyful, or compassionate), I will

____

____

____

____.

When others feel afraid (angry, sad, joyful, or compassionate), I will____

____

____

____.

Put the contract in a place where you can see it. Practice daily to cultivate this new relationship.

Spirit

Allow yourself to know that your emotions can be tools of the spirit. Draw a picture of how your fear (anger, sadness, joy, or compassion) serves you and your spirit.

Altar

Make an altar to your fear (anger, sadness, joy, or compassion). Find things to offer from nature or life, or make things to honor your sacred emotion.

Creativity

Invent a practice that helps you cultivate a better relationship with your emotions or with one particular emotion. Spend time doing this practice regularly.

Experiencing Wholeness in Your Emotions

Turn your attention to your emotions, or to one particular emotion you may be feeling strongly right now. Bring your awareness to your whole body—your feet, head, front, back, and sides—at the same time, and to your breath. Allow your body to be a container for that emotion, so the emotion you feel exists within the vast space of your whole self. From the large container of your whole body, allow yourself to be aware of that emotion. Send your breath and mindfulness to it. Say to it, "I know you are there." From the space of your more expanded self, bring compassion to your emotion.

Chapter 3
The Realm of Mind

The "realm of mind" is the third aspect of our wholeness. For the purposes of this chapter, it includes our thoughts, images, memories, attitudes, assumptions, expectations, beliefs, meanings, and philosophies. These are the *mental constructs* that comprise what we know and tell ourselves about ourselves and the world.

If we pay attention, we sometimes notice that the same thoughts cross our minds over and over. These recurring messages exert a huge power over the quality and content of our lives. Unfortunately, many of our thoughts are based on what we learned about the world in childhood, through faulty information and untested assumptions. Furthermore, most of the time the activity of our minds operates below our everyday awareness. Our unconsciously held mental constructs can be expansive or limiting, creative or destructive.

The job of the mind is to know, distinguish, make judgments, discriminate. Your mind divides the whole, and gives the parts names and meanings. As you practice in this realm, you will not be trying to stop your mind from doing this—this is the natural function of mind and, like your emotions, not likely to go away. What you are trying to do is to become aware of how your particular mind works—what informs its attitudes, judgments, and meanings—and to practice expanding your range of mental activity to include meanings, thoughts, images, and beliefs which may be outside of the familiar but which enhance your spiritual unfolding.

Basic Life Questions*

When we are born, we know very little about the world. As infants and young children, we absorb information very rapidly. Many of the attitudes and beliefs that shape our mental constructs come from our family, culture, and personal experiences. In addition, these mental constructs arise around a number of basic psychological questions we ask and find answers to in our early development. (All of this happens automatically in our prerational mind.) What happens to us at these early stages of development affects us deeply throughout our lives. Though often not consciously accessible to us, these experiences form a basis for our attitudes and beliefs about ourselves and the world.

Belonging

The first question that we unconsciously ask is whether or not the world is safe for us. Is it okay to be alive? Is there space for us? Because in the earliest stages of development we are merged with our environment—undifferentiated—we do not see the division between "in here" (within ourselves) and "out there" (the world around us). The information we receive about the world being an okay place also tells us whether or not we are okay. If we have good experiences, if our initial experiences with

*My thanks to Phil Del Prince, Senior Trainer for the Hakomi Institute. This section is based on his teachings on Character (see *Resources*).

the world are safe, comforting, and welcoming, we unconsciously conclude:

> *It is okay to be alive, to be human.*
> *Being in a body is good; so are my feelings.*
> *The world is a good place.*
> *There is space for me.*
> *I'm welcome and safe here.*

If our experiences are not so great, if we are treated harshly or feel unwelcome, we acquire mental constructs such as:

> *The world is dangerous.*
> *There is something wrong with me.*
> *I don't belong.*
> *I'm bad.*
> *Being human is bad.*
> *My thoughts, feelings, or sensations are dangerous.*

I have worked with people who feel that they were born to the wrong parents or on the wrong planet. When we have these feelings, we are expressing a basic lack of safety in belonging. This core belief that the world is not safe, or that it does not hold a space for us, is profound and deeply affects our ability to live full and happy lives. When this belief is strong, we withdraw—from life, from our feelings, from the sensation of the life force in our bodies, from the unknowns of relationships, from the thrill of our creativity. Sometimes being alive is so painful, we wish to die.

Laurel was born prematurely, spent several months in an incubator, and was subjected to invasive medical procedures which saved her life. At the time Laurel was born, medical doctors believed that infants were not sensitive to pain because of their relatively undeveloped nervous systems. As an adult, Laurel had recurring dreams and an intense fear of being tortured. She was exquisitely sensitive, and although she had a richly developed spiritual and artistic life, she was irritated by being "earthbound," as she called it. She bristled at the physicality of daily living, like deciding what to wear or eating regular meals. She experienced the world as basically hostile and was deeply horrified by cruelty, violence, and ecological destruction, often dwelling on these as proof of how depraved humans are. Connecting with people was difficult. She had the feeling of being separated from the world by a "wall of glass" and joked half-seriously that she was from another planet.

When I worked with Laurel, I told her that even if she is from another planet, she is spending her current lifetime on this one. In answer to my offer to let me show her how to relax in her life here on earth, Laurel began to learn Primary Contact: *You are here. You are welcome. I am here with you.* In Primary Contact, your being is acknowledged by another. Your existence is a joyful event, witnessed by another and mirrored back to you without demands or expectations. Primary Contact is the essential bonding experience, the fundamental basis for our sense of self and belonging in the world.

Much of our work together was to enable Laurel to feel this sense of safety and connectedness with herself and the world around her. I worked with her slowly, over time, offering gentle, soothing touch, mindful attention, and soft words. Because many of her emotions and bodily sensations had been misnamed, left unnamed, or critically judged, I helped her relearn the names of feelings and experiences. I introduced her to the experience of comfort, to bringing things into her life with which she felt an affinity. As she had these new experiences, Laurel learned that there is safety and comfort in the world; she slowly began to find activities that interested her and people with whom she could connect. She came to tolerate her feelings and bodily sensations, found that she was stronger than she had thought, and acknowledged that life contains both horror *and* beauty.

Laurel is still learning, she says. Her sense of being from another planet has shifted to feeling that she is simply living in the wrong culture. Her practice now is learning to channel the energy from this feeling of alienation into creating the kind of culture that values sensitivity, safety, and interconnectedness.

As you practice becoming aware of belonging and what it means to you, you have the opportunity to explore some of your core beliefs and attitudes. *How do you feel about being alive, about being human? What is your relationship to your planet and to the other people and beings on it? How connected to others are you? Is the world a safe place for you? Do you allow yourself to feel fully alive, or are you having a "near-life" experience?*

As we examine our beliefs and attitudes, and begin to understand their origins, we can start collecting new data based on new experience. If we notice that connectedness is missing from our lives, we begin to seek connections. We discover what stops us from acknowledging the ones we already have. We begin to feel the life force within us and explore the interface between ourselves and the world.

My client, Laurel, had to learn to bring her awareness to the surface of her skin to feel the edge between herself and the world. At first, occupying this interface felt uncomfortable, making her nervous and panicky. With practice, she was able to experience this edge as soothing, to sense comfort in the air around her body. In this way she accessed the feeling that the world could be a welcoming force. This helped her to find her place in it.

Nourishment

Early in life, we are totally dependent on the care and attention of others for survival. Our caretakers must be able to read our signals and attend to our needs, without much help from us. Though we are not able at this early stage to appreciate all that our caretakers do for us, we do sense unconsciously whether or not our needs are taken care of. If our caretakers are accurately attentive to what we need, providing care when needed, providing enough for our needs to be satisfied, without many negative messages to us, we form beliefs such as:

The world is a nurturing and supportive place.
I am worthy of support.
My needs are met.
The world provides for me.
There is enough for me.
I can be satisfied.
When I experience and communicate my needs, they are met.
The abundance in the world is available to me.
The nourishment I get is related to what I need.

If our caretakers are not comfortable with our dependence—if they give us what they think we need when they think we need it without reading our signals, if they neglect our needs, or only give us a portion of what we need, or make judgments about our neediness—we form beliefs such as:

I can't get my needs met.
There is not enough for me.
I am not worthy of support.
I'll never get what I want.
It's bad to need.
I should never show my needs to anyone.
The world is a bleak, empty place.
There is abundance in the world, but it is for others, not for me.
The nourishment I get is not related to what I need, but to what others think I need.
I'll never be satisfied.

As we get a little older, the support we get from others often becomes more conditional. We receive messages about what we have to do to win others' nurturing and support. "If you are a good boy, I'll make you pizza for dinner." "If you clean your room, I'll buy you a toy." "If you don't know how to stay clean, I'm going to stop buying you nice clothes." We still need our caretakers to provide us the essentials for survival, and our caretakers teach us what we have to do in exchange.

Sometimes the things we are asked to do in return are nurturing themselves, as they teach us to be self-supporting and competent, such as: "Help me cook dinner." "Why don't you mow lawns to help pay for that new bicycle you want?" "Hard work is rewarded." Other times we get messages that don't really make sense or are more about control than support, such as: "How can you be angry at me, after all the things I've done for you?" "How do you expect to earn a living if you can't spell?" "If you don't tell anyone what I am doing to you, you can be my special friend."

These messages form the basis of our beliefs about what we have to do to get what we need. A child who gets her needs met based on unquestioning obedience learns compliance, even at her own expense. A child who is manipulated or ignored when he expresses his needs, learns how to manipulate others or to conceal his needs.

I have worked with many clients who have been abused by their caretakers. The message they received as children was that abuse goes along with caring. Not surprisingly, they often find themselves in relationships which mirror their previous experience. Because of childhood sexual abuse, one client I worked with had learned to give herself sexually to people who were supposed to be helping her. She became involved with her teachers, her doctor, and even the lawyer who was helping her divorce her abusive husband. In her mind, care meant sex.

Though unlearning this was difficult, over time she was able to cultivate relationships with men who helped and cared for her without taking advantage of her sexual vulnerability. After seeing that this was an important step for her, I referred her to a male psychotherapist who had uncompromisingly clear boundaries. She made tremendous progress with him in learning how to receive care that was not sexual.

As we become older children and are able to move about, to be aware that we want things, to ask for and go toward those things, we get messages about whether or not the surrounding environment supports our new independence and will help us become self-supporting. Sometimes we are well-supported by our caretakers, but as we move toward self-support we begin to lose their blessing. Or we may be pushed toward self-support before we have the tools to really succeed. What we are looking for in our lives is a balance between self-support and support from the world.

If we are given good information about self-support, we arrive at conclusions such as:

I am competent.
I can take care of myself.
If I can't do it all myself, I can get help.
I can cooperate.
I can work on a team, and my contribution is valuable.
I can go after what I want, and find the resources to help myself.

I worked with a marvelously talented, competent woman, Celeste, who realized that even though she could do many things for herself, she did not know how to get help. As long as she stayed with situations where she did not need anyone's help, she was fine. But invariably she ran into circumstances wherein she had to enlist the help of others—a group project at work, for example—a situation which was usually disastrous for her. Her motto was: "If you want something done right, you have to do it yourself." Celeste did not know how to delegate responsibility or let others know when she was in a bind. She took on huge tasks, did the work of others, and generally exhausted herself to avoid the difficulty of learning how to work with the help, support, and talents of others. Some of Celeste's underlying beliefs about asking for help were:

You can't count on anyone.
People don't really want to help me.
I don't want to bother anyone.
Asking for help displays weakness.

Fortunately or unfortunately, the events in Celeste's life unfolded so that she had to practice receiving help from others. She experienced a car accident that left her immobilized for eight weeks and in recovery for six months. She needed others to dress her, feed her, grocery shop for her, and drive her places. At work, the important projects she felt only she could do had to be delegated to others, and she had to rely on the abilities of her coworkers to do a good job on these assignments. Although a difficult and painful time, she learned that she could rely on other people, that her friends were happy for the opportunity to help her, and that her vulnerability did not mean that she was not strong.

In contrast, Kara, had never been trusted to do much on her own. Her family had been so supportive and protective of her that they had not given her the resources to do things for herself. Even though no one had ever told her she was incompetent, she had inferred that she was because no one ever let her do anything they considered important. Even though she was educated and intelligent, she did not learn to support herself financially, instead relying on the money her father gave her until she married. Her husband was a successful businessman who replaced her father as provider and decision maker. After twenty years of marriage, against her husband's wishes, she enrolled in massage school where I met her in one of my classes. Learning for the first time about her talents outside her role as a homemaker, she began to discover what she wanted in life and to take the risks to pursue her goals. Her fellow students encouraged her to trust her own sense of what she needed and challenged her when she deferred to someone else's authority.

Needless to say, this initial period of doing things for herself after a lifetime of dependence terrified her; she had to look at many long-standing beliefs that she had about her own competence. Nonetheless, she persevered and learned that even though help was available, she didn't always have to take it. She learned to say "thank you" to others for their advice without having to follow it. She began to develop an inner sense of self-support and knowledge based on her own achievements.

As you practice becoming aware of your own mental constructs about nourishment, you learn about your thoughts and attitudes toward caring for yourself, caring for others, and receiving care from others. *What are your thoughts and beliefs about receiving? Is the world a nourishing place for you? Do you feel worthy of the care and attention of others? What are your beliefs about caring for yourself? About doing the things that are good for your physical, emotional, and spiritual well-being? How do you feel about caring for others? About your dependence upon other people and the planet for life? How do you feel about the good fortune of others? How do you avoid opportunities to take nourishment into your life? What is your relationship to gratitude?*

As we work with our beliefs, attitudes, memories, and images about nourishment, we begin to realize that all life on earth is comprised of interdependent relationships. The very earth itself supports our existence. Everything in our lives, whether naturally occurring or synthetic, comes ultimately from the earth. We are dependent upon it for our sustenance, and upon our fellow people, animals, plants, and minerals for the essentials of daily life. Nothing on earth has a separate self. No matter how independent, or self-sufficient, or alone we think ourselves, *we are not.*

Both giving and receiving are sacred acts. The practice of giving and receiving nourishment deepens our lives, and the relationships we have with people and things in our world. We can examine our relationship to nourishment and learn to experience the world as a satisfying place, replete with allies and opportunities for nourishment and support.

Power

As we become more independent and self-supporting as children, another question arises, this one concerning our power to affect the world around us. Previously, we had been learning what we had to do to win the support of others. Now we are learning how others will accommodate or change for us. At this stage we are testing our independence: *Can I be different? Can I say "No"? Can I disagree with or go against the wishes of my caretakers and still be loved? Do others respect my personal boundaries?*

At this stage, parenting is a delicate balance between allowing the child to have independence and power, and setting realistic boundaries and limits for the child. As children, we need to experience our power, to learn to say "no," to feel free to be different from others, to have our bodies, personalities, and needs respected, to know love is not conditional upon obedience and that other people will change somewhat for us. We also need to learn that there are limits to our power: Sometimes our caretakers know more than we do about what we need; the needs of other people are important, too; and our behavior can affect other people. If our caretakers are able to allow us to have power and independence without crushing us, then we develop attitudes such as:

I can have an effect on the world.
I can be myself.
My personal boundaries are respected.
My anger is not scary.
I can be strong.
I can assert myself.

Unfortunately many parents do not understand and have difficulty with this stage of development. They may be heavy-handed, making it so that any expression of independence is seen as defiance. They may try to break the child of this so-called defiance, engaging in rigid power struggles with him or her, where the parents are always right or always win. When our caretakers consistently squelch our power or abuse their own power in relationship to us, we come to believe such things as:

I am powerless.
It doesn't matter what I do or say.
No one respects me.
I must give up myself to be loved.
I can't be myself.
I must hide my true feelings.
People will hurt me.
I must always obey authority, even when it is wrong.
Nobody ever listens to me.
I can't make a difference.
It's hopeless.
Nothing will ever change.

I visited a family who had adopted a six-year-old girl, Marianne, whose birth family had abused her both physically and sexually. While we ate dinner together, Marianne said "no" to everything asked of her and refused to share, much to the embarrassment of her parents, who thought a child should not be defiant, especially in front of a guest. Since I was consulting with this family to help them with Marianne's adjustment, I explained to them that saying "no" and "mine" were important for Marianne since she had come from a family that had blatantly disregarded her personal boundaries; she had not been able to go through the stages of self-assertion and independence that children of two and four naturally experience. In fact, I explained, it is recommended as a means of preventing sexual abuse in children that blind obedience to authority not be taught.

As Marianne's parents learned to be more relaxed about her need to assert herself, they were able to recognize that her ability to say "no" and "mine" were important life skills, and were able to aid her in this process of finding her power.

On the other end of the spectrum, some parents allow themselves to be bullied by their child's anger or assertiveness, and give in to tantrums or to the child's persistence. This gives a child the message that there are no boundaries strong enough to contain his anger, needs, or behavior. Children know that adults are more powerful, so if a child is allowed to consistently be more powerful than adults, the resulting message is terrifying and confusing.

When my daughter, Lisa, was about four years old, she decided she wanted to eat a whole bag of marshmallows. While she was convinced this is what she needed ("I need to, Mommy!"), I reminded her that it was my job to take care of her, and insisted that eating a whole bag of marshmallows was not a healthy thing to do. Lisa persisted, got mad, had a fit, and the tantrum ended with her declaring that she hated me. Although it was not easy, I calmly gave her the space to be angry, but respected my own authority to know what was healthy for her. About an hour later, after she had calmed down, she told me, "Mommy, I don't really hate you. I just was so mad, I didn't know what else to say. I know you know about what is healthy to eat." Over time, Lisa was able to learn appropriate things to say when she was "so mad."

If we have caretakers who are afraid of our power while we are children, we learn to manipulate others with our power. We learn to avoid our vulnerability and to take advantage of the vulnerability of others. We become unable to acknowledge or take responsibility for the effect we have on other people.

Bill, an attractive and charming man, was referred to me by

his wife. She complained that much of his behavior showed a disregard for her needs or feelings. As Bill began to work with me, the question of his effect upon other people arose. I asked him to mindfully turn his attention to what happened inside of himself when I said the words: "You affect me." Bill had an instantaneous response which surprised us both. He was filled with a murderous rage, aware that when I said those words to him, he literally wanted to strangle me. He had never felt such a strong sense of anger before and it scared him. He liked to think of himself as a nice guy, and wanted others to see him that way. As Bill worked, he discovered that he was afraid of himself—afraid and confused by the power he had over others.

Bill had come from a family where his father was absent most of the time, and his mother was overwhelmed by the task of rearing three boys. The youngest, Bill was left to his own devices and soon discovered that if he stayed out of his mother's way, he could do whatever he wanted. When confronted by her about his behavior, Bill lied and his mother believed him, no matter how outrageous the lie. He grew up to resent his parents for letting him get away with all that he had as a child, for never seeing through his lies, for letting him run the show. Relieved that this not-so-nice part of himself had finally been seen by someone else—someone who was unafraid of it—he is now learning to practice setting limits on his behavior, and experiencing some comfort in these limitations.

Bill is fortunate. Because he truly cares for his wife, he has been able to learn to use his power in ways that allow him to experience love and a mature relationship. Because our culture rewards power without much regard for its effects, most people who abuse their power do not examine their attitudes or behavior. Indeed, many abusers hold powerful positions in our society. In order to protect ourselves and our children from being abused, we must find our own power, and teach our children to find theirs. We do this by knowing our needs and personal boundaries, expressing ourselves, disagreeing when necessary, speaking our truth, observing the effect we have on others, and allowing our children to do the same.

As you practice learning about power, you come to know your thoughts and beliefs about your effect upon others and their effect upon you. *How do you feel about your own power? What are your thoughts about your vulnerability? About the vulnerability and power of others? What attitudes do you have about limits? Do you know what your personal boundaries are? How they feel when intact? When violated? Are you aware of the boundaries, limits, and feelings of others? Do you give your power away? Do you always need to be in control? What are your attitudes about authority? Are you overly compliant? Automatically rebellious? Do you acknowledge, empower, and follow your own inner authority?*

With power comes responsibility for our actions, acknowledgment of realistic limits, and respect for our own boundaries and the boundaries of other people. A cause for celebration in my work comes when adult clients who were formerly victims of someone else's abuse of power begin to examine how they continue to allow abuse in their lives. This is a sign to me that these clients are finding their own power. While we are not responsible for the actions of abusers, we can be responsible for our own actions, making changes in our lives that protect us and others from abuse. A further step in our empowerment lies with recognizing the potential abuser that lives inside all of us, and taking steps to understand our power to affect others.

As we practice being in our power, we learn to care more deeply for ourselves and others. We learn that we can have an effect on the world, constructive or destructive. We learn that we don't have to take abuse, that we can speak our truths, and that with right use of power, we can change the world for the better.

Worth

Our experiences at previous stages of development with belonging, nourishment, and, to some extent, power give us ideas and beliefs about how others feel about our *being*. As we grow and begin to explore, assert our power, and take action in the world, a different set of questions comes to the fore, about *doing*. At this stage of our development, we are trying new things and learning new skills. We have started school, and our lives outside of our families have begun to develop. Our caretakers' responses to our efforts at this time in our lives form the basis of how we think about doing. We need to know that our ideas and creativity are valued. We need to be seen and heard. We need to know that our efforts are enough, that it is okay to make mistakes, that we don't have to be perfect. In addition to support and validation for our efforts, we also need to know that we are important simply for being, that it is okay to rest and relax, and that the process of doing is as important as the product. If in this stage we are responded to with attention, support, and encouragement, we form ideas such as:

I am a good person.
I am respected.
I can experiment and explore.
I don't have to be perfect.
People love me for who I am, not just for what I do.
My work is good enough.
I am loved just the way I am.
People pay attention to me.
My self-expression is valued.

However, we live in a culture that judges our worth largely by our achievements and that values accomplishments in some areas of life more than others. If our learning during this stage of development does not support our sense of inherent worth, we can learn, for example, that boys are more important than girls, that we get attention only when we do something outrageous, that the most important thing in life is getting straight "A"s, or that having a job is more important than caring for a family. As with the other basic life questions, there are a multitude of mental constructs which develop from our experience of worth. These thoughts, attitudes, and beliefs affect the quality of our daily experience.

Over-emphasis on achievement, for example, robs us of the present moment. We lose contact with the actual experience of our lives and live for and in the future. Years go by unappreciated as we seek what is just around the next corner. Even as we close in on an accomplishment, rather than savoring it, we're already looking to the next.

Keith came to me needing treatment for exhaustion. When we talked about his lifestyle, it became clear that providing Keith with more energy would not necessarily improve the quality of his life. He was working twelve-to-sixteen-hour days, a pattern established years ago in school. Being at the top of his class had gained Keith entry to a prestigious and competitive high school, where for the first time in his life he was surrounded by others academically stronger than he was. Keith was shocked to have to put in long hours studying and he always felt like he was behind. A time came every semester when he thought he was an utter failure, a phony who would soon be found out. This pattern was perpetuated by the fact that no one ever did find him out; he went on to a prestigious college where he graduated with a 4.0 grade point average and an ulcer.

Keith's job reinforced his school experience; his coworkers were as bright and competitive as he was. Though rewarded for his hard work by being one of the top people in his division, he never felt satisfied with his accomplishments. He feared that if he didn't keep up the hard work, someone else would outperform and replace him.

As if to balance himself, Keith had married a woman who

enjoyed the simple things in life. She did not desire more money than they had, or a bigger house, or nicer cars. She only wished that Keith had more time to spend with his family relaxing, going on outings, taking walks in the park, enjoying what he already had. Yet when Keith tried to relax, he felt haunted, as though he were forgetting something important. His idea of relaxation was to run ten miles or to read while watching TV. By the time he came to me, he was behind in several projects, utterly exhausted, and unable to sleep.

In the slow process of his recovery, Keith had to learn how to really rest. He became aware of the beliefs that kept him going at such a frantic pace:

> *If I stop, I'll miss something.*
> *If I slow down, everything will fall apart.*
> *My work is everything.*
> *People won't think much of me if I'm not the best.*
> *Things will be better when this project is completed.*
> *I'll rest in August when I have my vacation.*
> *To be good at what I do, I have to sacrifice quality time with my family.*

Keith began to see the toll these beliefs were taking, and the message he was communicating to his children about their own worth. He learned he could work with less than 110% of his energy and still do a good job. Because sitting still was difficult for him, he began to take Tai Chi, a moving meditation and Chinese martial art with no belts to earn. He is teaching himself to slow down, do one thing at a time, and let himself feel the satisfaction of his accomplishments.

In order to create a feeling of worth in her life, Jean had a different strategy. She had to have the most unique clothes, the most interesting stories, the most intense relationships, and the biggest crises. Her life was one major life change after another—to her this meant that she was "really living." She came to see me because she heard I was "a very powerful healer." Our first session together was like a whirlwind—full of big emotions, sensational revelations, and momentous insights which she provided without much assistance from me.

As we continued to work together, Jean discovered her belief that if she did not have a compelling story for me week after week, I would not pay attention to her. Of course, this was not true, but it was what she had experienced in her family, where attention was given only to enormous dramas or crises. Somehow, though, she could never make her life big enough to get the attention she needed. Some of Jean's central beliefs were:

> *No one understands me.*
> *If I'm really sick, then they'll show they care.*
> *People only pay attention to big feelings.*
> *I'm "too much" for most people.*
> *No one will ever love me.*
> *Everyone else is better (happier, smarter, prettier) than I am.*

Jean was starving for attention, but not the kind of attention she was used to getting. Jean needed to be listened to, to have understanding reflected back to her, to have the subtle aspects of her life noticed and appreciated. Like Keith, she had to learn to slow down, but her specific practice was to learn how to calm the whirlwind of emotions and events that kept her life in a constant upheaval.

Being alive is nothing short of a miracle. Each of us is born with a particular configuration of energy uniquely our own. As you practice learning about worth, you come to know your thoughts and beliefs about your own worth: the worth of your being and the worth of your actions. *Do you feel your own worth? What stops you from feeling it? Do you value the worth of others? Or are you in competition with others? Do you need to be better than others?*

Do you give your worth away to others? What do you truly value? Where did you learn your values? Do your values serve your true self? Are you able to see the richness of the present moment? Or do you live in the past or future?

Our practice of worth can bring us into alignment with our true self, and the true selves of others. As we practice cultivating a relationship with worth, we come to see the value of life—what we bring to our lives and what life brings to us.

The Role of Personal History

Our personal history—the events in our lives and what we learn from them—forms the basis of what we think about the world. It is the blueprint for our life, the foundation of our rules for living. Our life experiences inform the beliefs, attitudes, and thoughts we have about ourselves and the world around us. Our particular definitions and understandings of what a mother, a father, a lover, a partner, and a child are, of who we are, all are in some way shaped by the events of our lives, as are our understandings and relationships to hope, faith, love, freedom, commitment, responsibility, sex, money, values, the sacred, and the meaning of life. What we are told, how we are treated, and how we see others treated during our development shape our connections to ourselves, to others, and to the world.

Kate, for example, is intelligent and talented, the only child of a couple who wanted a son. In his disappointment, Kate's father believed that nothing useful could be taught this girl child. He did not believe she could have a worthwhile profession or manage money. Even though Kate took an interest in the family business, her father never encouraged it. It was not until she was almost 50 that she began to make her own financial decisions, and she still battles doubts concerning her talents, which are obvious to everyone but her father and herself.

Mick's experiences as a child with a schizophrenic mother

make it inexpressibly difficult for him, as an adult, to trust the normal emotional fluidity of his female partners, even though he is drawn to emotionally sensitive women.

Ann was led to believe that she was crazy because her ideas and goals differed from those of her parents.

Robert was taught to hate people he had never met because of the color of their skin.

More dramatic are cases involving overt physical abuse. We have read in recent years about thousands of people recovering memories of devastating sexual and physical abuse. While there may be a backlash of doubt about the veracity of these memories, there can be no doubt that physical, psychological, and sexual abuse do occur and deeply affect both the victims and the perpetrators. A writer who was physically punished as a child for speaking up can suffer agonies trying to use her gift. A man who sexually abuses children is so distressed by his compulsion he has no memory of the acts, which are rooted in his having been abused as a child.

Unhealed physical and sexual abuse can be damaging to future relationships. Abuse is passed on to the next generation, when the adult survivor, having an impaired ability to choose positive relationships, picks another perpetrator for a partner.

People live what they know. I worked with one woman who was so used to being beaten as a child she felt fortunate to find a partner who "only" abused her emotionally. Even though she was unhappy in her relationship and longed for someone to treat her kindly, it was difficult for her to imagine having something different than what she knew. Only after her first child was born was she able to understand how emotional abuse is damaging.

Our personal history never goes away—what happened to us in the past will always have happened to us. Nor is it ever truly forgotten, even if we consciously can't remember it. My work in Oriental Medicine has shown me that physical symptoms often carry within them old wounds, neglected longings, and spiritual anguish. People have begun to review their pasts in order to understand the choices they've made and for guidance in interpreting the circumstances of their present lives.

As a parent, I know that nothing brings personal history up to the forefront more rapidly than having a child. I have been shocked to hear admonitions coming out of my mouth that have little to do with my conscious belief system and much to do with what I heard as a child. In times of stress, I unconsciously take action from my own family repertoire. Until I choose to practice conscious change, my responses are informed more by what I know from my early personal experience than from my ideals, psychological knowledge and insights, and spiritual beliefs.

Along with wounds buried in our personal histories, there is also the potential that was not recognized or cultivated; there are parts of ourselves that were neglected and remain undeveloped. People scarred by their past long for tools to heal so they can begin to live lives directed by their spirits. When people come to me afraid of what they might remember about their past, I remind them that they already know what happened to them, that the knowledge of their personal history and the wisdom and the strength to survive it already exist inside them.

The wounds of our childhood can heal. In fact, it is possible that we unconsciously recreate hurtful situations in order to recall our wounds, tell our story, and find a way to wholeness. My friend, Sandra Ingerman, author of the beautiful books *Soul Retrieval* and *Welcome Home—Life After Healing*, believes that because we Westerners have such a tenuous connection to our familial and cultural histories, our personal histories offer us an important means of connection to the past and to the wisdom born of our experiences. Sometimes our personal histories come back to us in dreams, physical symptoms, flashes, insights, compulsions, or in destructive behavior. Other times, we are able to purposely remember and examine what we experienced and the beliefs that arose from those events.

In reviewing our history, we often come in touch with rightful anger, fear, and sorrow—emotions that convey to us that the abuses and neglects were meaningful. However, blaming others for what happened to us is not the purpose of mindfully spending time with our personal history. We bring our personal history to consciousness in order to truly understand our core beliefs and attitudes, to bring compassion to our limitations and longings, and to allow ourselves to heal unhealed wounds, so that we may grow toward wholeness.

In the course of this practice, we find our strength—the wisdom gained from our experiences. While what happened to us in the past cannot change, our relationship to the past and the meanings we ascribe to it does change. As our relationship to the past changes, as we practice bringing to it our insight and compassion, we discover and reconnect with qualities of ourselves left behind or forgotten, which can now be used for our spiritual growth.

Family Limitation

In the course of working with clients and their personal histories, I have discovered a useful tool to help them understand their past in a larger context. As people uncover limiting core beliefs, they may become angry at their family members for passing on such attitudes. Though anger at injustice is a natural and healthy emotion, it can also be a block, a sticking point that prevents us from growing. A larger understanding is necessary for healing and empowerment. A tool we can use to gain this understanding is the Family Limitation Map:

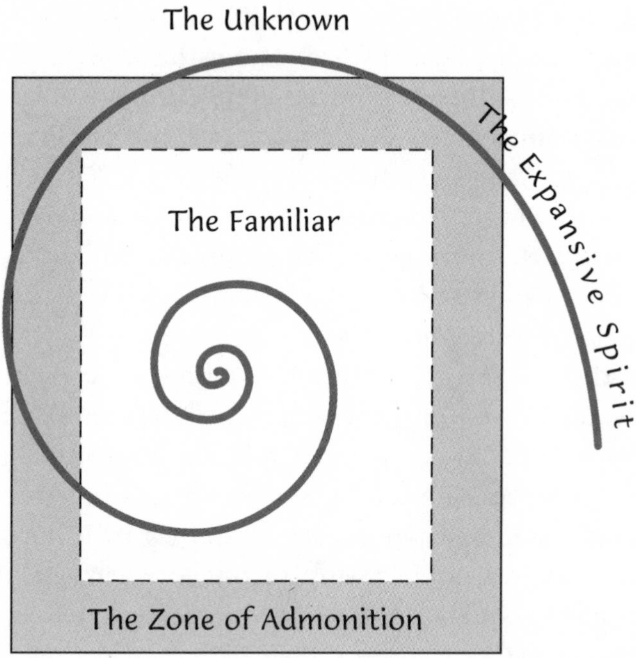

Our spirits guide us to seek wholeness. Wholeness is an expansive quality which includes limitation and moves beyond limitation. When we are born, we are naturally expansive beings—the acts of growing and learning about the world are expansive. Our families teach us what they know about the world, about ourselves—about our body, emotions, mind, spirit—and about other people. Up to a certain age, our families teach us how to be in the world. Generally, this information is passed on from generation to generation along with new information. All of this is in the box labeled *The Familiar*.

Every family has limitation. For some, it is the inability to express emotion. For others, it is that physical violence is used to handle anger. Other families are limited by their inability to express love, to tolerate differences, to connect spiritually, to be creative, to communicate deeply, to truly see each other, to be gentle, to allow for greatness, to respect boundaries, or to cope with reality. In some families, the limitation is expressed abusively; in others, through neglect. The child, intrinsically curious and expansive, will often sense there is something wrong. He or she will naturally seek out and try to go beyond the boundaries of these limitations.

Beyond the boundaries is the unfamiliar, the unknown. A child in a family of bankers wants to become an artist, or one in a family of artists wants to be a computer programmer. An emotionally sensitive child is born into an emotionally stifled family, an angry child into a family afraid of anger. Intellectual parents, who have little sense of their bodies, have a child more interested in athletics than in books. A family who has perpetuated sexual abuse for three generations has a child who actively seeks to break the cycle. This is not just rebellion; this is our natural spiritual tendency to seek the whole. In the best of all circumstances, the family sees these transgressions of the known as something positive that adds to the wholeness of the family, and the child is encouraged and protected as she explores this new territory.

But many times, something else happens. As the child approaches the unknown, the parents may issue warnings or reprimands, directly or indirectly, which prevent her from exploring the unknown. This is usually not malicious. Our parents have little experience with and are afraid of the unknown; they are trying to protect us. Or because they were abused and neglected themselves, they do not know how to give us what we truly need to be healthy and whole.

"You'll break your neck." "That's stupid." "Don't be a baby." "Nobody cares about your feelings." "It's too scary." "It's too hard." "Who do you think you are?" "You're all alone." "You're hurting us." These are all messages the child may sense as he goes after adventure, safety, respect, emotion, greatness, or any of the things his family cannot give him. These admonitions may be told explicitly to us, or they may be implicitly picked up by how we are treated or how we see others behave.

When a family cannot support exploration beyond its limitation, a space between the known and the unknown forms which I call the *Zone of Admonition*. An admonition is defined as a "warning to correct some fault; a rebuke; reprimand." I imagine the Zone of Admonition to be like something in a science fiction novel: As the explorers approach the perimeter of the space colony, alarms and buzzers sound, lights flash, a computer voice repeats, "Warning! Danger! You are leaving the safe area and entering a restricted area. You are not safe beyond this point." In families, as we approach what lies beyond the familiar limits, warnings and reproofs may be issued.

These admonitions become so well-ingrained by the time we are adults that we are usually unconscious of them. Then, we habitually avoid the unfamiliar, even when we know it contains what we want. When we work to make deep changes in our lives, as we move into the unknown, we are sure to hear some of these admonitions and feel fear and dread. I call this the *Holy Dread*, holy because it signals our surrender to the spirit's unfolding. We may experience a sense that we are violating some unwritten law, and even perhaps a sense of impending doom. These feelings are the normal consequence of expanding beyond our family limitation and crossing the Zone of Admonition into the unfamiliar.

On the following pages are a few examples of the Family Limitation Map filled out by people working on important issues in their lives:

Chris, a person longing for a relationship that works:

Committed relationship
Love doesn't last.
Most marriages are horrible.
People break promises.
You're responsible for other people's feelings. Other people are more interesting than you.
Other people's feelings are more important. Other people know better. Your ideas are stupid.
You can't trust anyone.
You have to be alone.
Those you love will hurt you.
Not losing myself, mutuality
Knowing what I want
Trust, someone who will truly love me

Jade, a woman dealing with a history of childhood physical and sexual abuse:

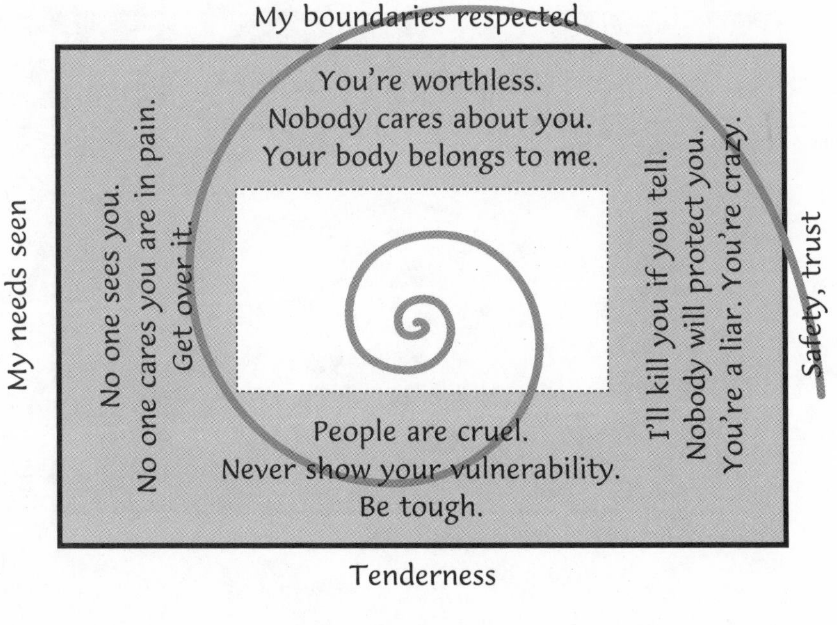
My boundaries respected
You're worthless.
Nobody cares about you.
Your body belongs to me.
No one sees you.
No one cares you are in pain.
Get over it.
I'll kill you if you tell.
Nobody will protect you.
You're a liar. You're crazy.
People are cruel.
Never show your vulnerability.
Be tough.
My needs seen
Safety, trust
Tenderness

Paul, a young, gay man struggling to accept his sexuality:

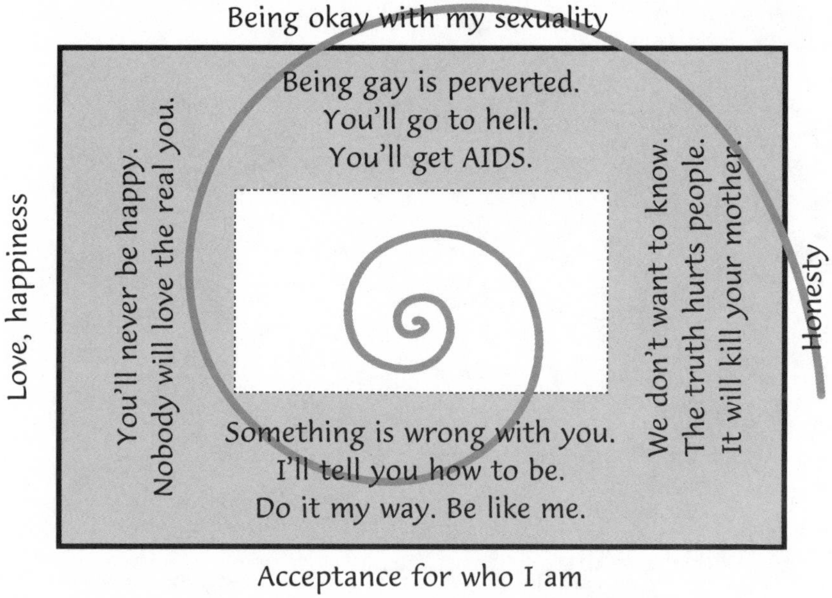

Me, as I realized that I was going to write this book:

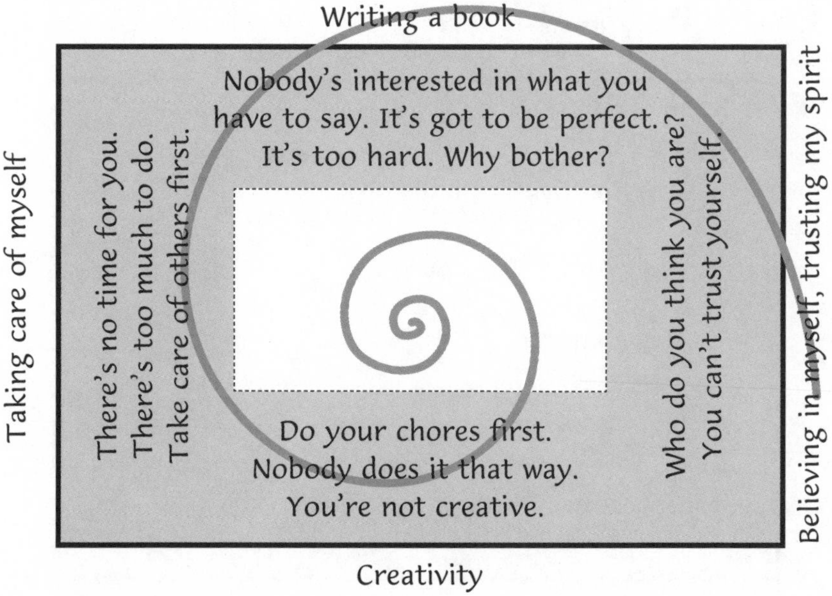

We need to realize that every family has limitation. Limitation is built into the human system. This is not necessarily bad; in a practical sense, it is necessary since we can't do everything at once. Sometimes limitation gives us something to push against. It motivates us, puts us in touch with what we want, and with the qualities and gifts our spirits want us to manifest.

Due to my own personal history there are things that, for all of my best intentions, I will not be able to teach my child. I hope she will seek them out. I hope what I tell her as she explores this unknown territory will not damage her, but will support her in her exploration. I know she will go beyond my abilities, and then we must rely on resources outside our family system.

As I learn to relate compassionately to my own family's limitation—which in different periods of its history has contained a range of dysfunctions common in our culture (alcoholism, physical, emotional, and sexual abuse, abandonment, neglect, perfectionism, racism, sexism), I see that my ancestors, usually without malice, did the best they could with what they knew. This does not mean I have not felt anger, sorrow, or despair at my family's limitations. I still do at times. But as I practice stepping out beyond my own inherited Zone of Admonition and living more and more from a sense of my wholeness, I come to feel compassion.

Compassion, "to suffer with," is rooted in our understanding and ability to be with our own suffering. Compassion occupies the bigger space of the spirit, beyond limitation. Mine has helped me to see that although my family's history has contained unhealthy elements, it has contained functional ones as well, including: love, courage, inspiration, commitment, sacrifice, perseverance, humor, curiosity, willingness to change.

People commonly state that the vast majority of us come from dysfunctional families. That may be true, but it is also true that our awareness as a culture of what is functional has changed. So an aspect of family limitation is cultural limitation. We have raised our standards, which is a good thing. We know more now; we have more resources. I am grateful for these resources, and can be understanding in my attempts to go beyond my family's limitation. I know—from my own and others' experience with this work—that even with resources, even with knowledge, this is not an easy process. It takes willingness to know all the parts of ourselves, the noble as well as the not-so-pretty. It takes willingness to go into the unknown. And more than anything else, it takes commitment to daily practice.

The Leap—Beyond Personal History

Our Relationship to Time

"The past is over; why dwell on it?" Many people react this way when they are asked to explore, or see others exploring, their family histories. In that it cannot be changed, the past *is* over. Yet time is a funny thing. Though we are alive in the present moment, how many of us really live here? Most people live in the past or the future; very few of us truly inhabit the present with our full awareness or attention. If time looks like this:

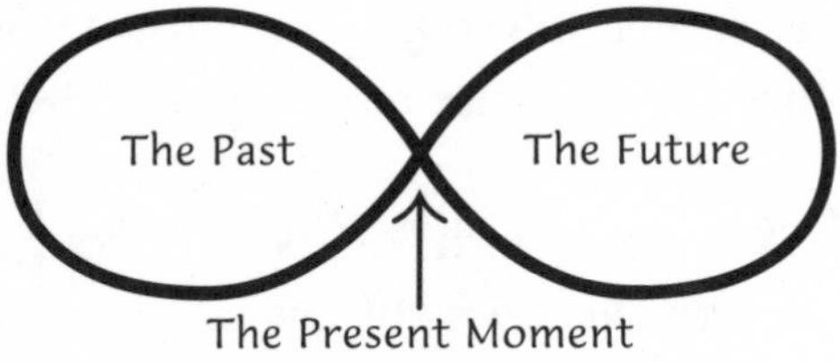

Then some of us live like this:

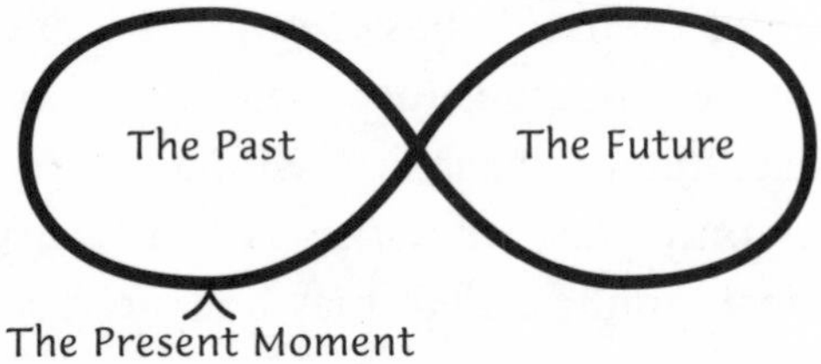

We think we are in the present moment but we are really in the past, maybe absorbed by some unhealed wound, or perceiving the present with the lens of past experience. We may even construct the present moment to look like what we know from the past.

Others of us live like this:

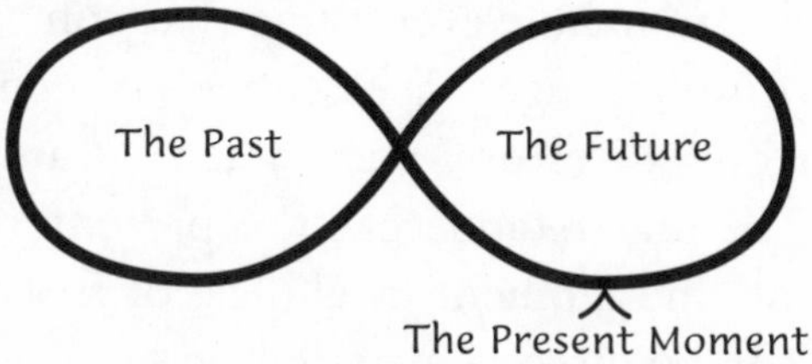

We live in what is going to happen—when I get my raise, when I go on vacation, when I finish school, when I'm through with this book, when I work through my issues, when I find my soulmate, when I paint my masterpiece—always expecting to find happiness at that point. We barely notice where we are now, and when we do, it may be only to find ourselves dissatisfied.

Either way, we miss the direct experience of our own lives. The present moment is right now. As I type this, it is the light falling through the window, the trees blooming outside, the sound of birds singing, the feel of my body against the chair, my dog lying next to me. It is your sense of yourself as you read this, your awareness of your breath, your body, your feelings, your thoughts, your spiritual longings, the room around you, other people, your place in the world.

If we take the time to practice returning to the present moment, to a sense of ourselves in the present moment, to really be with what is happening right now, a different world opens up for us. We find that the present moment has depth. We learn to tolerate, even love, ourselves and our experiences. We are filled with peace. We learn to perceive our needs and to make small adjustments to meet them. We find we are connected to everything around us. We learn that nothing bad is usually happening to us. We discover that the future unfolds before us one step at a time.

We also learn that when we plan a future while deeply connected with what we need and intend in the present, things work out better for us. Instead of trying to control everything that happens to us, we learn that we have the resources inside and outside of us to handle everything that comes up. Our relationship with time changes. We see we are connected to the past, through our ancestors, and to the future, through our descendants. We understand that the present moment is the pivotal moment, the moment of choice, of free will—the only moment that can be directly experienced.

The ability to live in the present moment does not occur on its own—it must be cultivated. We forget to be mindful and must return again and again to the practice. As we practice, with time, our ability to live deeply and directly grows. We are more fully present after one week of practice, after one year, ten years, fifty years. Don't wait to practice until you are healed, or have time off, or are done reading this book. Being in the present moment is the essence of mindfulness practice. The time to start is now.

Affirmations

Affirmations are positive statements we repeat to ourselves to counteract the effects of negative mental constructs. For example, if I believe the world is an unsafe place, I practice saying the affirmation: "I am safe." If I am tired of struggling for money, I could do the affirmation: "I am prosperous."

When I practice psychotherapy, I sometimes give my clients potentially nourishing statements such as the ones listed in this chapter in the section on Basic Life Questions. Such statements, like affirmations, may be outside of a client's current experience or belief system. I say these things to my clients not to make them feel better, but to help them study, in mindfulness, what happens automatically when they hear particular nourishing words. When we slow down enough to notice what happens when we hear a nourishing statement from outside our known experience or current belief system, we find that we have a variety of responses: rebuttals, admonitions, bodily reactions, strong emotions, memories, insights into why this can't be true, and so on.

In my experience, affirmations are valuable when we use them to study the echo—the automatic, previously unconscious response we have to the affirmation. If, for example, we spend days saying the affirmation "I am lovable" without listening for the part of ourselves that *doesn't* feel lovable, our affirmation will probably not have a long-term effect. In fact, the part of ourselves that feels unlovable may get stronger!

The part of ourselves that feels unlovable, like all of the limiting parts of ourselves, is there for a reason. These parts are usually wounded or neglected and have a story to tell. They need our loving attention. If we deny our experience, if we continue to neglect or contradict these parts, like any other kind of symptom, they will grow louder until they get our attention. These parts want healing, and healing means "to make whole." Becoming whole entails embracing the whole of our experience, all of ourselves. If we practice giving loving kindness to the parts of ourselves that feel unlovable, listening with compassion to our own grief and anger about the circumstances that created this belief, letting ourselves take in the love of others, we will soon have a felt sense of our own lovability. That felt experience exceeds any verbal affirmation we can give ourselves. Rather than pushing away or denying the parts of ourselves that hold negative beliefs, when we work to understand them, bring compassion to them, and acknowledge that they exist for a reason, we begin healing and come closer to wholeness. In time, when we hear the affirmation, it will be received and truly nourish us.

The same has proven true in my work with clients who are

trying to let go of an addiction. Colette came to me wanting to quit smoking. As I worked with her, she became aware that her smoking was related to the sadness and anger she felt over letting people walk all over her at work and in her relationships. She felt herself a pushover and became so upset in these situations, she smoked. I asked her to let me speak to the part of her that liked to smoke. As she gave that part a voice, Colette discovered, to her surprise, that this part was very fierce. In fact, it was angry and did not want to quit smoking. It was as if all of Colette's strength was hidden in the part of her that liked to smoke. If I had sided only with the part that wanted to quit smoking, we would have missed this important information and perhaps sabotaged the process by causing this part of her to battle us.

In order to help Colette reach her goal, I had to know about Colette the smoker—what she wanted, what purpose she served—so I could help her better meet her needs. Colette was happy to know she had such a strong part to herself. Her goal became to channel some of this strength into interpersonal relationships. As she learned to show her power, her need for cigarettes disappeared.

Another important aspect of working with affirmations is to practice noticing when our affirmations are true. A colleague of mine, Phil, tells this story:

I have a basic core belief that help is not available in the world, that I must do things myself. For a long time, I chose friends who believed this, too. I have been working with this belief for some time, working on changing it to the more realistic belief that "help is sometimes available." One day my car was having problems and, though I enjoy working on cars, I was not able to find what was wrong with it. I knew I needed to get someone to help me, so I walked over to the college campus near my house to look for my friend who also knows about cars. I found him and he said that although he thought he could figure it out, he didn't have time to help me until the following week because he was studying for an exam. I said okay (His unavailability did not surprise me!) and started back home. As I was walking home, I ran into another friend of mine who also knew about cars. He said, yes, he probably could figure it out, and asked me to call him to set up a time for him to work on it. By the time I got home, even though I had a pristine memory of the conversation with the friend who turned me down—what he was wearing and so on—I literally couldn't remember what my second friend had told me. Could he help me? Did he want me to call him or was he going to call me? My whole memory of this potential help was fuzzy!

A metaphor I use to describe this selective memory is *The Token Basket.* When we have a limiting belief, we have a psychic token basket that corresponds to it. If we believe no help is available, every time we are in a situation where our belief is confirmed, we unconsciously say, "Ah ha, see, I was right," and we put a token in the "No Help Basket." What we do not have is a "Help Basket;" when people help us, we have nowhere to put tokens to mark the event. The world contains "Help" and "No Help," but we forget to be mindful of the positive half of our experience.

We need to use our mindfulness to weave a second token basket for our experience. When our present reality differs from a limiting belief, we can put a token in the second basket and notice, "Oh, someone offered to help me today." "Oh, people seem concerned about me and willing to help." My colleague says, "It's not that nourishment is not available in the world; it's that we somehow have a barrier to taking it in." *We will even go out of our way, unconsciously, to construct a world that looks like our beliefs.*

If we understand that the world contains the whole spectrum of experiences, if we can create a space for the possibility of what we don't expect and allow ourselves to notice evidence of it—sometimes there's help and sometimes there's not, for example—we can have more choice about the kinds of people and situations we allow into our lives.

Not Knowing

People come to me who have been working with their personal histories for some time. What I see, as they continue to collect evidence of their wounding (retrieving memories, finding lost parts), is that they must eventually go beyond their histories into the unknown. "More evidence doesn't change the verdict," I tell them as they bring in yet another memory of a particular wound. It is as if we think that with all of our memories intact, we will finally believe ourselves. But believing ourselves is a practice; it does not come with more evidence.

We may believe that when we have all of the evidence, all of the insights, our lives will automatically change. But this is not how it works. In my experience, only a small percentage of major transformation comes from insight. What really happens is, at a certain point in our process, we come to a fork in the road: We can explore further how we didn't get what we needed, how we were hurt, and all the feelings and memories and beliefs that go with this, or we can explore what it is like to go toward what we want. Both explorations are important. But they are different.

To explore going toward what we want means going through the Zone of Admonition into the unknown. This is a scary process. As we cope with our personal histories, sometimes what happened to us as children, bad as it may have been, seems more comfortable than not knowing what will happen when we step beyond the familiar. This is also hard work because it goes beyond insight into the realm of practice. As we move into the unfamiliar, the practice is one of becoming comfortable with not knowing. The first step is to become familiar with our thoughts, feelings, and attitudes about not knowing.

Take a minute to think about how you do beginnings.

Everyone enters new situations in their own way. The way we encounter newness tells us a lot about our relationship to not knowing. Over and over in teaching, I find students who are embarrassed that they don't know what they have come to class to learn. This is especially true with the more educated students, as if they expect themselves to know at the beginning what they can only know through experience and practice. Often students will be embarrassed about letting me see them work, because they do not want me to see them make mistakes. They are afraid to ask questions when they are lost because they don't want to seem stupid even though, as a result, they are wasting me as a resource.

In our culture we are precocious. We hate not knowing. We hate being rookies. We want everything now, sometimes before we are truly ready. We go to weekend workshops expecting flashes of insight to turn us into masters overnight. I call this *The Heartbreak of Precociousness*, because precociousness doesn't allow us to take our time to experience all the steps. In other cultures, mastery only comes with practice over a long period of time.

The Practice of Wholeness is hard work because it does not come in a flash of insight. It requires taking the steps. Returning, returning, returning to the practice—no matter how we feel or what we think—is a deep commitment that takes work. But it is a very satisfying process. The changes we experience as we do this work are enlivening and empowering. As we practice, we discover that there is no need to wait to become a master in order to experience and live from our wholeness. In fact, true mind, our spirit, is available every step of the way.

Practice in the Realm of Mind

Check In

Several times a day, practice checking in with your mental constructs—the thoughts, images, memories, attitudes, meanings, assumptions, expectations, beliefs, and philosophies which may be present in you at any given moment. Notice what kinds of things you tell yourself throughout the day. What kind of attitudes do you bring to the situations in your life? What kinds of beliefs do you have toward the issues central to your life right now? What meanings do you give to the experiences you are having?

Rules

List at least ten rules, attitudes, and beliefs you learned in your family about:

belonging
nourishment
power
worth

These rules can be things you heard overtly ("You're no good." "You can be anything you want to be.") or things you learned by observing how other people dealt with these issues or how they dealt with you regarding these issues. Mark an "E" for explicit rules and an "I" for rules learned more implicitly (by observation). Keep this list in a place where you can add to it as you discover more rules.

Relationship

Draw a picture of your present relationship to:

belonging
nourishment
power
worth

Free Writing

In your journal, free write about a time when you:

belonged

felt truly nourished
felt powerful
felt your worth

Token Basket

Pick a limiting belief that you have about belonging, nourishment, power, or worth. Throughout the day make a point to acknowledge when things happen to challenge or contradict your limiting belief.

Dancing Your Needs

Without trying to control your movements, let your body freely express yourself without direction from your thoughts. Do a dance dedicated to the basic human needs of:

belonging
nourishment
power
worth

Notice what your body tells you about these basic needs.

Altars

Make an altar to belonging, nourishment, power, or worth. Find things to offer from nature or life, or make things to honor these basic human needs.

Family Limitation Map

Redraw the Family Limitation Map on the next page using a large sheet of paper.

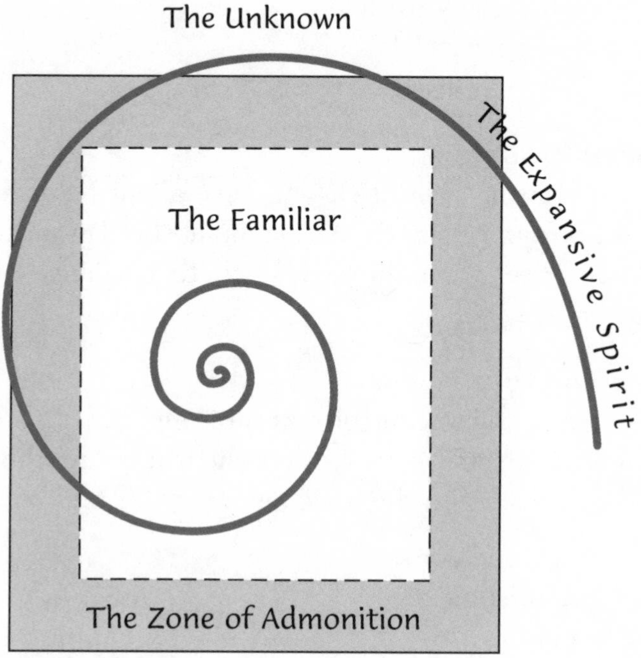

Fill in the Family Limitation Map. In the area marked "The Unknown," write a few personal goals—things you are currently working on in your life. These goals may be physical, emotional, or spiritual. (For example, finding a new job, being more creative, getting more exercise, having more joy).

In the box marked "The Familiar," describe how your family related to these goals. What role models (positive or not) existed in your family with regard to these aspirations?

In the shaded area, "The Zone of Admonition," write the rules or warnings you learned (overtly or by example) in your family about these particular goals. How do you live out these rules and warnings in your life? What messages might be more supportive? Write these messages next to your goals.

Relationship to Time

Throughout the day, notice where you are in time. Are you in the past? The present? The future?

Write your life story in the third person. (Use "he" or "she" instead of "I.") What places or situations in your past are most significant?

Write a summary of your future. What are the most important elements of your future? What do these tell you about your hopes or aspirations?

Write a summary of your present life. What are the most important elements of your present life? How do these relate to the past? How do they relate to the future?

Present Moment

Dedicate a day to returning to the present moment. When you notice yourself lost in the past or future, return to the here and now. Feel yourself in your body; breathe in and out deeply, slowly, and mindfully. Look around you. Take in the details of what is going on inside you (feelings, thoughts, sensations, aspirations, quality of well-being) and around you (light, colors, textures, sounds, and other beings).

Write a description of the here and now.

Find a place inside of you that feels at ease in the here and now. Notice what that place feels like. What does this place say to you? Practice returning to this place of ease throughout the day.

Not Knowing

Free write a page or two about "beginnings," noting what you do and how you feel when you are in new situations. List some of the physical sensations that your body experiences. List the emotions that come up for you most often, as well as some of your thoughts, attitudes, and beliefs about new situations or beginnings. List some of the rules that you learned about new situations or beginnings. Notice how these rules compare to the experiences you have when you are in new situations.

Practice Not Knowing

Practice tolerating the sensations and feelings of not knowing. Breathe in and out mindfully, allowing your awareness to settle into your body. Bring breath and loving attention to feelings that come up, making space for those feelings in your body.

Your individual thoughts, attitudes, and beliefs are a small part of the vast potential of your true mind—the unbroken wholeness that is reality. Practice calling in the element of curiosity in your life situations. Rather than jumping to conclusions, let yourself gather information. Notice your judgments and don't stop there. Ask yourself, "What else can this situation show me?"

Creativity

Invent a practice that helps you cultivate a better relationship with your mind or one aspect of your mind. Spend time doing this practice regularly.

Experiencing Wholeness in Your Mind

Turn your attention to your mind—the part of you that sorts things out, categorizes, judges, thinks, believes—or to one particular mental construct you may be aware of right now. Bring your awareness to your whole body—your feet, head, front, back, and sides—at the same time, and to your breath. Allow your body and your awareness to be a container for your mind, so that your mental constructs are held within the larger consciousness of your whole self. From the large container of your whole self, allow your consciousness to acknowledge your mental constructs. From the space of your more expanded self, bring compassion to your mind.

Chapter 4
The Expansive Spirit

Wholeness is the realm of the spirit. Rather than being separate from our bodies, our minds, and our emotions, our spirit pervades and unifies all of our parts. It is the glue that holds us in this form, allowing us to maintain the integrity of our being—our seeming individuality, our humanness—and at the same time letting us be part of the unbroken wholeness of the universe.

Spirit, from the Latin *spiritus* or breath, encompasses the part of us that embraces all that is within and outside us. Through the spirit we are vast, expansive, connected with something larger than our individual selves.

David Bohm, the physicist, describes reality as "unbroken wholeness in flowing movement." Buddhists believe the separate self does not exist. Our spirit understands this language and seeks to show us all that is beyond our self-imposed limitations. Our spirit seeks to show us our capacity to resonate within the matrix of unbroken wholeness of which everything is a part.

The word "heal" comes from the Old English word *hal*, which means "whole." In my work as a psychotherapist and a practitioner of Oriental Medicine, it has become apparent to me that all illness has spiritual as well as physical, mental, and emotional components. In Oriental Medicine, it is understood that all parts of ourselves are infused with spirit. Just as there is no separation between mind and body, so there is no separation between mind, body, and spirit.

Much of the malaise I see in my work comes from neglect of our spiritual selves. In our culture, because the spiritual dimension is often ignored, we have lost the tools for cultivating a daily relationship with it. Because of this, many people experience, along with physical or psychological symptoms, an emptiness, despair, or intense longing for connection with something bigger than themselves.

In the course of my work, I have found it increasingly difficult to ignore the spiritual dimension. I listen closely for expressions of the spirit from my clients, for it is these expressions that guide our work together. Our spirit is what enables us to survive the horrors in life, to challenge limitations, to transform ourselves. Our spiritual longing motivates us to seek help; it responds to the books, teachers, and healers that are appropriate for our growth. It is the spirit which directs our journey when we move through the Zone of Admonition into the unknown. Our spirit guides us to healing, to wholeness, to knowing our true nature.

The spiritual work I do with my clients takes the form of exploration and does not come from any particular religious dogma. Religion is a form of spiritual practice, invented by humans, but it is not spirit. Direct experience of spirit is available in all aspects of life—in nature, in human interactions, and in daily activities.

Exploration begins with an examination of our feelings, thoughts, and attitudes about spirit—where these feelings, thoughts and attitudes come from, and how they manifest themselves in our lives. Next, we form the intention to invoke spirit on a daily basis. This involves acknowledging the presence of spirit within and around us, and surrounding ourselves with elements which help us remember spirit. Finally, the work involves cultivating a form of spiritual practice that resonates with us, including perhaps a spiritual teacher and a spiritual community.

Examining Our Relationship to Spirit

As with all aspects of ourselves, our relationship to spirit is learned from our culture, family, and personal experience. Our ideas about what the sacred is, and the ways that we practice being in touch with it were taught to many of us at a very early age. Attitudes about what happens after death, about humanness, about our inherent worth are included in our religious upbringing, as are rules for how to live. Others of us have had no spiritual orientation. There was no talk of the sacred in our families.

In both cases, our family's underlying attitude toward the spirit is informed by our culture, a culture which separates the spiritual from the secular, and gives the secular an inordinate amount of time and energy. This split is evident in how we live, and in many of the symptoms which have manifested in us as individuals, families, and society.

My clients and students often find what they consider the most spiritual aspects of themselves—their inspiration, creativity, sensitivity, compassion, generosity, gratitude, wonder, curiosity, sense of justice, wisdom, and love—have not been acknowledged in their families or life experiences. Most of us feel tremendous pain and grief at having the most expansive, healthy, vibrant parts of ourselves left unrecognized and unnurtured. In fact, the most painful consequence of abuse is that spirit, the part of ourselves most capable of transformation, healing, understanding, and compassion, has been neglected.

It is important to know that our spirit—because it is, by nature, unbroken wholeness—is *never* damaged. What is damaged by abuse and neglect is *access to spirit*. It is our relationship to spirit that can be harmed. What often needs to be rebuilt—and this is the work of healing—is the connection to spirit. What need to be strengthened—and this is the role of practice—are the access roads to spirit. Fortunately, these are many and our spirit is always here waiting to be acknowledged.

Invoking Spirit

Although spirit may show up spontaneously in our lives in wonderful and miraculous ways, we can also cultivate a day-to-day relationship with it. This initially consists of setting the intention to contact spirit on a daily basis. The nature of everyday life makes it easy for us to forget about our connection with the unbroken wholeness of the universe. Because of this, we must make a commitment to remind ourselves of this connection.

One way to help with this endeavor is to surround ourselves with things from the world that *re-mind* us of the spirit. (The word "mind" has roots in the Greek *menos*, which means "spirit.") Mind refers not only to our capacity for perception, thinking, and memory, but also to our capacity for consciousness. In Oriental Medicine, the word *Shen* also means "spirit" or "mind," and refers to the creative, spiritual manifestation of energy in an individual—true mind.

In my treatment room, I display art, objects from nature, and gifts from others that remind me of the gifts of spirit—particularly beauty, mindfulness, and compassion. When I look at these objects, I am connected to the expansive parts of myself and my clients. This helps me do my work. I use the objects in my office to connect me with my consciousness or mindfulness of spirit. To me, they are actual manifestations of spirit.

In our culture, we often equate happiness with the

acquisition of material things. We typically do this in ways which are void of consciousness. We find ourselves buying things we think will bring us happiness only to find them stuffed in our closets, forgotten, a few weeks later. Instead of mindless acquisition of things which ultimately do nothing for us, we have the choice to become more mindful of the meaning of things in our lives, and surround ourselves with those things that further our spiritual awareness and true happiness.

Because spirit infuses all things in the world, anything can be a reminder of spirit. In the realm of spirit, everything is useful. When my clients find objects in the world to use in the cultivation of spirit, what they find is very individual—objects from nature, spiritual sayings, works of art, photographs of loved ones or inspiring people. For them, these things become truly sacred—infused with spirit.

I ask my clients to listen to the messages they get from these sacred objects, to consciously use these objects to remind them of these messages, and to listen for new messages as their relationship with spirit grows. Their sacred objects are reminders of courage, truth, transformation, love, compassion, generosity, justice, beauty, or of any of the thousands of manifestations of spiritual qualities in the world.

When we do this practice, we discover that our need for things is really rather simple. Instead of needing new things to make us happy, we simply need to deepen our relationship to spirit, and let the things around us remind us of this relationship. Then throughout the day, we take the time to remember our connection with spirit, and to notice how it moves in our lives, in ways both mysterious and ordinary.

Spiritual Practice

In the spiritual journey, we eventually move from spiritual insight to the need for ongoing spiritual practice. Realizing this has changed my life; this book is dedicated to it.

In the beginning, when we first make the commitment to invoking spirit in our everyday lives, we are often greeted with wonderful, lucid manifestations of spirit and with great spiritual insights which serve to reshape our lives. It seems all we have to do is ask, and spirit is there guiding us, laying the path before us. Our life may seem to be filled with magic or synchronicity, which makes us happy and motivates us to continue. Usually though, as we continue on our spiritual path, such visible and distinct manifestations of spirit are less available, and the mundane aspects of life seem to overwhelm us. At these times, we may feel despair, disconnected, and lost. We may lose our motivation to keep spirit in our lives, but it is during these times that spiritual practice is very important.

Spiritual practice done on a daily basis cultivates our relationship to spirit. Practice includes performing specific spiritual forms such as meditation or prayer, developing a relationship with a spiritual teacher, as well as becoming part of a spiritual community. While it is easy to do spiritual practice when we strongly feel spirit, it is essential, though much more difficult, to continue our spiritual practice when spirit seems less accessible.

Spiritual practice serves many purposes. It helps us cultivate spiritual attributes such as mindfulness, serenity, and faith. It helps us hold spiritual energy in our bodies and activate it in our lives. It provides a means for further spiritual development. Spiritual practice teaches us that spirit is available no matter what we feel. It is a constant—unbroken wholeness in flowing movement.

Consistent spiritual practice becomes a container which holds the normal flux of our consciousness, devotion, inspiration, connectedness, and faith. By returning, returning, returning to our spiritual practice, we learn to recognize ourselves and our path. We learn forgiveness, perseverance, courage, and commitment. Some days we easily relate to our spirituality, other days we don't, but it is regular practice that helps us deepen and mature in our spiritual life.

The Role of a Spiritual Teacher

A spiritual teacher helps us by giving us access to spiritual wisdom, by providing spiritual guidance and consolation, and by being an inspiration and role-model for us. Our spiritual teacher helps us to map out the territory of our path, showing us from his or her experience the landmarks along the way. By being a mirror for us, he or she can reveal to us our deepest and most expansive selves.

My spiritual teacher, Thich Nhat Hanh, has been practicing for over fifty years. Inspiration and comfort emanate from him due to his long and devoted practice. Through him I feel a connection with both a spiritual tradition comprised of thousands of years of practice and the practical wisdom that comes from such deep spiritual habits. His teaching focuses on bringing spirituality to everyday life, by engaging our spiritual practice with the problems that face our families, societies, and planet.

I am also inspired by the work of many Tibetan Buddhist teachers who have mapped out the territory of consciousness and transformation in detail; by teachers such as Mother Meera who are manifestations of the Divine Mother; and by the many teachers from various religions who have made strong and visible practices of the spiritual teachings of love and service. I am grateful for the teachers from my Christian roots, for planting the seed of spirituality in me at an early age. The generosity of these spiritual teachers in devoting their lives to our liberation fills me with gratitude and hope.

Spiritual Community

A spiritual community provides support for individual practitioners. Within the community, we discuss spiritual teachings, encourage practice, work out difficulties, share experiences of our spiritual journey, offer service, and build a common spiritual context for being in the world. I find that practicing with others makes my practice easier and more consistent. Spiritual communities offer strength and comfort in their numbers, reflecting the powerful energy of group commitment to spirit. Spiritual communities also offer us the opportunity and challenge of learning to live what spirit is teaching us, to release our sense of aloneness and separation, and to become part of a larger whole.

Thich Nhat Hanh's community, Plum Village, is an ongoing monastery during the year, but every summer it opens its doors to hundreds of lay practitioners from all over the world. When they arrive, they find they must create almost from scratch a spiritual community which serves as a means of practicing Thich Nhat Hanh's teachings of mindfulness in everyday life. The summer retreatants must help with meals and all of the ongoing chores of the village. At Plum Village, we learn about the role of spiritual community not in a lecture hall, but by actively practicing community. We learn as we work together about the challenges of community—how to be sensitive to the needs of others, how to work out difficulties. We learn how easy or how hard it is for us as individuals to be in community.

A functioning spiritual community enables us to learn, grow, and undergo deep transformation. We can smooth the rough edges, heal the wounds, and right the erroneous mental constructs which imperil our relationships with others. Though not easy, participating in a spiritual community provides a forum for practice.

There are many kinds of spiritual practices, spiritual teachers, and spiritual communities, just as there are many access roads to spirit. The important thing is to find ones that work for you, ones that put you in touch with the realm of spirit, and with the deep sense of happiness and peace that comes from spiritual connection. Find ones that help you to develop, grow, and deepen as a spiritual being; ones that offer you support and solace, and challenge the mental constructs which keep you from experiencing your true nature. We can learn about spirit from anyone, but an ongoing spiritual teacher is invaluable. Find someone who inspires you, who has compassion for your humanness, who practices what he or she preaches, who lives the kind of life that is, inarguably, of the spirit.

Spirit and Everyday Life

It is also important to remember that spirit is not separate from humanness and daily life. It is not separate from going to work, taking care of our children, doing our household chores, paying our bills, expressing our feelings, attending to our psychological development, and taking care of our bodies.

It is possible to cultivate what appears to be a spiritual practice while neglecting the physical, emotional, psychological, and real world aspects of ourselves, such as our relationships, families, or jobs. Dean, a client of mine, was a perfect example of this. He was a devoted spiritual practitioner for years, but was unhappy nonetheless. When he came to me he seemed lonely, depressed, and in pain. However, he could not admit this, as it was very difficult for him to feel his emotional and bodily needs.

He used his spiritual practice to leave the world—a world that he thought painful and horrific. He used his spirituality as an excuse to leave a job ("too materialistic"), to reject lovers ("not spiritual enough"), to find fault with almost everyone and everything around him. His spiritual practice often got in the way of his ability to have intimate relationships, and ironically, affected even his physical survival. He had created this "spiritual" world as a teenager, and to help him cope with an extremely painful family situation. But built into this world were unhealed parts of himself that his brand of spirituality had helped him avoid for years.

As we worked together, Dean began to realize that his spiritual life was frozen, based on attitudes and feelings that were no longer functional. He began to recognize that authentic spirituality is vibrant, expansive, and full of life. He let his true spirit heal his painful personal history, and stopped struggling with what he had called the "non-spiritual" parts of himself—his physical body and his feelings. The practice of being whole became his spiritual practice.

Michelle came to me because she had read of special acupuncture points that activate spiritual energy. Listening to her history, it became clear that she had spent much of her life as a spiritual seeker without really ever feeling satisfied. She had tried meditation and channeling, read many books on spirituality, took workshops, joined churches and various spiritual groups. It was hard for her to stick to any one practice—she gave up as soon as things felt uncomfortable or ordinary. She seemed unable to ground her spirituality in her body or in her daily life; in fact, her idea of spirituality involved leaving her body. Michelle's difficulty in sticking with her spiritual practice kept her spirituality from deepening.

Instead of using the esoteric acupuncture points that Michelle had suggested, I worked with commonly used points which served to ground her and allow her to feel herself in her body. At the end of the treatment she was radiant. She related that she felt more connected to her spirit than she had known possible. Because inhabiting her body was the experience that had been missing, she now had a true experience of wholeness, one that connected her more deeply with her spirit while still being in her body.

Because our spirit is inherently whole, it often leads us to become more well-rounded, to cultivate parts of ourselves that are undeveloped or neglected. Most of us live in one part of ourselves more than in others. Some of us are in our heads; others of us come from our feelings; others live primarily in our physicality. When I work with people, I look for the parts of them that are undeveloped and then help these parts grow. Similarly, our spirit leads us to attend to our bodies, to understand our feelings, to be mindful of our mental constructs. It seeks to make us know our completeness. This is difficult work because it is easier to stick with what we already know, even if we are miserable. Few people enjoy the feeling of exploring the parts of themselves that are hidden, neglected, or hurt. Nonetheless, cultivating wholeness, we are truly healed—"made whole."

The true measure of our spiritual practice is the extent to which we can be in the world, embrace our humanness, and bring all of ourselves to our spiritual journey. Human spirituality does not require leaving the world. It entails learning how to *bring spirit to the world.* It is, I believe, the essence of our work—to understand form, to understand limitation, and to embrace and embody spirit within form and limitation. Our work is to learn to tolerate the sensation of spirit in our bodies, to allow spirit to inform our emotions and our minds, and to know form as a miraculous conduit for spirit, and spirit as a magnificent matrix for form.

Practice with the Expansive Spirit

Check In

Practice checking in with your spirit every day or several times a day. Take a few moments to stop and return your awareness to your spirit—your spiritual aspirations and spiritual gifts. What is it like for you as you bring your awareness to your spirit? What message is your spirit giving you? How does your awareness of spirit change how you go through your day?

Definition

Fill in the blank:

Spirit is____.

Relationship to Spirit

Draw a picture of your relationship with your spirit.

List ten attitudes or rules you learned about spirit from your family.

Tell the story of your spiritual history in the third person (using "he" or "she" instead of "I").

List people, things, and experiences that have nurtured your access to spirit. How have they done this?

List people, things, and experiences that have damaged your access to spirit. How have they done this?

Describe the role of spirit in your daily life.

Describe the relationship to spirit to which you aspire.

Invoking Spirit

Surround yourself in your home, office, and car with "sacred objects"—things that remind you of spirit and spiritual qualities. Listen for the messages you get from spirit through these things.

Dedicate a corner of your house to spirit and spiritual practice.

Altar

Make an altar to your spirit. Keep this altar alive by developing a relationship to it. Visit it regularly; add to it or take from it as your relationship with spirit changes and develops. Let the altar speak to you; listen to what it tells you.

Honor

Take a day off in honor of spirit. See where spirit takes you. Or dedicate a workday to spirit. Notice how this changes your work.

Spirit Within

Describe what it is like when you are in touch with spirit within you. How do you feel in your body? What kinds of emotions do you have? What are your thoughts, attitudes, and beliefs? What qualities does spirit within you have? How does spirit act through you and express itself in your life situations?

Throughout the day, take the time to get in touch with spirit within you. Allow spirit within you to speak to you and listen to what it has to say. Allow spirit within you to act through you.

Spiritual Practice

Spiritual practice is what we do on a daily basis to cultivate our relationship to spirit.

Describe the role of spiritual practice in your daily life.

Dedicate a portion of your day—even ten minutes can be enough—to some kind of spiritual practice. Some examples: meditation, prayer, contemplating nature, cultivating your spiritual gifts, invoking spirit, visiting your altar, going to church, doing service, creating ritual, reading spiritual works, connecting with the larger world around you, doing the exercises in this book.

Explore spiritual practices that are unfamiliar to you. Try one that calls to you in some way.

Creativity

Invent a practice that helps you cultivate a better relationship with your spirit. Spend time doing this practice regularly.

Experiencing Wholeness with Your Spirit

Turn your attention to your spirit. Bring your awareness to your whole body—your feet, head, front, back, and sides—at the same time, and to your breath. Allow your body to be part of your spirit—your spirit's physical expression. Know that your spirit is woven into every cell of your body and is not separate from any part of you. Experience what this awareness feels like in your body.

Part 2
The Elements of Transformation

When I first began practicing psychotherapy and Oriental Medicine, I noticed that while many people made changes, not everybody, not even a majority of them, made what I would call genuine core transformations. Everyone had insights. Everyone was able to identify their needs, to understand their problems, to see what changes were necessary, but not everyone made the kind of changes that lasted beyond insight. Only a portion of my clients transformed their insights into actions and responses that helped them live their aspirations. For the people who did make the jump, new actions and responses became second nature, fully integrated into their daily lives.

So I began to ask, "What is psychological or spiritual transformation? What do the people who are able to make significant changes in their lives do that the other people don't do? What are the elements of the transformation process?" The word "transformation" comes from the Latin *transformare* which means "to form over." After years of observing and participating in this process, I noticed that people who underwent deep transformations felt as if they were indeed new people. I have found that the transformation process contains certain consistent elements which occur in the lives of those people who have made remarkable progress in their spiritual and psychological work. These next chapters are dedicated to what I've discovered.

Chapter 5
The Door to Transformation

Insight brings us to the door of the transformation process. In psychology, insight is the awareness of one's own mental attitudes and behavior. The tools to insight are mindfulness and meaning.

Simply put, mindfulness is the practice of being aware of what we are doing, feeling, thinking, and saying in the present moment. Our mindfulness is a neutral witness that watches without judgment. We can apply our mindfulness to our physical bodies, our emotions, our mental constructs, and our spirits. We can uncover the relationships we have to these elements of our wholeness, and come to understand the basis of these relationships.

Meaning forms the basis of the relationships we have with ourselves, the world, and the events in our lives. The meanings we give to events, both internal and external, are important in determining what we do with these events. Meaning is a powerful tool; it affects how we feel about ourselves and the world around us. Research has indicated that the meanings we give to what happens to us can have a dramatic effect on our health and well-being.

Meaning is also personal. We see the world through our own special filters. Many of us have experienced the retelling of an event in our family history through the eyes of different family members and been shocked to see how differently each person remembers the same incident. Our own personal meanings or interpretations contribute to how we see and remember. We accumulate the meanings by which we define our whole lives.

Deluged with information, many of us have lost the ability to glean meaning from the events of our lives. We can't read our own minds, hear our bodies' signals, or understand what other people are really saying to us. In many people, this loss leads to numbness, denial, and despair. They may come to psychotherapy to "find themselves"—to uncover their true selves, and to cultivate a relationship with themselves that helps them live full lives. Many of us come to therapy because the ways we live our lives no longer feel satisfying or are downright destructive.

While much of psychology is geared toward helping us find insight, very little core transformation comes solely from insight. Often in the course of therapy, we have marvelous insights—know how and why we do things—and we still do not change. Insight is simply the first step in the transformation process. Insight gets us in the door of transformation; it is our admission ticket.

Denial

Denial is the opposite of insight. It is a psychological defense by which we keep ourselves from knowing what is really going on inside or right in front of us. When we are in denial, the aspects of ourselves which allow us to be mindful and find meaning—our senses and bodily sensations, feelings, thoughts, and spiritual guidance—are not available to us. Denial is a useful tool when it helps us cope with information that seems too painful to bear, or to deal with pain which cannot be adequately addressed or healed at the time. But in a healthy, functioning system—one which welcomes new information—denial is retained only until we find the resources to cope with our pain. In the light of this new information, denial no longer feels comfortable, and the pain of separation from ourselves becomes more distressing than our perceived pain of the truth.

But much of our culture is based upon denial, and does not allow us to function in a natural or healthy way. In its cultural guise, denial can be a form of dishonesty, which keeps us confused and childlike and robs us of our power as mature adults. We see examples of this kind of denial everyday. The newspapers are full of denial of the obvious: the tobacco industry saying that cigarettes are not harmful, government officials lying about their involvement in illicit activities, Hollywood executives denying that the constant barrage of graphic violence in movies and on television affects us and our children. We are asked to believe these official statements, ignoring our own senses and inner wisdom. We become so accustomed to this denial that we do not see how this constant diet of lies feeds our feelings of hopelessness and disempowerment.

We carry this cultural denial into our families where the popular practice of "ignoring the elephant in the living room" is passed on to our children, undermining their sense of truth, intuition, inner guidance, and hope. We have grown to believe that "what we don't know won't hurt us." We don't see our denial as a defense but the normal, socially correct way of being in the world. We believe if we don't allow ourselves to see or think about what is really going on, we will not have to feel it or deal with the consequences. If we ignore the fact that our spouse is an alcoholic, for example, or that we or our children are being abused, or that we are really unhappy in our work, we believe we can avoid feeling this pain. But our spirit knows the truth and will somehow communicate this information to us.

We feel it with general malaise, a lack of energy, numbness, powerlessness, or hopelessness. We find ourselves acting out in ways that are compulsive, angry, and destructive. We develop physical symptoms. We experience constant anxiety. We forget our dreams and aspirations.

Children cope far better with the truth, if it is told with sensitivity to their needs and stages of development, than with denial or lies. Children know something is going on in their families, whether or not they know all the details, by the general atmosphere created by the events in their family life. Children from families with addictive patterns, or where the parents are unhappy with each other, or where one child is blamed for all the problems, or where there is ongoing abuse, feel that something is wrong. A child can take on the unspoken dynamic and act it out for the whole family with nightmares, tantrums, physical symptoms, fearfulness, unruly behavior, withdrawal, or by being extra good.

I saw a heart-wrenching example of this while I was working in an agency that counseled children and their families. One of my clients, Danny, an eight-year-old boy, had cancer and lived with his father who was addicted to drugs. Because the father could not be counted on to bring Danny in for his chemotherapy treatments, members of our staff picked him up and drove him to the treatment center. One day, when I arrived at his house, Danny's father was passed out in the living room. Usually cheerful and upbeat, today Danny was depressed. We talked about how sad he was for his father, that he knew his dad did drugs, even though his dad tried to hide it from him. Danny talked about how he knew he might die from his cancer and wished his dad had more time for him. I asked Danny whether he wished his dad would come with us when he went for his chemotherapy treatments. Danny's reply moved me to tears: "I'd love it if my dad came with me, but I can't ask him to. It's so hard for him to see me like this. I think it would kill him."

Children are naturally good-hearted. They want to help. Many of us, as children, took on our family problems, worked hard to be good, or felt that we had to be the adult in the family, so our families would be better and our parents would be happier.

Children are usually relieved when the truth is openly discussed because it helps them bring meaning to what they have been sensing all along. While children don't need to know all of the gory details of adult problems, simple acknowledgment that "mommy or daddy is having a hard time, it's not your fault, and we are working to change this" can be enough to reassure them, and to free them to be children.

In more severe cases of familial denial, the child is asked to participate directly in the denial or lies. This can be confusing or devastating for a child, as it undermines his or her sense of what is fair and right, making the child a pawn in a dysfunctional system and teaching him or her that it is better to lie. The child also learns that there is no hope for coping with the truth or changing what needs to be changed.

Our denial can be minor ("I'm okay, I'm just under a lot of stress") or severe ("I am not an alcoholic.") But no matter the level, denial is a form of self-protection that ultimately does not work because it cuts us off from parts of ourselves, keeping us from cultivating the resources and developing the skills to truly deal with life.

Typically, the basis of our denial is fear. We may be afraid that if we face the truth, we won't be able to bear it. While fear of the unknown is normal, denial-based fear comes from our experiences of how the truth was handled in our personal histories. We may be afraid to know ourselves—what we actually feel and think, and who we truly are. We may have been taught that the truth is bad, or that we are bad for having our feelings, thoughts, bodies, or our unique manifestations of spirit. We can run from ourselves, but we can't hide. We are always with ourselves; our efforts to conceal parts of ourselves from ourselves and others only drains us of the energy we need to fully live our lives.

Once we undo the denial and air the family limitations we are able to pass through the Zone of Admonition (see *Chapter 3*). We feel relieved and empowered to finally know the truth of our situation. We discover parts of ourselves that have been imprisoned, waiting to be contacted, developed, and loved. We are now free to find the many resources available to help us deal with what is true, both inside and outside of ourselves.

Garbage

I hear often from my clients when they first come to me: "I want to get rid of my (psychological or emotional) garbage." I ask them, "What do you want to do with your psychological garbage—throw it away? What happens when you throw away real garbage; where does it go? To the dump. What happens to garbage in the dump?"

An archeologist, William Rathje*, began studying the contents of landfills in 1987. He found, contrary to popular myth, that our garbage does not biodegrade. Digging with machinery deep into landfills, he found whole steaks from the early 1970's, a twenty-year-old mound of guacamole, raked leaves from 1964, and countless perfectly preserved hot dogs! Without air circulation, fluid, and regular mixing, the garbage that we throw into landfills goes nowhere, piling up in the earth.

The only thing to do with garbage, really, is to compost it (chop it up, add fluids, and give it air) or recycle it. This is precisely the process of transformation. Without carefully and attentively applying the energy of transformation, what we call our "psychic garbage" pollutes us, others, and the earth.

---

* William Rathje, "Once and Future Landfills," *National Geographic*, May 1991, pp. 117-134.

In reality, no part of ourselves is garbage. There are parts of ourselves that are undeveloped, parts which are wounded and need help healing, parts that are neglected and need attention, and parts which no longer serve us. But these parts are all there for a reason, having served us at one time, and their energy can be used for change. Even our pain, when transformed, offers us the gifts of wisdom, knowledge, and compassion. We can learn to listen to all the parts of ourselves, to cultivate a deep relationship with them. They tell our story, the story of our journey toward wholeness. While we can't be anyone else but who we are—with our strengths and limitations—how we behave because of our parts can be made conscious; then cultivated, or transformed.

Inviting All the Parts of Ourselves

Once we have agreed to come out of denial, to find mindfulness and meaning, the next work at the door to transformation is inviting all our parts to participate in our healing. The basic elements of our wholeness are our bodies, our emotions, our minds, and our spirits. These parts of ourselves contribute wholeheartedly to our transformation and healing—we cannot truly change without them. Transformation means "to form over," and transformation that is integrated and lasting involves a different sense of ourselves in our bodies, a change of heart, fresh attitudes, thoughts, beliefs, and feelings, and a reconnection and active relationship with spirit.

This step of allowing all our parts to become visible or conscious is often difficult because of our legacy of denial, abuse, and neglect. We have been taught to think of some parts of ourselves as good and other parts bad, or best left alone. We may love our bodies but not our feelings. We may live in our feelings but cannot clearly use our minds. We're in our heads but we forget to feel. We spend time "being spiritual" to the neglect of our bodies or emotions. We may like our strength but hate our vulnerability. We love our intelligence but we dislike ourselves when we make mistakes. We appreciate our assertiveness but we are not so sure about our sensitivity. We feel uncomfortable with many qualities in ourselves that are childlike, vulnerable, uncertain, unskilled, undeveloped, or needy, because these parts may not have been treated well by our caretakers, whose attitudes and examples of neglect and abuse get passed on to us.

Just like an athlete who warms up using only the stretches which are the easiest for his body to do, we dislike visiting the parts of ourselves that are pained, troublesome, neglected, or wanting. We like to feel competent and sure of ourselves. Unfortunately, if we stay only within our competence, we limit ourselves to a narrow range of living.

Being willing to invite all parts of ourselves into the healing process is an important step at the threshold of transformation. We know our wholeness is made up of our bodies, emotions, minds, and spirits, and we welcome these parts in. We know there are parts of ourselves that are hurt, neglected, undeveloped, unskilled, and vulnerable, and we make room for these parts. We practice welcoming ourselves—all parts of ourselves—greeting them with the words of Primary Contact: *You are here; you are welcome; I am here with you.*

Through this practice, we become aware of how we have been torn apart, fragmented, led away from our wholeness. We feel the pain of this separation and experience the emotions involved in this pain—fear or shame of our hidden parts, anger and sadness for our plight, joy and curiosity at the unfolding process, and compassion for ourselves and the human condition. We begin to understand how we really think. We invite our attitudes, beliefs, and "mental chatter" into our consciousness. We listen to what we have to say about our personal history, needs, aspirations, and wounds.

We have now crossed the threshold, entrusting our spirit to lead us on this amazing journey toward wholeness.

Giving Up the Fight with Ourselves

Most of us are accustomed to a war raging on inside of us. Daily I witness people fighting parts of themselves they feel are bad, lazy, irrational, weak, or stupid, without really knowing these parts, where they came from, or what purpose they serve. Most believe if they don't battle their baser instincts—thwart their desires, bury their feelings—they will be out of control, lost, or doomed to a life of evil.

While I believe self-control is a useful skill that we want in our repertoire of responses, my experience in working with people over the years has shown me that few people are truly evil. Most people are lost, cut off from access to spirit. Most are influenced and distracted by messages that have led them away from knowing their true selves. Throughout our lives, we internalize these messages: "You're lazy." "Men want just one thing." "You're too sensitive." "You'll never get anywhere with those ideas." "What you want is crazy." "You 'gotta' be tough." "You're too serious." "You're too frivolous." "People who are not like us are bad." "You must be practical." "You're always in your head." "Women are irrational." "Other people are what's important." "It's better not to depend on anyone."

We begin to think these ideas are who we are and what the world is about. Because none of us is just one of these qualities, we assign them to different parts of ourselves. The sensitive part gets assigned to our artistic nature and is pitted against our practical, logical side. Our heart is pitted against our head. Our need for independence fights our desire for connection. Each of these parts has rules and ideas about the best way to be, so they battle within us, pulling us one way then another. Sometimes the stronger parts completely cut us off from the less developed parts. The battleground often resembles our family environment and reflects its limitation.

This battle takes place below the level of consciousness. Its manifestations appear as ambivalence, indecision, chaos, fear, anxiety, never completing anything, never starting anything, inability to take action, lack of commitment, blame, projection, bigotry, confusion, frustration, arrogance, self-hatred, destructive behavior, violence, depression, or despair. We are usually unaware of the underlying causes, beliefs, and attitudes which fuel these behaviors.

When we bring this battle to our consciousness we find mental constructs such as:

I can't believe I'm 45 years old and I still don't know what I want.
I thought I dealt with this issue.
I'll never be good enough.
I should be able to do this for myself.
My process is too slow; it's not happening fast enough.
Why do I have to feel these feelings?
I should know better.
I shouldn't feel this way.
I hate this part of me; I wish it would go away.
I'm trying to transcend my anger (fear, sadness, or other "negative" emotion).
I'm afraid of what I'm going to find inside of me.
If I just banish these thoughts, my life will be better.
I've gone beyond that.

When I hear these statements from my clients, I know they are manifestations of the fight they are having within themselves. My clients have invited the parts of themselves in and they don't like what shows up. Statements like these reflect the idea that there is something wrong with us, that we are somehow broken and need to be fixed. They represent our shame with ourselves—our misguided perfectionism. These are parts we may not like, parts we may be afraid of, that were hurt and don't trust that they now are welcomed and can be healed, parts we are ashamed of or embarrassed by, or that are undeveloped or unskilled. We may even be afraid or ashamed of our best qualities, especially if these qualities were troublesome for or neglected by the people in our lives. I have worked with people who were at odds with their power, sensitivity, compassion, intelligence, artistic abilities, strength, intuition, happiness, or desire to help others. It is as if they were keeping these qualities a secret to ward off hurt, instead of cultivating them and finding empowerment, support, and respect.

Instead of acknowledging that transformation is a process which naturally unfolds as we do our spiritual work, these beliefs infer that transformation happens only when we possess certain qualities. Like parents who expect their children to exhibit more mature behavior than they themselves are exhibiting, we expect ourselves to change on the basis of how we think we should be, or how we think the transformation process should take place. And when things are not how we think they should be, we assume there is something wrong with us or the process. Treating ourselves as though we do not need to be fixed, but only guided, assisted, or allowed to develop, is a practice that teaches us patience, compassion, and steadfastness.

The first step in this practice is to acknowledge the battle within us. In the course of writing this book, I have been constantly aware of the part of myself that had a certain idea about how the writing process should go. I hear my self-criticism when I don't keep to my schedule. Some days the writing has been easy; other days I've resisted it, procrastinated, climbed the walls. My friend Sandy, the author of several books and one of my allies for support and encouragement in writing this one, called one day when I was in the middle of a writing crisis. I had not been able to write for several weeks and felt guilty and hopeless. She gave me some of my own best advice, telling me not to fight with myself and to trust that even though I am not writing, if it is my intention to write, some part of me is working on the book. With her help, I practiced trusting my internal schedule for writing, instead of the one I had fabricated in my mind. I found writing came more easily, and I wasted less time and energy berating myself.

I ask the students at the beginning of some of my classes to make a simple statement, without a lot of explanation, about who and where they are right now. As each student speaks, the rest of the class just listens. I ask them to refrain from offering condolences, advice, their own stories, or congratulations. We all practice just sitting in compassion with where each person is—knowing there is nothing to fix or add, that who and where the speaker is right now is okay. Members of the group make statements such as:

I'm excited because I set a date for my wedding.
I'm struggling with my addiction to cigarettes.
My grandmother died; she was the member of my family I was the closest to. I'm very sad.
I just found out my lover has AIDS.
I don't know what I am going to do after I graduate. Everyone is pressuring me to know what to do next, but I just don't know yet.
I feel so open to everything that is happening in my life right now. It's like life has become magical.
I found a lump in my breast. I really want to avoid dealing with it.
In therapy, I'm working with memories of sexual abuse. It's overwhelming sometimes.
I'm in love!
I'm really confused about my life right now. I feel stuck—it's so frustrating.
I'm pissed off at my girlfriend. I really don't feel heard by her.
My work is going really well; I'm finally learning to feel my power.

The rest of us just listen mindfully and absorb where each person is. At first, this practice is difficult. We think if we are not responding demonstratively in some way we are cold or uncaring. We practice not stopping at any judgments about what is being said. In mindfulness, we notice that we naturally have judgments, feelings, or impulses to take some kind of action, but we don't have to give these entities any energy beyond noticing them. We don't need to get stuck in them and miss what is really happening with the person in front of us. We can say to ourselves, "I am having a judgment (feeling or impulse)" and return to being present with the person. We can just allow what is happening for that person to simply be.

The result of this practice is powerful. Week after week, we tell each other where we are. Some of us are doing well; others are struggling. Some of us change quickly in our process, others much more slowly. Sometimes we are elated, other times, stuck. We tell the group what has inspired or thwarted our process during the week, and the group holds the attitude that there is nothing to fix, creating space for trust in our spiritual unfolding.

As a result, a deep connection forms among the members of the group. We learn how to tolerate each other, and then how to be present for each other in a deep way. This helps us contact the spirit in each person. We learn that life is change, sometimes painful, other times pleasurable. We learn to trust ourselves, and to not feel shame about who and where we are. Because we practice giving this presence and deep listening to others and receiving it from others, we learn that we can give the same to ourselves and receive it for ourselves from others.

The single most important thing that 100 per cent of the people who make core transformations do is this: *they give up the fight with themselves.* These people come to a point in their healing process where they feel that who and where they are *right now* is okay, even though it is unfinished, imperfect, in process.

This self-acceptance and forgiveness is a momentous occasion in healing.

From this point—the place where we are no longer fighting with ourselves—our transformational journey becomes very different. It does not always become easier, but it does become more joyful and more engaging. We come to trust in ourselves, in the unfolding of our lives, and in our spirit. We use our energy to work with rather than fight with ourselves. When my clients come to this place, I rejoice, because I know they can more easily use the tools and resources available both within and around them.

Your life has brought you to this moment, reading this book, in your current situation. You may like some things about where you are; some things you may not like. But you are here. You are who and where you are right now, and this is all that you can be *right now.* While you can to some extent consciously direct where you want to take your life from here, "You can't get where you're going until you know where you are."

The practice of knowing and accepting who and where you are right now is the practice of compassion for yourself. It is a pivotal point in the transformation process. If you want to take yourself somewhere else in your life, if you want to truly change, you must bring yourself with you—all of yourself—your mistakes, wounds, personal history, visions, hopes, gifts, and aspirations. Knowing and accepting who and where you are right now frees you to be with yourself. It helps you trust and align yourself with your spirit, your wholeness—the expansive aspect of your being that directs your journey.

Practices at the Door to Transformation

The Door to Transformation

Contemplate a transformation you would like to make in your life. This may be a change in some external circumstance, or an internal change—physical, emotional, mental, or spiritual. Write your intention for transformation down.

What will be different about your life when this transformation occurs? Name the qualities that your life will have.

What does making this transformation mean to you? What does not making it mean?

Meaning

Name five major events in your life that you consider positive. For each one, write a sentence that summarizes the meaning that event has for you. Do the same with five events you consider negative.

Denial

List the ways your family of origin used denial.

List the ways you use denial. What purposes does your denial serve? How does your use of denial affect the goal for transformation you stated above? Does it block or slow transformation? Ease it?

Inviting All Parts of Yourself

Thinking of your goal for transformation, list five parts of yourself that can aid you in achieving this goal. (These parts can be physical, emotional, mental, or spiritual.) Pick the three that are most important.

List three that hinder or get in the way of achieving your goal. Pick the two that are most important.

On a large piece of paper draw a large circle. Divide the circle into five equal parts as if cutting a pie. In each piece of the pie, draw a picture of the parts you named above. (Three parts which help you achieve your goal for transformation, and two parts which seem to hinder you.)

For each picture, write down what you are:

doing?
saying?
wanting?
needing?
avoiding?

Giving Up the Fight with Yourself

For each of the five parts named in your pie drawing above, write one word that summarizes your relationship with that part. Assuming that giving up the fight with yourself is a crucial part of the transformation process, what kind of relationship would you like to have with these parts?

For each part, write a story about how that part came to be, and what its job is.

Write a dialogue between two parts that seem in conflict. Let these parts discuss the transformation you want to make; have them ask each other questions, be curious about each other, get to know each other better. Have them ask each other what they can do for each other. What kind of nourishment does each of these parts need? What kind of nourishment is each capable of giving?

Practice Being Who and Where You are Right Now

Once a day, make a simple statement to yourself about who and where you are in your life. (See examples on page 134.) Don't try to explain or make excuses; let the statement stand on its own and be okay as it is. Notice what you tell yourself about who and where you are.

Practice letting other people be who and where they are right now.

Altar
Make an altar to giving up the fight with yourself.

Creativity
Invent a practice that helps you at the door to transformation—to come out of denial, to find mindfulness and meaning, to give up the fight with yourself, to be who and where you are right now. Spend time regularly doing this practice.

Chapter 6
Getting Stuck

The hardest point in the process of transformation is the place where my clients feel stuck. They feel they aren't going anywhere, that nothing is happening. In my experience, all people who have made core transformations in their lives come to a place like this. How they handle feeling stuck has an effect upon the outcome. Sometimes our feeling stuck can arouse our curiosity. We want to know what is going on, how we got here, and what we can do about it. Other times, we experience depression, frustration, and despair—times I call true *stuckness*, because we don't yet have the automatic responses with which to offer ourselves compassion and curiosity.

If we cultivate the habit of approaching our stuckness with compassion and curiosity, we can learn what it has to teach us. We find that sometimes we are stuck because we need to accept where we are, to stop a while and integrate. Or we are stuck because we are fighting with ourselves and the unfolding of our process. Or there is some part of us that needs our attention before we can go on. Or we simply don't have a resource we need in order to change.

When a client complains of feeling stuck, I pay close attention because, frustrating as it can be, being stuck indicates great potential for transformation. I have come to liken this point in the process to "going through the eye of the needle." It is a difficult place because we feel like change is impossible. We feel like giving up and must reckon with hopelessness and despair.

But I know from experience that when we reach this place—if we recognize and acknowledge it, learn from it, call in our resources, and hang in there—we make it through the eye of the needle and are released into the more expanded space that landmarks true transformation.

Our Relationship to Change

Life is full of change. Our relationship to change affects the meaning that it will have in our lives. For some of us change is so frightening we would rather remain unhappy than experience it. We are stuck in unsatisfying lives because we do not know if we can handle, or if we are worthy of, circumstances being different. We project into the unknown all our fears based on negative past experiences or future predictions.

On the other end of the spectrum are those of us who fill our lives with change because we are afraid of stability. Our lives are in constant flux with one crisis or major life change after another. We make sure we don't let ourselves get too comfortable because we have given stability a negative meaning.

We learned to be the way we are because it was the best way to be at the time, given the resources we had. Resistance to change is the result of our protective mechanisms doing their jobs. These protective parts know that if we move toward transformation into the unknown, we will have to cross the Zone of

Admonition, a potentially painful place. We will have to hear the old warnings again and re-experience when we first heard those messages. We may even have to feel the pain again. The role of our protective parts is to keep us from this pain—even if the source of the pain is no longer operational.

The ways we resist transformation are many: we procrastinate, get distracted, engage in fantasy, become impatient and perfectionistic, overwhelm ourselves by taking on too much at once, or create crises which divert us from our goals. We may be unconsciously drawn to other people who reflect our resistance for us. Underlying this resistance are our fears of the unknown and the messages at the Zone of Admonition, which feed our limiting beliefs about ourselves and our possibilities, and keep us from moving into the unknown, the realm of transformation.

However, our spirits compel us to seek wholeness, and therefore cause us to pursue what is missing in ourselves and in our lives. Sometimes transformation comes from making major changes in our life patterns; other times transformation comes when we can ground ourselves and find stability. As we move toward transformation, we feel less comfortable, even if we are moving toward something we want. Our lives are organized around what is familiar—what we learned about life in our families and through our experiences. We are generally more comfortable with what is familiar than with the unknown. The journey of transformation takes us away from that comfort zone.

Most people who undergo core transformations in their lives enter a period of destabilization. Here, the way they are used to being no longer works or feels good. Yet the new way of being is not yet established, and feels awkward and tentative—uncomfortable—to most people. Our ability to tolerate the discomfort created by change has a direct effect on the outcome. When we can't tolerate this discomfort, we get stuck: not satisfied with where we are and not able to change.

Our practice here is to become aware of our relationship to

change, and conscious of how we act out this relationship. It helps to bring mindfulness to the core beliefs that form our relationship to change, to know where these beliefs came from and whether they serve us.

It is also helpful to know that change often happens in stages—in its own time. First, you are in denial; you don't know that you need to change. Second, you are aware you've done something you would like to do differently next time. Third, you are aware you are doing that something right now, but you don't know how to stop yourself because it is a habit. Fourth, you see yourself about to do that habitual thing but you make a different choice. Finally, that behavior is only one of many options and you don't choose it. Each of these stages takes time. It helps to practice being patient with ourselves and to cultivate a relationship with the discomfort that accompanies change.

Healing Despair

The Wall—Recognizing Our Despair

Fear of our despair is a strong obstacle to the transformation process. We don't like feeling our despair. We don't like thinking about it or telling other people about it. It's even a secret we keep from ourselves. Feeling despair makes us feel "crazy," "weak," and "out of control." Of all the parts of ourselves we must learn to stop fighting, this is often the most challenging. We would much rather ignore it.

Yet nearly every person I have worked with has found themselves having to deal with despair in some way. Until we make our despair conscious—begin to know when we are in it, understand how it affects us and what beliefs go with it—we have little opportunity to recognize it, become aware of the role that it plays in our lives, and learn what resources to bring to it.

I do an exercise in my classes that helps us recognize what our stuckness looks like and to understand the automatic, unconscious ways in which we handle it. I call this exercise *The*

Wall, and it was inspired by watching my clients being stuck. After students hear about this exercise, they come to it with a great deal of dread, because little encouragement exists in our culture for making our despair explicit, learning from it, or letting others see it and help us with it.

Students work in pairs. One person (Person A) places him or herself, literally, up against a wall. The Wall represents something immovable, something which feels like it is never going to change or which, in reality, *is* never going to change—actual limitation. For example, The Wall could represent a parent who will never give their approval, a physical disability, someone who has died or gone away, an event which cannot be undone, a limiting life circumstance, a habit, an addiction, or a personal trait that one dislikes. Person A feels the presence of The Wall, begins to sense what The Wall is for him or her and listens for messages from The Wall. Person A tells these messages to Person B. Person B takes the role of The Wall, and expresses these messages over and over to Person A.

This exercise allows Person A to explore his or her relationship to this immovable limitation. How does he feel about it? What does she do with it? What messages does he get from it? Where did these messages come from? How do these messages make her feel?

Here are some of the messages people in my classes experienced in this exercise:

> *It's no use.*
> *Why bother trying?*
> *You'll never get rid of me, no matter how hard you try.*
> *You're bad (stupid, lazy, not enough, ugly, useless, etc.).*
> *No one will ever love you.*
> *It will never change.*
> *It will never work.*
> *You'll never get what you want.*
> *You can't trust anyone.*

No one understands.
No one cares.
You can't trust yourself.
Life is a drag.
The world is an awful (unsafe, dangerous, horrible, lonely, violent) place.
It's not worth it.
People leave you.
You're all alone.
You're trapped.

Here are some of the things people report they do at The Wall:

Work harder.
Push.
Fight.
Center myself.
Strategize.
Get frustrated (angry, sad, afraid).
Give up.
Get curious.
Plan.
Persuade.
Blame myself.
Blame other people.
Want to die.
Seduce.
Deny.
Collapse.
Ignore it.
Get apathetic.
Rage.
Distract myself.
Isolate myself.
Make it bigger.

Minimize the impact.
Pretend it doesn't bother me.
Pray.
Let it take over my life.
Wait.
Ask for help.

When we do this exercise, we come face to face with how we deal with limitations. We learn whether the limitations are real or created, but, most importantly, we learn the mental constructs we have fabricated around these limitations. We also see what responses to limitation we have in our repertoire—which ones are automatic, missing, or need to be cultivated.

When they do this exercise, many students learn that The Wall is really made up of admonitions and lessons from childhood; it has little to do with present reality. Others learn that The Wall involves missing resources—information they didn't receive or lack of support at crucial times in their lives. Still others learn that The Wall represents the real limitation life brings us (death, sickness, physical limits, loss) and the mental constructs we create around these real events.

For Susan, The Wall involved messages she got as a child about not being good enough. Unconsciously competitive, she was always comparing herself to other people. The Wall represented this fact: There was always someone better than her. When Susan explored what she did with this idea, she learned that she harbored resentment for being constantly compared to her older siblings, a resentment which stopped her from trying very hard at anything. At The Wall, she was filled with frustration and anger, hearing messages about how she would never amount to anything. As she worked, she saw fleeting glimpses of the things in her life she would like to pursue. Because these conflicted with the messages, she felt an attitude of "why bother?" and a sense of hopelessness, which caused her to collapse into a state of dull apathy. Susan came to understand how The

Wall manifested in her life: in lethargy, sitting around all day watching television shows she did not enjoy, not trying hard at work, letting other people take credit for her ideas.

Daniel noticed he was fine, as long as he faced The Wall. While facing The Wall, Daniel felt the need to push and that he never let anything stand in his way. He was angry at the idea that The Wall was relentless, that it was limitation, that it could possibly never change. He was mad at me for suggesting that some things are not changeable—that sometimes the only thing we can change is our relationship to these things. The message he got from The Wall was he wasn't trying hard enough, that he just needed to work harder.

Daniel reported this as his basic orientation to life. All problems could be solved with hard work, nothing was insurmountable, and he was willing to fight to prove he was right. Indeed, Daniel was adventuresome, daring, and quite successful in his work. He liked to mountain climb, sky dive, and play competitive sports. He was successful at everything except his intimate relationships—one place where his aggressive, "can do" attitude did not work. He was recently divorced after the death of his baby son because he could not deal with his wife's grief. He was angry at her inability to "get on with her life."

When Daniel was not squared-off with The Wall in a confident, confrontational stance, a different scenario unfolded. When I had him put The Wall behind or next to him, he became anxious and afraid. The Wall felt like a shadow that was always with him, one he could never get rid of, no matter how hard he tried. The messages he heard had to do with people: how he could never trust anyone, how he would always be disappointed, that no matter how successful he was, he would never really have love—people would always hurt and leave him. He felt the sadness in this attitude and the reality of it in his life. Daniel was surprised to find these feelings lurking so close to the surface (it was not how he consciously viewed himself) and he began to explore where the experiences and messages behind them had come from. He was able to see that his despairing attitude about relationships had limited the connections he had in his life—and had even limited what he thought was possible for him in relationships.

For Ross, the Wall was his drug habit. He saw what was beyond The Wall—the things he longed for in his life—and he saw that his drug use prevented him from having these things. He had tried many times to quit doing drugs and drinking, but his resolve never lasted. He gave up as soon as a buddy came by with an interesting offer, and ended up feeling depressed and weak because he had given in. As Ross worked, he approached The Wall with fierce determination—literally trying to push himself through. I asked Ross to let The Wall be his will to do drugs, and when I asked him how strong his will to do drugs was, he surprised himself by answering "very strong." I let him show me how hard he would have to push to overcome that will; he pushed himself into exhaustion and had to lean against The Wall for support. "See," he told me, "I'm just not strong enough."

I told Ross his will to do drugs was a part of him and marveled at how wonderful it would be to have such a strong will working with him instead of against him. If he could somehow befriend The Wall and use it as an ally, he'd have that strength on his side to get what he wanted in life. Ross pondered this idea and, as he was leaning against The Wall, he began to feel it as support and stability. He realized some of his drug use was a rebellion against stability—which had been extremely rigid and authoritarian in his family. He found it ironic that this rebellion was the most stable thing in his life. He acknowledged his mistrust of support, which he never felt to be for him, but an experience of what other people wanted from him. Drugs were the way he fiercely held on to his individuality—his sense of self—at the expense of building stability in his life. Ross went away from the exercise acknowledging his strength and considering how he could find allies who supported his true self and help him deepen his life goals.

Our despair comes in many forms and arises from many sources. We apply it, unconsciously, to our attitudes about ourselves, other people, and the world. When we take the time to become conscious of how our despair manifests in our lives—in our bodies, our thoughts, our feelings, our spirituality—we come to recognize it, and bring to it compassion, resources, and healing. In the process of transformation, our spirit makes our despair available to us so that we may come to a deeper understanding of ourselves, and offer ourselves the opportunity to deeply heal.

Compassion—Orienting Ourselves and Finding the Bigger Space

The despairing part of us needs our compassion. We may not like this part and may even treat it harshly. However, my experience with my clients at The Wall has taught me that we need to cultivate a compassionate relationship with our despair. It is important to cut ourselves some slack, knowing that getting stuck is a normal part of the transformation process, and imperfection is part of the human experience.

The first step in the practice of compassion toward our despair is to acknowledge that whatever it is that makes up our despair is not all of who we are. *Finding the bigger space* takes practice as it does not come automatically. In fact, despair, by its nature, actually hinders us from doing so. But finding the bigger space is the practice of evoking a part of us that is bigger than, or outside of, our despair.

Once when I was feeling stuck and despondent, a friend of mine, Steve, asked me how I was doing. I told him I was not doing very well, and what he said in response surprised me. "Lorena," he said, "life is like a brilliant light—radiant and full.

You see one dark spot in your life and you think that this is who you are, or that this is what your whole life is about. You need perspective. If you had perspective you could see how large your spirit is."

Needless to say, this is not the kind of commiseration I expected to hear, and at first I didn't like it—it felt like a negation of my suffering. But oddly enough, I've heard this message again and again from different teachers throughout my life. It was as if everyone could see this but me! Eventually, even I've come to see the obvious, but the habits and workings of my despair make this an ongoing practice, because the nature of my despair is to lose perspective.

When my students ask me about despair, I liken us to a landscape. Outside of my window are beautiful desert mountains dotted with large rocks and small plants. We are like these mountains with many components—rocks, canyons, caves, plants, trees, sand, water. When we are walking along on the mountain trail and come across a boulder in our path, it may seem an insurmountable obstacle. But from a broader perspective, it is just a part of the larger whole—a big rock, yes, part of an even grander landscape. Similarly, we must remember that our despair is not all of us, just a small part of the large whole that is encompassed by our spirit. We can use our knowledge of our despair—how it feels inside of us and how it works in our lives—to orient ourselves to where we are on the landscape.

When we are face to face with overwhelming despair, we can practice orienting ourselves and stepping back to inhabit a bigger space. We can do the practice of the Token Basket (see *Chapter 3*), where we remember to recognize the times in which the present moment differs from our despairing perceptions. If we are feeling that we are not safe, that people don't understand us, or that we are failures, we can practice recognizing the moments when we are safe, people do understand us, and we are successful. We can practice gratitude for the gifts that we do have in our lives, and recognize that there are always people less fortunate than ourselves. We can practice invoking spirit—remembering and calling forth our wholeness, our true self, which embraces all of our parts.

Once we find the space in ourselves that is bigger than despair, we know we don't have to get swamped by our despair. Instead of getting caught in it, we can turn that larger space—our spirit—toward our despair. We can make a space for our despair and explore it, learn what it has to say to us, and talk to it. From this bigger space, we can treat our despair with compassion—as if it were a small, lost child needing our patience, comfort, and guidance.

One of my clients, Eva, had her own metaphor for her despair. She likened it to a deep, dark pit. In it was no room to move, no light. It was lonely, isolated from the world around her. Eva had lived in this pit for long periods of time with no idea of where she was or how to get out. As she worked to recognize her despair, she learned to recognize the pit with its attitudes, feelings, and sensations. She began to recognize when she was in the pit before too much time had elapsed, and that at the slightest obstacle in her life, she flung herself into her pit of despair.

As she worked, she learned to bring resources into the pit, to bring light, other people, even a ladder! As more time passed she learned to recognize the landscape around the pit, and to stop herself from leaping in. We joked about putting a guardrail up around it and, for quite a while, we practiced viewing the pit from a safe distance behind the guardrail.

As Eva spent more time out of the pit, she began to explore other parts of the landscape of her life. In the big picture, she knows the pit is there—"over by that rocky place where things start to go not so smoothly"—but she knows now it is only one of many places in the larger landscape. She now feels she has choices about visiting it, how much time she wants to spend in it, and what resources to take with her when she goes. Just as she had to learn to recognize when she was in the pit, she also had to recognize when she was *not* in the pit.

Eva, a woman who spent ten years of her life depressed, says she now gets depressed sometimes, but usually only for minutes instead of years. During those minutes, the quality of her depression is the same as it was for all those years—the same thoughts and feelings, the same bodily sensations. The difference is she now knows this is just a small part of herself, instead of who she is. It takes up a small part of her life, instead of being what her whole life is about. She also knows she has more resources for dealing with these feelings and sensations, and it is her practice to remember to call upon those resources.

Getting Help—Calling In New Resources

Living systems are open systems, which means we are capable of taking in new information and resources and using them to heal, change, and grow. One quality of despair is that it blocks out new information and resources. This happens mainly due to how our core despair arises.

As children, we are curious, inquisitive, trusting individuals. We have a sense of the larger whole, of when things feel right, and of how things could be. We have hopes and wishes. When something is wrong, we naturally seek to heal it. If we are repeatedly exposed to experiences which don't allow us to be curious, inquisitive, and trusting, which don't feel right or, most importantly don't allow us to heal when something is wrong—we feel despair. We are relatively helpless to bring in new resources, although we do our best with the available ones.

Our core despair places us back into a primal situation wherein we think that what is happening is all there is, that it represents the whole world. Even though things may be different now, they don't feel different when we are in despair. We don't know there are other resources available or, if we know they are available, we feel they aren't for us, or we don't know how to call them in. We learn to mistake our despair for the whole.

When this happens, we need help.

Our relationship to getting help is critical. In some families we were taught that needing help is a sign of weakness, or that it is wrong to go outside of our families for help, or that we don't deserve help. Or that the help that was available wasn't really helpful. Or that we are a bother and should be able to do this for ourselves. Clients constantly tell me they should be able to do "these things" (the things I do for them) for themselves. I reply, "Who says?"

We learn to take care of ourselves because someone has taken care of us. We give to ourselves what has been given to us. I am able to give you what is in this book because it was given to me by others—people and things outside of me. It is a mistake to think we should be able to do everything for ourselves. *It is impossible to undergo deep transformation alone.* Core transformation does not occur in a vacuum but is inspired by the world around us, and the people and things in it. In fact, it is the inspiration from other resources that permeates our wall of despair, and calls us to the bigger space of spirit and wholeness.

While I was writing this chapter, my friend Diana called, very depressed. She felt stuck in a relationship pattern in which she set herself up to feel incompetent and abandoned. I told her I was writing about despair and we talked a little about what hers might be. Two days later, without knowing what I had written, Diana called me to say that she was doing better. I asked her what had changed for her. This is what she told me:

I've been thinking a lot about despair and I seem to have gotten some perspective. I realize my depression is anger. I wrote in my journal: "Despair is never having forgiven yourself, never putting yourself in the center, never having a private space." I'm angry about being made to feel wrong and always having to give myself up for love. Yesterday, I got an acupuncture treatment and saw my therapist. The acupuncture stopped the downward spiral and opened me up to new information, which my therapist helped me understand. My therapist also had me put colored stars up around my house to remind me of the things I am learning.

Without consciously knowing the process, Diana had identified and acknowledged her despair, found the bigger space (perspective), and called in her resources. It was a breakthrough for her to address her despair directly, hang in there with it, and to let the wonderful resources she has cultivated work explicitly with this issue.

So, the practice at this stage of the transformation process is calling for help. In many spiritual practices, calling upon a divinity or teacher for help is the only way out of certain spiritual crises. We can indeed call upon spirit or upon our teachers. But we can also call upon our friends and the multitudinous resources available in the world today—videos, books, classes, healers, our inner resources, the wisdom of the human condition, the wisdom of our planet earth.

One of my clients, after reading this, wrote:

I think it is also possible to call for help without having the faintest idea whence it comes. I do not believe in a god but have experienced help from who knows where? Not knowing is okay. Also you don't have to believe help is available—you only have to ask for it. Since you told me to try it, I said, "What the hell!" So during my most recent attack of despair I asked, despite the fact that I could not imagine help coming. But it did. So those with a crisis of faith can still ask for help. Though I do think sincerity, really wanting help, might be necessary.

When we call for help in earnest, many helpers become available. We only need to be willing to recognize them.

Like finding the bigger space, calling for help takes practice, because in our despair we believe that no help is available. But help *is* available. It is all around us. The way beyond the wall of our despair is finding this help in new resources. We are fortunate to live in a time abundant with them.

A favorite motto of mine is: *Everything is useful.* Anything can be used in the service of healing. Healing has its own time frame, and sometimes it does not look how we expect it to look. This is why we must practice being open and patient, learn to work with our emotions and mental constructs, and practice staying in contact with the bigger space that is spirit. In our despair, we need to call for help with all of our deepest sincerity, and look around and inside of ourselves. Help will come—for our spirits guide us toward healing (wholeness).

Knowing how to deal with our personal despair gives us the resources to help others. We live in a time of widespread cultural despair that has us acting out in many ways—in apathy, hatred, suspicion, violence, desperation, and addiction. Our young people, ever sensitive to societal malaise, make our cultural despair explicit in their music, attitudes, clothing, and behavior.

There is much to grieve in our society. In one group I worked with, we had a day of sadness practice. During one incredible practice, we did a group grief dance where we found our tears and the physical shapes of our grief. As we danced, we called out the things we were grieving and added them to our dance: broken families, child abuse, destruction of our planet, war, killing of other species, global atrocities, racism, homophobia, sexism, torture, greed, violence, the pain of our young people, the abandonment of our elderly, and the loss of our connection with the earth and with spirit. To say the least, it was a powerful and moving experience.

Our dance left us feeling acknowledged, empowered, and united. We lovingly named ourselves *The Crybabies* in honor of the wounds to our sensitivity: "Don't be a crybaby." We fantasized that instead of marching on Washington in anger, someday Crybabies, 100,000 strong, would bring our grief dance to Washington, where we would grieve for all the sorrowful events in our world. We would make public our societal grief—long denied or hidden under our anger and fear— and we would be on every TV channel, in every living room across the country. "We are crying for you. We are crying for all of us" We felt it is our grief that could unite us as a country, for who among us does not have something to grieve in these troubled times?

Denial affects us—denial that anything is wrong, denial of our grief, denial of our longing for healing and wholeness (and the accompanying message that there is nothing we can or should do) contributes to our feelings of cultural powerlessness and despair. We learn we are helpless, so we don't develop the resources for transforming our despair. We never have the experience of this transformation, so we don't know it is possible.

As we learn how to accept our despair and navigate through its realm, we begin to understand the gifts our vulnerability gives us—trust, acceptance, patience, strength, comfort, connection, compassion, and wisdom. We learn that we can enter and leave this realm more freely than we had previously thought. While we *are* affected by the horrors taking place in our world, it is also true there *is* much we can do to help. Learning how to recognize and heal our personal despair gives us the strength, power, and resources to help with healing the cultural and societal despair so prevalent in our time.

Forgetting

During the process of transformation, we experience many glorious moments of insight, clarity, and inspiration. We feel these in our bodies and know they are real and true—and then we forget. We have all been touched and inspired at workshops, in our spiritual practices, by books and talks, only to have that inspiration dissipate with time.

Many people who come to me have a clear vision of what they want to change, of the new energy they want in their lives. They have had glimpses, tastes, a felt sense of what it would be like to live the new way. They have been able to hold on to this new felt sense for minutes, hours, even days. It inspires them, but then it goes away. Because they cannot hold on to the feeling, they become discouraged.

Some of my clients are surprised and frustrated when they must hear me say the same things over and over. They feel they should "get it" in one try. They feel that once they have the insight, the new message, they should remember what they have learned and change permanently. When they don't, they feel stupid and embarrassed. I tell them, "Remember, you are going to forget."

I tell my clients not to feel bad that they have forgotten. It is my job to remind them. I am happy to do it as many times as it takes. Why should we just hear these messages once? All of our lives we have heard, again and again, messages that were inaccurate, messages that damaged us. Why should we not hear the helpful messages over and over? There is comfort in letting ourselves do this, in letting ourselves be reminded.

This process of forgetting what we have learned—losing touch with our aspirations, the felt sense of change, the new messages—is a normal part of the transformation process. It is as if the energy it takes to hold and incorporate the new information into our life is not yet there. We are creatures of habit, so to integrate new information into our daily lives takes the establishment of new habits. This is what practice is all about. Practice is the cultivation of habits that support our transformation.

At this stage in the transformation process, the practice is to return to our intention. When it gets hard, when we forget, we need to remind ourselves of our goals. If we know we are going to forget, we can enlist the help of everything around us to remind us. A client, Nancy, was trying to end an abusive relationship. She knew, because of her fear of being alone, it would be hard not to call her ex-boyfriend, or to engage with him when he called her. When she gave into this temptation, it was disastrous. She was left feeling confused and hurt, and in worse shape than if she had just stayed with her loneliness. In order to help remind her of her intention not to continue a relationship that was clearly harmful to her, I had her make a big sign which simply said "NO!" and put it next to her telephone. Every time her loneliness compelled her to phone her ex-boyfriend to explain one more thing, to try to "just be friends," she would be confronted by the sign. The "NO!" was a reminder of her will and determination, helping her when she had forgotten that feeling.

After the sign was up for a few days, Nancy realized that saying "no" was really difficult for her—and not saying "no" got her into a lot of trouble. The sign worked so well that she began making other signs to remind her of the other new parts of herself she was bringing into her life.

A couple of years ago while doing my own work with a wonderful therapist, Dee Pye, I had a new experience. Dee performed a ritual for me and, for a few minutes at the end of the ceremony, I had a feeling I had never had before—a felt sense of the unbroken wholeness and of being inextricably woven into it. I could feel my body part of the fabric of the whole universe—part of everything in it. I only got a small taste of this marvelous feeling, but it changed me deeply. It was as if I had gotten a glimpse into a whole new realm—one of true wholeness, of pure spirit. Of course, I could not hold on to that feeling and, since that experience, I have forgotten about it many times. But when I remember to remember it, it serves as a guide for my spiritual practice. It has led me to expansive experiences and teachings, which have given me a whole new sense of myself in my daily life. I feel those moments were a gift from my spirit, inspiration and encouragement for doing difficult things, nourishment for writing this book. Even though I have had that feeling again only a few times as strongly and clearly, I can remember it often. And I know what I do in my life can prepare me for one day being able to hold that feeling in my body for a longer and longer time.

We can make signs. We can write ourselves notes or hang inspirational pictures on our walls. We can reread sections of books over and over. We can find reminders anywhere—but we must remember to look. And once we find them we must remember to use them. What helps us remember is knowing we are going to forget.

Transformation is like entering foreign territory; learning the messages of transformation is like learning a foreign language. We hear the messages again and again and eventually we understand, we become fluent, we begin to think and dream in that new language.

Doing What is Difficult

The process of transformation is difficult. We face our limitations, move into the Zone of Admonition, experience our despair, go through the eye of the needle, make leaps of faith, and have dark nights of the soul. Transformation means we are learning something new. We are in new territory and, as a result, we are not in a field of our competence or expertise. So exploring our relationship to doing what is difficult is very important.

I learned about "doing what is difficult" from watching my daughter Lisa learn to play the flute. When she was six years old and told me she wanted to play the flute, the flute teachers I contacted said she was too young and would have to play the recorder until she was ten. So I bought her a recorder and she half-heartedly began playing it. When she was seven, we happened upon a quartet playing Christmas music in a store. Lisa listened intently to the flutist and burst into tears saying, "The flute is so beautiful, Mommy, I really, really want to play it." Moved by her dedication, I found a flute teacher who would begin her on the flute immediately. After her initial shock at not being able to make the flute sound the way she heard it in her head, she dedicated herself to practice. I have learned so much by watching her in her daily practice. Some days it is difficult, some days easy, some days she is distracted, some days stuck, some days inspired. Some days she says, "It's too hard." On these days, she needs encouragement.

Lisa was not content with a rote "you're doing great" from me. She needed me to pay attention, to really listen, to really be there with her. There were times when she didn't know what she needed so we had to experiment; we had to hang in there. Encouragement was a new concept for me. In my personal experience, you were congratulated on the things you did well but if something was too hard, you just didn't do it. I was astonished by how much energy and attention it took for me to learn how to deal with these difficult times. This kind of energy and attention was not part of my repertoire. I was not used to applying myself that way and had to learn how to give Lisa the encouragement she needed to make it through her struggles.

The word "encourage" means "to give courage, hope, or confidence to; embolden, hearten; to give support to; be favorable to; foster; help." How we were encouraged as children has an effect on how we do what is difficult now. Our relationship to doing what is difficult is formed, like all our core beliefs, in our personal history. Some of us are still waiting for a particular kind of encouragement we never got. What we need in the way of encouragement when things are difficult is a very personal thing, something important to discover.

The kind of encouragement we need at a given time can be very specific. Yesterday my friend, Rich, told me a touching story about his six-year-old godson, Ian, who is on a beginning soccer team. The kids run around en masse kicking the ball, the play so exciting and absorbing that sometimes they kick it to the wrong goal. During one game, as they were running and the parents cheering, Ian ran up to his mom and said, "Hey Mom, can you yell out 'Go, Ian!'?"

We all need encouragement. We like the feeling that someone is rooting for us. The specific kind of encouragement we need can take many forms. Here are some kinds of encouragement the students in one of my classes said they needed for doing the difficult things in their lives:

Kind words.
Clear limits.
Permission.
Role models.
To be reminded not to struggle so hard.
A gentle push.
To be shown how.
To be told, "You can do it."
Someone to just be with me when it's hard.
Someone to validate that it is hard.
To know that I am not crazy to want what I want.
Other people doing it, too.
Someone to remind me of my goals.
Someone who believes in me.
I need to be made to do it.
I need someone to play the devil's advocate so I can feel my determination.
To be told that it's going to be okay no matter what happens.

Although encouragement is a form of help that initially comes from outside ourselves, as we experience this help over and over, we learn to internalize the practice of encouragement. Because my daughter Lisa has practiced going through difficult places, she is better able to trust herself when the terrain gets rocky, and to trust that resources are available to help her handle whatever comes up. Internalizing encouragement imparts self-confidence. It allows us the core beliefs that someone is rooting for us, that help is available, that we can do it, that we are not alone.

The practice at this stage in the transformation process is to discover our specific needs for encouragement—and to find the resources, allies, and helpers that can give us the encouragement and inspiration we need. To do this, we need to know how we get stuck and what our particular despair looks like. We need to know that our despair is created by the feelings of hopelessness and helplessness which first developed when we were too young to have perspective and didn't know other resources were there. We need to recognize that we are no longer so young; we have grown up and it is a different world—a world full of ideas and resources that can be enlisted in the service of our wholeness.

Practices for When You are Stuck

Check In

When you are stuck, frustrated, or feeling despair, practice checking in with yourself. This may be different from your normal habit, since feeling stuck doesn't feel good to most of us and we normally like to avoid rather than explore this feeling. Check in to what your body is doing. Notice your emotions and your thoughts. Notice what kind of behaviors you exhibit when you feel stuck. Ask yourself what kind of resources might help you when you feel this way. What happens when you bring the stuck part of you in contact with resources?

Relationship to Change

When things in your life are changing or in flux, how does your body react? How do you feel in your body? What kinds of emotions come up for you?

List ten attitudes you have about change.

List ten rules you learned in your family about change or transitions (overtly or by example).

List ten things you do when you are in transition or feeling destabilized.

List ten things you do when someone else is in transition.

Relationship to Stability

What is your relationship to stability? How does stability feel in your body? What kinds of emotions come up for you?

List ten attitudes you have about stability.

List ten rules you learned in your family about stability (overtly or by example).

Relationship to Being Stuck

List what happens in your body when you feel you are:

stuck?
struggling?
despairing?

List the emotions that come up for you.

List ten rules (overt or by example) that you learned from your family about getting stuck.

List ten things you do when you are:

stuck
struggling
despairing

List ten things that you do when someone else is:

stuck
struggling
despairing

The Wall

This exercise is easier to do with two people, although it is possible to do alone. This is a potent exercise and works best after you have done the preceding practices in this book. The person who works with you should be someone you trust and who is willing to explore your despair with you in an open and curious way.

Place yourself up against a wall. Think of something in your life right now that feels immovable, like it is never going to change, or think of something that *is* really never going to change. This could be a limiting life circumstance, a personal limitation, or a limitation in someone else. Let The Wall represent this thing.

As you feel the presence of The Wall, notice your relationship to it. Have your partner slowly help you explore this. How does it feel to be up against this limitation? What does it feel like in your body? Where is the impact of The Wall felt in your body? What kinds of emotions do you have? What kinds of thoughts do you think? What do you wish for? What kinds of messages do you get from The Wall? (If The Wall could talk, what would it say to you?) Have your partner repeat these messages to you. What happens inside of you when you hear them? What do you do when you hear these messages? What messages do you wish you could hear? What would nourish you here?

Take time with your partner to discuss what comes up for you. Try not to act on the urge to solve or make it better; just use the time to gather information about how you experience this limitation, and to notice from the inside what kinds of things might be helpful for you.

Take it slowly. Try not to push yourself into any particular place. If emotions come that feel strong or overwhelming, slow down and take care of any exposed hurt parts. These parts may believe they have no resources because there weren't any in the past, but resources are now available. Explore what these resources might be. Practice bringing resources to these parts, offering them your tenderness and compassion.

Compassion

The part of you that gets stuck needs your compassion. When you feel stuck, struggling, or despairing, practice being kind to yourself. Some ways to be kind to yourself: being patient with your process, being curious about your feelings, openly and attentively listening to your hurt parts, understanding that your unhealthy behavior exists for a reason, being gentle with your vulnerability, getting help when you are struggling, doing things that are truly nourishing.

Spend a day being compassionate with yourself. Notice what happens.

Practice Orienting Yourself

When you feel stuck, struggling, or despairing, it helps to know where you are. Becoming familiar with what you feel in your body, what emotions come up, what kinds of thoughts you think (as in the exercises above) when you feel stuck or despairing can help get you oriented. When you find yourself feeling these feelings or thinking these things, practice saying to yourself, "This is just my stuckness, my struggle, my despair coming up." Practice remembering that despair, struggles, or stuckness are not you, but only one part of who you are. Call in parts of yourself that have perspective. Ask yourself, "What is the larger context around my present feelings?"

Write a story in third person (using "he" or "she" instead of "I") about being stuck and the bigger picture you could not see.

Help

List ten rules you learned in your family (overtly or by example) about asking for help.

List ten internal resources (parts of you) available to others when they need help. (For example, your ability to listen, your patience, etc.)

List ten internal resources (parts of you) available to help you when you are stuck, struggling, or despairing. List ten that you actually use. How do these lists compare?

List ten external resources that are available for you when you need help. List ten that you actually use. How do these lists compare?

List the kinds of help that are genuinely helpful to you when you feel stuck.

Practice calling on internal or external resources when you feel stuck. Ask these resources for help. Be as specific as you can about what you need. Pick resources that work for you. Or experiment with just asking and noticing what kind of help makes itself available.

Forgetting

Recognizing that you will often forget the things that you are learning or practicing, use reminders to help you remember. These can be little signs you place up around you, objects, sayings, notes on your calendar, pictures on your bathroom mirror, asking friends to remind you, alerts on your computer screen, or entries in your appointment book.

Encouragement for Doing What is Difficult

List the kinds of messages that are encouraging for you when you are doing difficult tasks.

List the kinds of actions from others that are encouraging for you.

What kinds of actions from yourself are encouraging? Do these things for yourself.

Ask a friend or family member for encouragement. Let them know exactly what you would like them to say or do (and how often) to encourage you.

Altar

Make an altar to:

stuckness
forgetting
encouragement
gratitude

Creativity

Invent a practice that helps you when you feel stuck. Write down the steps to this practice in case your memory fails at the moment of need. Spend time regularly doing this practice.

Chapter 7
Integration and Alignment

When we understand that wholeness is not possible without including all aspects of our humanness—our bodies, our emotions, our minds, and our spirits—we are able to begin the process of integration which culminates in our alignment with spirit. As we become practiced in working with the elements of transformation—coming out of denial, evoking the parts of ourselves, giving up the fight with ourselves, getting stuck, healing our despair, forgetting and remembering our aspirations—a wonderful thing starts to happen. We become familiar with ourselves—how we are and how we act. This familiarity brings peace, comfort, curiosity, and a willingness to accept ourselves and life.

At this point in the transformation process, we begin to integrate aspects of our whole being which have been shut off, denied, or neglected. Our capacity to feel becomes integrated with our ability to reason. Our spirituality becomes integrated into our daily lives. The deepest sense of who we are allows itself into the world. As this happens, we start to align with ourselves. All of our various parts move toward alignment with our deepest, most expansive core self. The elements of our wholeness line up in service of our spirit. We begin to work with ourselves, to trust ourselves—instead of fighting with or being afraid of ourselves.

Integration

Integration is a built-in capacity of living systems. Our bodies are miracles of integration. Countless simultaneous activities are coordinated in our bodies—all out of our conscious awareness—to create of us a living whole. Our psyches integrate our experiences into meaning and a workable strategy for dealing with the world. When the strategies or meanings no longer work, we are compelled to integrate new information in order to find better strategies and new meanings—so we can change and grow. Integration is a natural part of the growth process.

In therapy and healing work, times come when it is necessary to stop taking in new information and start putting information together into an integrated whole. On a practical level, integration allows us to get used to our new lessons, to bring them deeply into ourselves and then out into the world.

We need to take the elements we are cultivating in our transformational work into the world to test them out. If we are learning to be more assertive, for example, we need to practice integrating our new-found boldness with the other aspects of ourselves. We let this quality inhabit our bodies, we notice our feelings about it, we update our beliefs and attitudes toward it to coincide with our current experience, and then we bring it into our everyday lives. This crucial process of integration determines whether what we are learning will stick with us and become a part of who we are, or whether it will be merely another insight.

I recommend that my students who are healers and therapists include time for integration in sessions with their clients. I remind them there will be whole periods of the therapy and healing process that will be about practicing integration. Many times, when clients have done psychological work in which they have uncovered and worked with different parts of themselves, they are left feeling fragmented until someone helps them to integrate these parts into a functioning whole.

Much of today's psychotherapy is aimed at uncovering many of our different parts. Janet, after years of such therapy, came to me feeling shattered and disoriented. She thought she might have multiple personality disorder. It became clear while working with Janet that many different parts of her were at war.

Janet was suffering from the same fragmentation that many people in our culture feel. She was afraid of herself. She had been taught not to feel her feelings. She was unhappy in relationships which she used to help her feel whole, but which never filled her emptiness. Memories of the past plagued her. Janet was in the habit of returning to these memories over and over to find clues to her lost and unhealed parts. She spoke about her "three year old," her "eight year old," her "adult" when referring to different parts of herself.

My work was to help Janet bring these parts together into one functioning adult—one spacious enough to embrace all of her parts. I worked away from Janet's tendency to go for more memories (more parts) and helped her cultivate the habit of bringing her parts back to the whole. Janet was so used to finding the painful and unhealed parts of herself that she had to be taught to find her wholeness—to find what was *not* wrong with her life.

Spiritually, we are already integrated; we are already whole. Our failure to recognize this—our separation from our inherent wholeness—causes us much confusion and pain. Our culture supports this separation, dividing things into pairs of opposites:

good/bad, us/them, men/women, black/white, liberal/conservative, rich/poor, beautiful/ugly, child/adult, body/spirit, head/heart, right brain/left brain, heaven/earth, life/death. We ascribe meanings to each half of a duality, ("The heart is better than the head." "Poor people are poor because they don't try hard enough." "Life on earth is hard; our reward will be in heaven." "The body is sinful; the spirit is our salvation.") and these meanings run our lives—often filling us with fear, confusion, anger, and blame.

This forced duality is actually an illusion. We cannot have beauty without a perception of ugliness, our perception of rich is relative to our sense of poor, and the differences we ascribe to other people are actually quite superficial when viewed from a spiritual framework—the matrix of unbroken wholeness. This false us/them dichotomy has brought much suffering into our lives—war, racism, homophobia, hostility between men and women, the generation gap, hate crimes, fear, alienation.

To live from the illusion of separateness is to live a lie that hurts us. This lie keeps us in isolation, estranged from our wholeness, keeping us ignorant of essential truths that affect our lives and the quality of life on the planet. Nowhere is this more obvious than in our reckless treatment of the environment. When traveling in Mexico in the early 1980's, I learned that a number of pesticides, made in the United States but banned there because of their toxicity, were exported to Mexico where they were sprayed on food that was then imported back to the United States. Our chemical companies' disregard for the health of our neighbors in Mexico affects our own health as well.

While few people knew about this twenty years ago, we now have many more examples of how our ignorance of interconnectedness harms us. In fact, it has become clear that our very survival as a species depends on our adopting a more holistic attitude toward our planet and everything on it.

Our need to see ourselves as separate, while an important stage in both human and cultural development, is merely that—a stage. It helps us have a sense of self, to know who we are, to stand out—something that is necessary at certain points in our psychological growth. Beyond these points—when we have a sense of our own autonomy, individuality, and power—the work becomes creating a space big enough to hold our perceived differences. We begin to feel the need to know ourselves as part of a larger whole: a partnership, a family, a community, a cosmos.

My spiritual teacher, Thich Nhat Hanh, talks about "interbeing," the principle which teaches us there is no such thing as a separate self—everything is interconnected:

*Just as a piece of paper is the fruit, the combination of many elements that can be called non-paper elements, the individual is made up of non-individual elements. If you are a poet, you will see clearly that there is a cloud floating in this sheet of paper. Without a cloud there will be no water; without water, the trees cannot grow; and without trees, you cannot make paper. So the cloud is in here. The existence of this page is dependent on the existence of a cloud. Paper and cloud are so close. Let us think of other things, like sunshine. Sunshine is very important because the forest cannot grow without sunshine, and we humans cannot grow without sunshine. So the logger needs sunshine in order to cut the tree, and the tree needs sunshine in order to be a tree. Therefore you can see sunshine in this sheet of paper. And if you look more deeply, with the eyes.... of those who are awake, you see not only the cloud and the sunshine in it, but that everything is here: the wheat that became the bread for the logger to eat, the logger's father—everything is in this sheet of paper....In the same way, the individual is made of non-individual elements.**

When we live from the principle of interbeing, we become aware that feelings of separateness that arise from dualistic thinking are fabricated. We ourselves are made up of many elements—our bodies, our emotions, our mental constructs, and

*Thich Nhat Hanh, *Being Peace* (Berkeley: Parallax Press, 1987) pp.45-47.

our spirits. These elements have all been supported and influenced by other elements—our environment, other people, our culture, and the times in which we live. All of these combine to give us a sense of ourselves. It is impossible to live without the influence, aid, and resources of other living and non-living things. Our very sustenance depends upon them. Even beyond mere existence, our complex lives are born of a web that interconnects us with and influences the entire planet.

Alignment

When we begin practicing integration, we gain energy. This energy, which we formerly used to fight with ourselves or keep ourselves fragmented or cut off from ourselves, can now be used in service of the spirit. The sense of all our parts working together in service of something bigger than any individual part is what I call *alignment*.

The experience of alignment has been described by my students in a variety of ways:

I feel intact, like I'm in one piece.
I'm not fighting with myself anymore—or at least when I do fight with myself, I know there is a bigger place that I can go.
I trust myself more.
I listen to myself more. I have a sense of deep inner guidance.
It's very exciting. I feel ready for anything.
My head and my heart actually communicate with each other.
I feel less afraid of life.
I find myself thinking nice things about myself. I guess I can say I like myself.
I'm less self-absorbed—more able to connect with the world outside of me. I notice that my prayers are less about me and what I want and more about concern for others and asking to do God's will.

I don't feel scared of what's inside of me anymore.
There's a different sense of myself. Like I'm bigger. Like a bigger part of me is directing my life.

When the elements of our wholeness are in alignment we have a feeling that we are in one piece, moving in one direction. We feel ready to meet life—its beauty and its challenges. An exciting time in the transformation process, we feel light, expansive, and balanced. We are receptive to both ourselves and to life. We feel we are supported by the world around us. We may experience a sense of magic or serendipity—wherein events happen which fit our needs perfectly. Seemingly remarkable coincidences—being in the right place at the right time, the chance meeting of someone who alters the course of our lives, randomly opening a book to a passage that exactly addresses our current situation, overhearing a conversation in a grocery store line that speaks to what is on our mind, receiving help from out of the blue—are the result of our receptivity.

Receptivity is a practice many people find difficult, because we live in a culture that says things are accomplished primarily through doing. This attitude creates a bias toward knowing, planning, and taking action, a kind of predatory attitude toward life—where we decide what we want, focus on it, and go for it at all costs. But how many of us have done this only to be dissatisfied with what we get?

During the past decade I have been repeatedly brought to this understanding. With my partner and daughter, I made plans to sell our house, move to a new state, build a new house, write this book, and get it published. Throughout this time, I've learned over and over that things don't always go the way I want. Many aspects of my life are out of my control—in the hands of others, timing, "fate." All the strategizing and worrying in the world doesn't help. It only makes me frustrated, anxious, and prone to headaches—because all of my energy goes to my head to try to figure out how to make things work out, without much success. Instead, when I change tactics and practice cultivating receptivity, I notice an immediate improvement. My energy leaves my head and centers itself in my abdomen. I am able to breathe more easily. I feel I have more space, as if my eyes are open to the world around me rather than narrowly focused on my goals, blinders in place. In general, I feel lighter, happier, and more trusting that things will work out. I am easier to be around and work with, people seem more willing to help me, and just as much is accomplished, with more ease.

When we practice receptivity, we enter into a relationship with life—one in which we receive the many marvels and gifts life has to offer us. Instead of relying solely on our will, receptivity allows us to feel the hand of spirit at work in our lives.

As they practice alignment, another thing people report is they become sure about how to be in their lives. They clearly know when something or someone is right or wrong for them. In the words of musician Chick Corea: "The truth is basically simple—and feels good, clean, and right."

Gina, one of my clients, explained it like this:

I have a sense that I have no choice anymore about how to live my life. This sounds weird since I place so much value on having options—my freedom has always been so important to me. But if I don't listen to myself and act from what is really good for me, I feel very uncomfortable—it literally makes me ill. I wasn't always like this; I used to numb out, and as a result, I got myself into many situations that were not good for me, or I did things without thinking about the consequences. It was like one part of me was saying "Go ahead," while another part of me was protesting "This is wrong." Now it feels like I have no choice but to listen for what is really good for me. It's actually a good feeling; it does not feel limiting at all. It feels very freeing, as I have freed myself from doing the things that are harmful to my spirit.

The feeling of having no choice but to act from integrity is a result of practicing alignment, of aligning all aspects of oneself with one's spirit. Integrity is defined as "the quality or state of being complete; unbroken condition; wholeness." It also refers to "sound moral principle, uprightness, honesty, sincerity." The spirit provides us with a measure for our lives. It lets us know—through our bodies, our feelings, our minds—how we must live. Our symptoms tell us when we are not living right, when our life is out of balance, when we are not in harmony with our true self.

When we operate in alignment, we feel good. We are healthy, flexible, happy, and expansive. When we have other emotions like fear or anger, a bigger context holds our experience. We are aware of this bigger picture, and not stuck in our emotions. We do not define ourselves by our smaller experiences but rather by the spirit that directs us. Our daily actions reflect an expanded consciousness of all parts of ourselves. From a sense of integration and alignment, our lives start to make sense.

Many people involved in spiritual or psychological work expect to attain a certain level of well-being and then live happily every after, never again having to suffer or face unpleasant events. While glimpses of alignment and integration come with doing the work of transformation—wherein we get little flashes of what it is like to feel whole and aligned with something bigger than ourselves—it is important to keep in mind that integration and alignment are ongoing practices, not just the result of doing our work. In other words, we do not arrive at a sense of integration and alignment and remain there.

To be in the world today is to never be free of the awareness of suffering or of circumstances that make us lose our balance. To regain balance in a constantly changing world requires evoking and cultivating integration and alignment. It is a daily, moment to moment practice.

What changes as we practice integration and alignment is our knowing that we have resources inside and outside of ourselves. Our bodies, our emotions, and our thoughts are all parts of ourselves and can be put in service of our spirit, which is capable of handling everything that life brings us.

Cultivating Integration and Alignment

A sense of integration and alignment among all parts of ourselves must be practiced. Many of the exercises in the previous chapters can be used for this purpose by adding the intention to cultivate integration and alignment. Here are a few more practices which also can help us do this.

The Present Moment

One of the most important of these practices is returning to the present moment. Fritz Perls, the founder of Gestalt therapy, said neurosis is not being able to be in the here and now. Indeed, many of us live in the future, rehearsing what may happen, or in the past, reviewing what has happened.

We pick our partners based upon their potential, rather than on who they are and what they are doing right now. Then we are disappointed when they don't live up to our expectations. We daydream about what is yet to come or reminisce about what has passed, and miss what is happening inside and around us right now. Our relationship with time is unbalanced. We feel rushed like there is never enough of it, or we feel as if time is passing too slowly and what we want will never arrive. But as Zen Master Taisen Dashmaru explains: "Time is not a line, but a series of now-points."

Bringing our awareness to the present moment puts us in the here and now. From within the present moment, we can direct our mindfulness inward toward ourselves and outward toward the world. Inside, we become aware of our bodies, our feelings, our mental constructs; outside, we become aware of our environment, other people, our effect on the world, and its effect on us.

In the present moment we become receptive to what the

world has to offer us and what we have to offer. We become aware of who we are and what we must do. At any given moment, we can call ourselves back from wherever we have gone from the here and now, and check in with ourselves in the present moment.

From the present moment, we can bring our awareness to ourselves as a whole. In the practice section of this chapter, there are exercises that help us develop a sense of our whole selves. Instead of focusing on all of the different parts of ourselves, we practice invoking a bigger self—our true self which holds all these parts. We use our conscious mind to find our bigger self, experience what this self feels like in our bodies, and teach ourselves to accept the sensations that come with this sense of self. We use our breath to relax into and savor these sensations, allowing breath and sensation into our abdomen where the root of the body's energy lives. The idea of integration is not enough. We must experience the felt sense of integration in our bodies.

In the present moment, we allow ourselves the time to savor the changes we are making in our lives, to feel them, to let ourselves be satisfied with them. We can sit quietly and let these changes fill our bodies, listen to their messages, allow them to express themselves through our dreams and creativity.

Many people, when doing healing and transformation work, don't remember to take the time to feel and savor the changes that are actually happening in them. Often my clients have to be reminded that they are really changing. They need to learn to feel the changes, to let them unfold at their own pace, and to honor plateaus as resting places.

What Is Not Wrong

Another thing we can do to cultivate integration and alignment is the practice of finding what is *not* wrong. Often, if we have done a great deal of healing work or psychotherapy, we are used to looking for the pain—what is "wrong" with us or our lives. Because nothing stays the same and we are never finished growing, we can always find our edge—the places inside of us that feel incomplete, unfinished. We also need to look for our wholeness—what is right, what is working—so that we can build a reservoir of resources within ourselves—a place of peace, joy, and gratitude for our unfolding.

I have a client, Ann Marie, with whom I worked about ten years ago and recently started seeing again. When I first met her, she had a great deal of physical pain for which doctors could find no cause. In the course of receiving acupuncture treatments, Ann Marie discovered a strong psychological component to what she was feeling, related to the severe abuse she suffered as a child.

While she had remembered most of this abuse, she had been unable to comprehend the tremendous emotional impact it had on her life. So her body expressed this pain for her. As she uncovered how the years of abuse affected her present life, she began the work of understanding how her relationships, her work, her feelings about herself, and her parenting were all informed by the negative messages she had received. She learned to become conscious of her previously unconscious motivations and beliefs, and made tremendous positive changes in her life.

In the years since I had seen her, she had done much work with several therapists to heal the effects of her abusive childhood. She had a variety of internal and external resources available to her as the result of her work. She was an excellent communicator, very clear about her feelings, and able to deal with people honestly and with integrity. As a teacher, she created a nurturing, safe, and spiritual environment for her students, and was able to help parents deal with their children's emotional needs in a healthy way.

Ann Marie came to me again because she was having some menopausal symptoms she knew would be helped with Oriental

Medicine. As we worked together this time, it became apparent that Ann Marie needed to practice finding what was not wrong with her life. She was constantly on "red alert," looking for the pain and problems so she could work on them. Basically, she was exhausted from approaching herself as a series of problems and was not able to determine which of her symptoms were part of the normal process of menopause and which were the result of her "extreme abuse." As one of her friends so succinctly put it: "Ann Marie has no idea how intact she is."

Ann Marie's work was to see her intactness, her wholeness. It was time for her to appreciate what all the work she had done over the past ten years had accomplished. It had not only helped her to heal her abuse, it had also helped her to become an emotionally healthy, strong, spiritually alive person, a model and inspiration for others. As homework, I asked her to spend some time every day being mindful of all the gifts in her life. She was to make an altar of thanksgiving to these gifts, to visit this altar every day, and to spend time meditating in front of it, allowing herself to feel the reality of these gifts in her body.

My spiritual teacher, Thich Nhat Hanh, highly recommends the practice of finding what is not wrong:

> *We should learn to ask, "What's not wrong?" and be in touch with that. There are so many elements in the world and within our bodies, feelings, perceptions, and consciousness that are wholesome, refreshing, and healing. If we block ourselves, if we stay in the prison of our sorrow, we will not be in touch with these healing elements.**

Allowing ourselves to discover and practice gratitude for the things not wrong, and to feel and savor the changes occurring in our lives as the result of our spiritual and psychological work, are necessary practices for transformation. Without an ability to sense what is right in our lives and feel satisfied with the small

*Thich Nhat Hanh, *Peace is Every Step* (New York: Bantam Books, 1991) p.77.

changes in our lives, there would be no point to transforming our suffering.

Prayer and Meditation

Prayer and meditation are two practices that can help us align ourselves with our spirit. Prayer serves many purposes. We can use it to ask for something for ourselves and others, to show our gratitude, to ask for forgiveness, and to honor and invoke spirit. While many people pray by asking for specific outcomes, one prayer that is useful to help us align with spirit is the simple prayer: "Thy will be done." In this prayer, we offer ourselves to spirit, and let the will of spirit work through us. Instead of praying for what we think we want to happen, we trust there is a larger context unfolding of which we are a part. The practice of prayer reminds us there is something bigger than our everyday selves at work. It activates a sense of the sacred in our daily life, and teaches us to trust the unfolding process.

Meditation also helps us align ourselves with spirit, as the practice of meditation enables us to calm our mind and emotions and rest within a larger context. Simple forms of meditation such as mindfully following our breath or repeating a word or sentence which has meaning to us, can help us to still the endless chatter in our minds. This kind of meditation helps keep us from being controlled by our emotions, and brings us back into the bigger picture. Other kinds of meditation where we mindfully follow the workings of our thoughts, sensations, and emotions teach us that these states are temporary. Our thoughts, emotions, and sensations pass; they are not the essence of who we are.

By practicing, we can learn to rest within spirit, which is larger and more enduring than these transitory states. We can train our mind and emotions to give way to the larger sense of spirit, so we can learn to listen to the voice of spirit in our lives.

Offerings

Another practice that helps us align ourselves with spirit is making offerings. Offerings take many forms, having their roots in different spiritual traditions. The practice of offering is based upon action, just as invoking spirit is based upon receptivity. In the practice of offering, we use our actions to give to spirit.

One way to use this practice is to make altars that honor something inside or outside of ourselves. Altars give us a living, growing, changing sense of the thing being honored. If someone is having difficulty with one of his emotions—fear, for example—he can make an altar to his fear. He can place things on the altar that somehow speak of his fear (drawings, dreams, things from nature, photographs, etc.). By working with the altar for a period of time, visiting it and adding to it, his relationship with fear changes. He makes offerings to his fear, not to appease it, but to truly honor and respect it, to use the altar to cultivate a living relationship with his fear. Within this relationship are resources for being with and understanding fear.

We can make offerings in many other ways—we can dedicate our time to people in need, we can dedicate specific works to others or to larger causes. This book is an offering to spirit—to remind me and you of the sacredness that is available at any given moment in our lives. I return to this offering every time I have anything to do with this book. I cultivate this offering in the arduous tasks of listening for the words, writing them down, rereading, revising, working toward getting this work published. I dedicate all of these actions to spirit—"Thy will be done"—and practice cultivating the trust that spirit has its own plans for this work, even after it leaves my hands and rests in yours.

As we cultivate integration of all aspects of ourselves and alignment with spirit, we are brought to the gate of The Mystery. The Mystery is the aspect of life that is truly bigger than us and beyond our understanding. Our capacity to live in The Mystery grows as our sense of self and spirit grow.

Practice for Integration and Alignment

Check In
Throughout the day, check in to see whether the parts of you are in alignment with each other. Is you head in alignment with your heart? Are your head and heart in alignment with your body? Practice inviting all parts of you to work together.

Alignment
Alignment occurs when the parts of ourselves are working together in service of something bigger than any individual part. Describe what alignment feels like in your body. What kinds of feelings do you have? What are your thoughts, attitudes, and beliefs? What spiritual goal are these parts of you working toward?

Receptivity
Spend a day with one of these attitudes:

Life is always giving me things to help in my spiritual growth.
Everything is useful.
All the people I encounter today are my teachers.

At the end of the day, record how this day has been different from the days when you don't maintain this attitude.

Invoking Your Wholeness
Your wholeness—your deepest, most expansive core self, your true self—is both a container for and the synthesis of all parts of you and all of your experiences. Your sense of your true self changes and deepens as your practice deepens. At the beginning of the day, practice inviting your wholeness or your biggest self into your awareness. When you sense it, practice using your breath to allow this feeling to spread through your whole body. Breathe into your abdomen, and allow the rest of your body to relax into the feeling of being in your wholeness.

Invite your wholeness or your biggest self to go with you through your day. Throughout the day, when you notice you have lost sense of your biggest self, practice inviting it back. When something stressful happens, practice inviting your wholeness to be available.

When you are being in or acting from your wholeness or biggest self, describe what it is like:

in your body
in your emotions
in your mind

Draw a picture of what it is like when you are experiencing and acting from your wholeness or biggest self.

Write or tell a story of a time when you acted from your wholeness or biggest self to solve a problem.

Change Inventory
Make an inventory of the changes that are happening in your inner and outer life.

Take time to feel where you are in this change process.

Note how you are different than you were:

last year
last month
since beginning this book

Let yourself savor the changes that are happening.

Finding What is Not Wrong
Make a list of all the things that are not wrong in your inner and outer life.

Spend a part of each day being mindful of the gifts in your life.

Prayer and Meditation

Throughout the day, offer a prayer of gratitude for the gifts in your life.

For a week, practice saying the prayer, "Thy will be done." Notice what happens.

Use prayer as a way to regularly communicate with the divine. Have a real dialogue; listen for answers.

Spend time at the beginning or end of the day in meditation.

A simple meditation:
Sit comfortably on a cushion or chair with your back straight but relaxed, or lie down. Follow your breathing with your awareness. Follow the entire length of your in-breath and out-breath. If your mind wanders, simply return your awareness to your breath. Do this for fifteen or twenty minutes. If it is difficult for you to keep your mind quiet, say, "Breathing in, I know I am breathing in," with each in-breath, and "Breathing out, I know I am breathing out," with each out-breath. Or count each breath, saying "one..." for the entire length of the first breath, and so on.

A calming meditation:
Do this meditation lying down. Follow your breath for a few minutes allowing it to become deep and slow. Become aware of your body. Send your breath to the various parts of your body—your sense organs, your internal organs, your muscles, your bones, your blood, your skin. Smile and send tenderness to these parts of your body as they come into your awareness. Become aware of your emotions. Smile and send your breath to your emotions. Become aware of your mental constructs. Smile and send your breath to your mental constructs. Become aware of your spirit. Smile and breathe deeply to your spirit, allowing your breath to carry your spirit throughout all parts of you.

Altars

Think about a spiritual goal. Make an altar to the parts of you that participate in your relationship with this goal.

Make an altar to the vastness of your whole self. Visit it daily. Make daily offerings to it from the world around you, or from something you create.

Make an altar that represents where your sense of wholeness is taking you. As you travel on this journey, make new offerings.

Make an altar of thanksgiving for the gifts in your life.

Creativity

Invent a practice that helps you have a sense of integration or alignment. Spend time regularly doing this practice.

Chapter 8
The Mystery: Entering the Unknown

Alignment with spirit brings us to the door of the unknown. No transformation is possible without a journey through this door. With change, we leave what is familiar and travel beyond the Zone of Admonition into unfamiliar territory. Scary and exciting, going into the unknown yields many wonders and surprises, beyond our imagination or expectations. As we take this journey, we learn about our strengths and resources, about delights and challenges, about the places where we are limited and need help.

Our practices thus far have prepared us to make this sojourn, and have given us the trust in ourselves and in spirit to provide what we need along the way. Because we have practiced knowing the elements that make up our wholeness, entering the door to transformation, acknowledging our stuckness and despair, and integrating and aligning with spirit, we know we have available resources—tools for entering the unknown and for helping us deal with what we find.

The Practice of Not Knowing

Most of us approach life through what we know. We value and prize our knowledge. We want answers; we seek the one true way. We look for these answers and provide them to others. To not know is to be uncomfortable. When we encounter this feeling, we pretend to know, fall back on what we already know, or despair that we do not know. Education has placed such a bigger value on coming up with the answer than on asking questions that often when we don't know, we feel stupid, ignorant, childish, and powerless. Most of us have not had good experiences with not knowing.

I listen all the time to how students, clients, and I limit ourselves when searching for solutions. Our mental constructs are full of "yes, buts...": "Yes, I want to quit my job, but the job market is so bad right now." "Yes, I want a good relationship, but I still have so much personal work to do." "Yes, I need a rest, but I don't have a vacation until next May." "Yes, buts" are the language of stuckness. When we use them, we can neither move toward what we want, nor be happy with where we are.

We are ever ready to embrace what we already know, even when it brings suffering. Why is this? Because stepping into the unknown is scary. But if we have a good relationship with our fear, it need not stop us. We have to practice, over and over, not choosing the familiar in an attempt to avoid experiencing our fear. Instead we need to accept fear as an inevitable part of entering the unknown. We must practice tolerating, and bringing resources to our fear.

Sometimes we think that when we are truly ready to change, the new thing we want will automatically fall into place. Sometimes it does. Usually, however, it just presents itself as one of the options. And we have to courageously choose it.

Old habits are strong. We easily assume we have not crossed over into new territory when we encounter familiar situations, but this is not necessarily true. We say things like, "He's just like my father," and then fall into old patterns of relating based on our old relationships instead of trying out new ways. It takes practice being comfortable with our uncertainty, with not knowing how things will turn out.

When my clients are ready to venture into the unknown, we know it. They are not content with covering old ground; they are restless, excited, scared, distracted, impatient. I teach them to orient themselves to the new terrain, to consciously commit to this part of the journey.

Not knowing can be a marvelous place—full of curiosity, wonder, and surprise. The important events in people's lives have often been beyond their wildest dreams. When we let go of needing to know how our lives will turn out, we open ourselves up to a vast range of possibilities. The practice of not knowing is the practice of unleashing our curiosity, turning toward our intuition, setting our intention, finding our sense of trust and faith, and seeking our allies and resources in this new territory.

Unleashing Our Curiosity

One of our most important tools for exploring the realm of the unknown is curiosity. The word "curious" is defined as "eager to learn or know," and the roots of this word include "care," "careful," and "diligent."

Our relationship to our curiosity is mediated by our attitudes and experiences. As children, we were innately curious, which served our need to explore and learn about the world. Yet the world's response to curiosity is mixed.

Synonyms for the word "curious" include "inquisitive, nosy, inquiring, inquisitorial, interested, meddlesome, peeping, prying, and spying." These synonyms give us some idea about our relationship to curiosity and the mental constructs we may have about it. Children's stories are full of examples where curiosity causes trouble and harm.

Our curiosity can be "meddlesome" or "interested," depending on our motivation. Combined with mindful attention and care, curiosity toward the unknown allows us to explore, to observe, to be open, to leave space for information to come in. It allows us to look deeply into the nature of things, which may be different from how they appear on the surface. Curiosity leads us to examine what may be difficult for us or hard to understand. It can relax, inspire, and excite us. It can be light and playful, bringing us back to our childlike innocence. Curiosity also has the capacity to convey mature wisdom and compassion.

The Return of Intuition

As we become more comfortable with taking ourselves into the unknown, we rely more and more on intuition. Intuition is knowledge that does not come from the rational mind. The dictionary defines it as "the direct learning or knowing of something without the conscious use of reasoning; immediate understanding." Many of us are not used to relying on intuition. We need hard evidence. That small voice inside of us, our intuition, is often overridden by a trained command to be rational.

We think if we give in to our intuition, we must forsake our rationality. But this book is about allowing all parts of ourselves to exist. We need our rationality, just as we need our intuition. They cannot be mutually exclusive because they exist within the wholeness that is us. I spent years being schooled in rational thought, and then years training myself to listen to my intuition. Why would I want to give up any of this?

Daily life is full of anecdotes of people's "non-rational" experiences—inspirations, premonitions, funny feelings, flashes of insight, coincidences, signs, surprises, synchronicities. These experiences are often spoken about as though they were out of the ordinary when, in fact, they are commonplace—and they greatly enrich our lives. It is important to know there are places in our lives that cannot be reached by rational thought and, not surprisingly, some of these places have to do with the unknown.

At a conference last summer, I took a walk with the intention of discovering what forms in nature I was drawn toward. The usual places did not compel me: water, sunny meadows, large trees. What drew me in on this particular day were bridges of all kinds: logs over streams, fallen trees, wooden bridges, and a beautiful metal mesh footbridge with rushing water visible through it. I did not know what attracted me to these bridges, but I allowed myself to spend time with them, sensing them, noticing how they were, standing on the midpoint between the two sides, crossing them.

The next day I was in a large group workshop where two sides in the group were struggling with their differences and hurt feelings. When the leader asked us to place ourselves on one side of the room or another, depending on which subgroup we felt more resonance with, I found myself in the middle. This place simply felt right. As the workshop progressed, I played the role of a bridge between the two sides. I had not consciously sought this role, but could sincerely understand what both sides were feeling. Had some part of me known the day before when I was drawn to the bridges in nature that I would play the role of a bridge? Or had my experience with bridges prepared me to step into a needed role at the workshop? A mystery. Nevertheless, I was delighted I had listened to my intuition; it opened me to lessons from bridges.

When we listen to our intuition we are often surprised at how wise it is! True intuition is connected to all parts of ourselves and to what is going on around us. It is not bound by the usual realm of mind—the mental constructs created by our learned beliefs. Instead, intuition is related to what my teacher, Dr. Yvonne Agazarian, calls "apprehensive learning," which she distinguishes from comprehensive (rational) knowledge:

We apprehend something and all of a sudden we know—we may not be able to explain how we know, or why we know—or even what we *know—but there is no doubt inside us. We know and we know we know....In comprehension we are a long way from apprehension. In apprehension we know we are right. In comprehension we have to prove that we are right.**

Learning to rely on intuition takes practice. Students ask me: "How do we know whether our intuition is right, or just fantasy or imagination?" This takes experience—learning how our imagination works, and what it looks and sounds like. Yvonne teaches that imagination comes more from our comprehensive self, because in our imagination we use our minds to conjure things up, but "intuitive images are not conjured up—they happen spontaneously and unpredictably."

Here is an example:

Imagine you are on a beautiful tropical island. It is dusk. A balmy breeze is blowing through the palm trees, and the ocean waves are lapping calmly on the shore. You are lying on the sand relaxing and enjoying the sunset, feeling very peaceful.

Or:

Let your intuition take you to a place, anyplace in the world, where you can be relaxed and peaceful. Fill in the scene, from your intuition, with images, feelings, sounds, whatever your intuition brings you.

The first experience uses imagination, the second, intuition. The first makes many kinds of assumptions: Everyone will find a tropical island relaxing and peaceful, lying on the sand is pleasurable, everyone has happy associations with dusk, or everyone can even relate to an ocean experience. In reality, there are people who are afraid of the ocean, who hate lying on the sand, who

---

*Yvonne Agazarian, "A Theory of Living Human Systems and the Practice of Systems-Centered Psychotherapy," Special Presentation at the 37th Annual Meeting of the American Group Psychotherapy Association, San Diego, California, February 15, 1993, pp. 26-27.

feel very sad in the evenings, or who have never experienced an ocean. While almost everyone can imagine themselves in the first scene, some people would not be able to really experience peacefulness in such a setting.

The second experience relies on each person's own intuition to fill in what would be relaxing and peaceful. If you did it from your intuition rather than what you already know, you may have been surprised about where your intuition took you. In a large group doing this exercise, everyone's experience is different. And everyone's experience is right for them.

Both kinds of experiences are valid. They just serve different purposes. Imagination is important in many creative processes. In the realm of the unknown, however, when we only make things up—from our imagination, or from our fears and projections—we miss life as it is unfolding before us. Intuition is born of the present moment; using it allows us to be surprised and delighted, to venture beyond what we already know.

My friend Laura has a prayer she says when she is on the edge of the unknown: "I pray I remain open to the universe resolving things in a way that is easier than anything I can imagine." She says this prayer because a great deal of her learning has come from difficult situations. Laura now understands that much in her life can come from ease as well as hardship. For her, struggle, conflict, and violence are familiar. She has developed resources for dealing with these, but has very little familiarity with ease, comfort, and gentleness. These things are hard for her to imagine, so she knows she must pray for them—invoke them—whenever she feels at the brink of the unfamiliar.

Setting Our Intention

Another tool for entering the unknown is the practice of setting our intention. Though a different process than using our intuition, it is often complimentary. While intuition is a receptive practice, setting our intention is active. Our intention reflects what we want. Intentions can be general or specific.

They serve the purpose of orienting us in the unknown to our needs and goals, which can be physical, emotional, or spiritual. Intention helps us know why we are doing what we are doing. At the beginning of any class I teach, I ask the participants to set their intention for the class. If you know what you want, I say, you are more likely to get it.

Setting intention is the practice of listening for what we want and need (an intuitive, receptive process), and stating it consciously to ourselves (an active process). It always surprises me how difficult it is for some people to do this step. They are not used to asking themselves what they want. More likely, they have been passive receptors of what life dishes out to them. But if we don't know what we want or need, how can we recognize it when it is there? How can we tell if a situation is toxic or supportive, relative to our needs?

Karen, whose intention is to have intimate relationships in her life, did not always admit this. When I met her she was a very active, successful person who knew a lot of people. She stayed busy and was quite social, but seemed lonely. This was hard for her to admit. She thought something was wrong with her for being dissatisfied with her life. She should be satisfied, she thought—she had good friends, a good job, a nice home. I asked her about the quality of her relationships and she said she enjoyed the people in her life; she had a lot of fun with them. "Is there anything lacking?" I asked. She admitted there was an intimate quality missing that she wished she had more of. I asked her to be more specific, to sense what the essence of intimacy would be for her. At first, this was difficult. But as she worked with the idea, she realized she wanted more tenderness, quiet time, and expressions of caring.

Getting specific helped Karen quite a bit. When she knew her intention was tenderness, she was able to cultivate this quality in herself and look for it in the world. She learned that to have tenderness, she needed to slow down a bit, notice things more, be quieter inside, feel her feelings. Her intention went from general (more intimacy) to specific (tenderness) and helped her see a course of action to navigate through the myriad of available options. During the time it took Karen to transition from her old relationship habits to new ones, remembering her intention helped her. Here are her words:

Sometimes it was so hard. Friends would call and want me to go out dancing or to a party. In the past, I would never say no, even when I knew what I really wanted was more one-on-one quiet time with someone. It was hard to say no and face the fear I would be alone. But I would remember my intention and know that this was important. And I would start to reach out in a different way to people—call people who liked quieter things like going out to dinner or taking walks. At first it felt weird, and I felt I was missing out on something. But then I realized I was doing what I really wanted, and slowly I started having friends who liked this kind of closeness.

As Karen experienced getting what she wanted, her intention grew to having a long-term, committed relationship that had these same qualities. This was new territory for her; up to now she had been happy with more transitory relationships. She realized her new ability to make a commitment to herself and to her intentions made her less likely to act from desperation. She was more able to say no to the offers that were not what she wanted, even if it meant facing her fear of being alone and the mental constructs that went with it.

I weeded out everything not good for me, relationship-wise. I stopped being ashamed of my need for something lasting. I scared a lot of people away, because I admitted I wanted depth and commitment. But I saved myself a lot of disappointment.

When we forget or don't know our intention, we lose a means to navigate through the unknown. When things get stressful or tough, we forget why we are doing what we are doing. We're easily distracted from our goals. Change can be difficult. It takes energy to break out of our old habits, often more energy than it takes to continue doing what we have always done, even if that has not satisfied us. Our tolerance for handling difficult situations is strengthened if we have a clear intention. Intention reminds us of what is important, giving us a place to start and a means to continue.

Allies and Resources

Often when we are in unknown territory, we get the feeling we are out there alone. It is lonely, even terrifying. This is because we are outside of The Zone of Admonition. We have gone beyond what is familiar, and we have not previously had support and comfort here. We find ourselves trying, with varying degrees of success, to explain to our families and friends what we are doing when we try something new. Then we have to cope with their reactions. In many intimate circles, there is great resistance to change. To the degree that we have doubt (a normal feeling in the unknown), we will find people to mirror that doubt back to us. Having to deal with all this can be draining and distracting. Therefore, it is essential when we are in the unknown to find allies and resources.

Resources, such as those discussed in Chapter 6 as a means of moving past our stuckness, are also available to help us know what is possible as we enter The Mystery. These resources show us the steps and remind us we are not alone, that our goals are not foolish. Resources help us know that others have also been down this path.

Fortunately, we live in a time of tremendous resources—books, classes, teachers, practices, and so on. Knowing what resources to use is a matter of finding what is available, using our intuition to know which resources seem right for us, and then trying some out. In my own experience, and in working with others, I have come to realize it is sometimes our relationship with resources—whether or not we know they exist—more than a particular resource itself, that is critical. Believing resources are available gives us support. When we act from this belief, we get very different results than when we act from the belief that we must go it alone.

We are open systems. Even on the cellular level, change is a matter of taking in new resources and incorporating them into ourselves. We are in a constant relationship with the world around us that changes us all the time, whether we are aware of it or not. By consciously knowing that the world is full of resources, we are poised to utilize them. As we practice finding the resources available in our lives, we discover they are not out of reach. Our very life experiences are full of things to aid us in our spiritual growth.

Allies are helpers, aids—people and things that are on our side. The dictionary defines "allies" as "a country, person, or group joined with another or others for a common purpose." Allies can be people, but they can also be things. In some spiritual traditions, allies are animals, elements in nature, or spirit guides, all of which serve to inspire, direct, and comfort us. Our spiritual allies are aligned with us for the purpose of our unfolding. They offer us inspiration and encouragement, and challenge us when we go astray. They make us practice what we are learning. Our allies can keep us from danger and teach us lessons that help us on our path. They sometimes appear magically, saying or doing the right thing at the right time, and then disappear. Or they can be constant and easily identified. Sometimes they are dramatic, other times, subtle.

Although in our rational culture we do not talk much about spiritual allies, there are countless stories of people who have been touched by them in earthly and unearthly forms. Spiritual allies affect our lives and change us for the better.

My friend Gretchen tells of the dog that she had as a child:

My dog's name was Rusty. Stunningly beautiful, he was a rust colored collie with white paws and a white tip on his tail. We were inseparable from the time I was five until I had to hold him at nineteen to euthanize him. He was the gentlest creature in the world. Birds ate at his feet around the bird feeder. He taught me how to observe, how to sniff, how to be still. He was my introduction to the world of sensuality. He was my first teacher and I credit my ability to give and receive love on a deep level to his presence in my life. He was the most magical, significant confirmation of my soul's worth.

When I ask people in my groups to name some spiritual allies, here are some of the things they mention:

I have a spirit guide named Michael. He has quite a sense of humor. He helps me laugh at myself and lighten up.
Once when I wanted to kill myself, a white light filled the room and a voice told me if I could kill myself, I could do anything. I think of that presence as an angel. Since then, angels have been very strong allies for me. Sometimes they appear in human form.
My animals, they teach me about unconditional love.
Jesus.
Acts of kindness and compassion always inspire me.
There is a particular spot in a redwood grove where I never cease to be filled with peace and a sense of quiet wisdom. All I have to do is think of that place and I am filled with these feelings.
Dr. Martin Luther King, Jr.
Bach. His music makes me happy to be alive.
My wife.
I like to think of the great spiritual teachers—Jesus, the Buddha, Mohammed, the prophets, and mystics—as spiritual allies for me. They make me know that it is possible to be a living spirit in human form.
I worked with this little girl who was dying of leukemia. She

was so present and loving, even up to the time she died. She is still with me. I will never forget her. She was a great inspiration. She had so much strength.
My aunt. She taught me I could do anything I put my mind to.
Great artists. They express the magnificence of the human spirit.
My minister.
My therapist.
Nature. I am really nurtured by it. I feel part of a bigger whole when I am in it.
Lately, my spiritual allies have been the hawks that fly around my house. When I see them, I feel light and free. They remind me of the vast, empty space when my life feels crowded with distractions. They help me get perspective.

One of my own strongest spiritual allies is my daughter. Because of my depth of love for her, I am compelled to be the best person I can be. She gives me strength and inspiration to struggle with my limitations, to show up for her in ways that push me past my Zone of Admonition. She demands that I be honest, that I take care of myself, that I practice compassion and kindness. I know I would be a different person without her—less available to the full range of human experience and, as a result, less joyful.

Our spiritual allies are everywhere. We must begin to look for them and let them into our lives. They can be the person next to us on a bus bench. The person writing the book we are reading. An animal that crosses our path on a trail and makes us stop and feel the beauty all around us. A teacher who recognizes our ability. A loved one who doesn't give up on us. A child who reminds us of our innocence and simple truthfulness. The apple tree blossoming outside our window. A person from another culture, or another time in history. People whose actions, life works, and very being inspire us and deepen our relationship with ourselves and the world around us.

Spiritual allies also come in forms we may not recognize: the homeless person who activates our compassion, a friend who tells us the truth about how he sees us hurting ourselves, an unfaithful lover who rejects us and forces us to clarify what kind of relationships we want, a boss who fires us from a job we hate, or a teacher who won't let us fake it and demands that we do our best.

The practice of recognizing our resources and spiritual allies fills us with wonder. We come to understand we are not alone in our unfolding. We are part of an intricate network of both allies and resources. We have helpers—people and things which intentionally and unintentionally aid and inspire us, and compel us to cultivate our true selves.

Encountering the Mystery

Experience

The Mystery makes itself available in many forms, allowing us to expand, to become bigger than we normally are. It penetrates our unconscious trances. It stops us in our tracks. It gently shows us the way. The Mystery makes us laugh at ourselves. It gets us out of our heads and our routine ways of perceiving ourselves and the world. In its presence we may feel a sense of expansiveness, aliveness, wholeness, peace, or wonder—in touch with our spiritual gifts and blessings.

Experiences that put us in touch with The Mystery do not have to be spectacular or unusual. They can be, and often are, very ordinary. In fact, many spiritual teachers tell us to look for The Mystery ("the kingdom of God") in the everyday world around us. When we practice letting go of our need to know what everything means and what will happen next, we place ourselves in the realm of The Mystery, even in situations and experiences that are, at first glance, extremely familiar.

Here are some things that people wrote when I asked them about encountering The Mystery:

I think of a time when I was pulled to haul myself out to Christ in the Desert Monastery outside of Abiquiu, New Mexico in February. I felt like I needed an official retreat (never having had one in the religious sense). My story getting there was an endless amount of irritating delays. After missing plane connections, I arrived at the stopover place outside of Albuquerque too late for any food, ten hours in transit from New York. The next morning I had a treacherous car trip driving alone in the desert trying to find the unmarked monastery and get in on the dirt road which they warned turned into mud by noon. At the monastery I was alone, the only woman with seven monks who seemed very uncomfortable with me. The next morning after living in the monk cell I was given, I went out in the cold and sat huddled in some outdoor spot, held my face to the sun...tears sprouting. I had a realization or was it a voice or an experience of seeing true mind? The words that came to me were something like: "Look what you have to put yourself through, how little love you have for yourself, thus how little love you can have for the Divine." It was a moment of deep internal shift and a letting in of all that was around me in what felt like very new ways. And, of course, profound gratefulness mixed with the tears.

-Leisha Douglas

The experience like this that I can remember most vividly was during the winter of 1974. I had been up all night visiting friends and, rather than trying to go to sleep, I decided to simply stay up. Early in the morning, just before dawn, I climbed a small mountain next to our home in Franconia, New Hampshire. When I got to the top, I remember resting in a little shelter that you could sit in and from there see the entire panoramic view of the White Mountains. A dog started barking and suddenly I felt myself experiencing all of time from way in the past to way into the future, all at once, in that moment, from that mountain top. I remember feeling right about it. As though I had suddenly acquired some intimacy with time. It felt good.

-Jaci Hull

down in belly,
bubbling cauldron
of rage and judgment
like a bowl
contained by force of will
by the familiar mind talk:
"Calm down. It's okay."
staying there in the cauldron
a few seconds longer than usual
I look in a mirror and see,
oh great sadness, not myself,
but my heroes, my "I should bes"
staring at me like pictures hung on a wall
in overwhelming grief
I return to the cauldron in my belly
I wait
it opens and begins to send its heat
up through my chest, into my heart
I am frightened that it will be too much
for my heart
heat will fry heart like a barbecue
check with heart
no, it's okay, this heat helps heart express itself
yes, weeping
look at the mirror again
through the heat in my chest
now it's me looking at myself, smiling
now, it's me looking around
seeing people in the room
with more depth, more distinct colors
tender
human
like me
compassionate acceptance of humanness
replaces rage and judgment

-Cedar Barstow

I had just caught my wife cheating on me. After being together for seventeen years, this was quite a shock. I felt so empty; nothing would go right.

On a particularly beautiful fall day, I had to take a long drive for my job. I was having car problems so I took my car to the dealer. He gave me a loaner car. I noticed the gas gauge was on empty. The mechanic reassured me the gauge was broken and he had just put gas in the car. I headed down the interstate, which in Vermont doesn't have many cars on it. Thinking about all the chaos in my life at that moment made me mad. The car I was driving started to sputter and jump, then it died! There I was all alone on the interstate with no car phone—the car was out of gas. There are no gas stations on the interstate in Vermont. Another nightmare. What a mess. Why me? I started to walk to the nearest phone about eight miles away. As I walked I got angrier and angrier with each step, until I became exhausted and sat down. As soon as I sat down I started to see things around me. The beauty of everything startled me. What a great day! It was the splendor of fall foliage and the colors were unbelievable. How lucky could I be? All those poor people in their cars driving quickly by all this splendor and only I had the opportunity to look closely at God's work. I got to enjoy a walk on a great day; how lucky could you get? Later, after I refueled my gas tank, I realized that God had just refueled my *gas tank. I thanked the mechanic—he probably thought I was nuts. After that day I knew things were going to get better. And every time I drive down the interstate, I have a good laugh.*

-Frank

Today in Tai Chi class I got an especially strong and clear awareness of both my groundedness and *my lightness. Experiencing both simultaneously gives me a sense of well-being, a unified feeling, a lengthening, an openness, a rootedness that allows lightness....When I did the form, I became exquisitely aware of not just my energy moving through space, but my* being *the space around me. No separation. And no necessity of giving up my inside presence in order to experience this! In fact, Hel, my teacher said: "You cannot have this experience* without *having your inner awareness." What a pleasant surprise!*

-Sally Crocker

Encountering The Mystery is not so much a matter of orchestrating a particular kind of experience as it is one of cultivating a certain kind of perception. If we think The Mystery is only available to the holy or the spiritually adept, or when we are living our lives in perfect harmony, we are missing out on one of life's great gifts. For our very life experiences can offer us an opportunity to directly encounter The Mystery.

Yet in our everyday state of consciousness, we are usually so preoccupied with our thoughts, emotions, and "to do" lists, that we don't experience what is before us. We need to practice recognizing the feelings and mental constructs that block our ability to sense the wonder around us. We need to invite The Mystery into our lives and allow it to work its magic.

Living from the Present Moment

I have suddenly realized that I have been so preoccupied with writing this chapter that for long periods of time I have forgotten to look out the window next to my desk. As I direct my attention outside I notice it is Spring. The huge apple tree in the field across from my window is in full bloom, its white blossoms luminous against the gray sky. How had I missed this gorgeous tree, its radiant presence offering me joy? It has obviously been blooming for several days, but where have I been? Do I believe the work I am doing is more important than experiencing this beautiful tree? Now that I have noticed, I can allow this tree to be a mindfulness bell—a reminder to come back to the moment, to look around me, to feel myself within my surroundings.

This is the practice of returning to life in the present moment. Due to our relationship with time we often find ourselves living in the past or the future. We are anticipating what will happen—with dread, neutrality, or excitement—or reviewing what has already happened—with satisfaction, neutrality, or regret. But where we actually are is right here, right now. To truly live here requires practice. We must repeatedly bring ourselves back, feel ourselves, connect with the world around us as it is right now.

The present moment is where we get real information about ourselves and the world. It is in the present moment that we can notice what we and others are doing, thinking, feeling, wanting, needing, or avoiding. It is here that we can update our mental constructs so they align with reality. In the present moment we can make clear, mindful choices that serve us, rather than habitual, unconscious choices that don't.

It is beautiful to witness a client when she sees she has a choice. This moment of experiencing the actual choice point—the fork in the road where we can go down the familiar path of habitual feeling, thought, or sensation, or go down a different path—is tremendously empowering.

Returning to the present moment is a powerful practice that helps us find peace. We notice we are here, and become aware of the refreshing and nourishing things around us and the resources inside us that we may not have seen before. We become aware that in this particular moment, as we read this sentence, nothing bad is happening to us. In fact, the possibility exists that, in this particular moment, we are being nourished. In the present moment we can let ourselves absorb this nourishment.

Although there is much horror and pain in the world, each day brings moments upon moments full of wonder and beauty, both inside and outside of ourselves. We must remember to acknowledge these moments, to find them and cultivate them. In doing so, we can come to experience the absolute gift that is our life.

The Dance of Change

We are changing every moment, for change is an element of life. Our bodies are continually in flux. Every day thousands of our cells die, thousands are born. Our thoughts and feelings arise and die down like ocean waves. We move, we grow, we age, we die. Our ongoing development brings us to different physical, emotional, and spiritual needs—and to different attitudes, ideas, and meanings. Mentally, too, we have the capacity to expand, grow, and learn. Stuckness, while part of the human experience, occurs primarily in our minds. In reality, we are always changing; we have no choice about that.

Having practiced the elements of wholeness and transformation presented in this book so far, we are already familiar with our relationship to change. At this stage in our practice, we can acknowledge and understand our capacity to change and we can do things to support that change. We also know that our lives unfold at their own pace, like a flower blooming. We can practice trusting our internal sense of timing. This trust in our spirit's unfolding can help us accept and soothe our impatience.

Change is dependent upon our ability to tolerate uncertainty and enter the unknown. In fact, there are those who believe that human culture is at a crucial point in its evolution; that in order for us to survive, we must leave behind old paradigms—ways of being, thinking, and doing that no longer serve us. As technology and media have made our planet smaller, we have become increasingly aware of our interconnectedness. We have come to see that our relationships with our environment, with people who are different than us, with the other beings on the planet—both animals and plants—affect the quality of our lives. Events half a world away have an undeniable impact on us. To deeply comprehend this interconnectedness will take major shifts in consciousness and in how we live our lives.

The dance of change is a deep practice—one of embracing the whole of life as it is—including death. To do this takes us far into life, beyond our superficial ideas and feelings about it. This practice reveals to us both the unavoidability of impermanence and that something remains after the bodies, ideas, emotions, and relationships we hold on to so strongly pass away. To engage in the dance of change requires willingness and will, trust and intention. It requires the ability to do, and to let ourselves be done to—to affect our own lives, and to be affected by life. Change asks of us curiosity and patience, to move and to be still. It asks us to open inward into ourselves and outward into the world. It asks us to let go of who we think we are and to delve ever more deeply into life.

Unfolding into the Future

The future unfolds from the present moment. I picture this like a walking meditation where we walk just to walk. We put one foot in front of the other, mindful of our breathing, our feet touching the earth, the things around us as we pass them, but unconcerned about arriving. After a certain length of time, we have arrived at the end of our walk, enriched by the things along the way we have touched with our mindfulness.

If we approach the future like this we will be sure to arrive whole. We will bring all of ourselves along and, most likely, we will be surprised at what we have achieved and who we are. We are part of the stream of life that began before memory and will end who knows when. Our place in this stream is determined not only by our wills but by history, by the development of human consciousness, by our ancestors and descendants. We are connected not only to our past but to things yet to come; and our actions and choices in the present moment affect both our past and the future.

I am often struck by how many of my clients unconsciously prepare early in their lives for a change that will happen far in the future. They are not aware of what that change will be, but some part of them is readying; they learn and experience, one thing leads to another, and the change occurs.

Recently, I found a journal I kept in my late teens. In it were threads of what I know more deeply today—ideas and feelings I had about relationships, about consciousness, about healing—fleeting glimpses into the me I am now, buried in the intensity that was my life then. As I read my journal, I was surprised by my observations. They seemed insightful, with a wisdom I did not know I possessed at nineteen. I was amazed by how much of my almost agonizing struggle to understand myself and my relationships formed a foundation for my present knowledge. And how many of the things I was unconsciously striving for—clarity, honesty, inner peace, solidity, love—are presently available in my life.

It was touching to see myself as I was then—more raw, full of pain and self-doubt. I was heartened to see how I have changed, and to acknowledge the people and events that have contributed to my transformation. And it was surprising to see that the essence of what I experience as me, my spirit, was present to such a degree then, guiding the process, however unconsciously.

Shortly after I had written the section of this book on despair, my dear friend, Darcie Silver, was murdered at age 27 by an unknown killer. This shocking, random event took me to the depths of my fear and despair. For many months, I grieved, raged, numbed out, and watched myself doing these things. I could find no meaning in this tragedy. *Why did it happen? What kind of world is this? How can I go on in such a place?* I could not find any explanation to soothe me. I had nothing to say any more; I believed in nothing. I stopped writing and for the most part stopped teaching. I spent my time feeling my feelings and slowly learning ways to take care of such a penetrating pain.

In the summer, I was to talk on healing and transformation as part of a public lecture series. Because of my state of mind, I found it difficult to prepare. Usually, I have at least an outline from which to speak, but this time I could not even come up with that. The time arrived and I approached the podium unprepared yet curious about what would come out of my mouth.

I began to talk about my experience with my friend's murder. I explained since nothing I knew or understood in my life up to that time could help me understand this event, the meaning of Darcie's death could only lie in how it brought me into the future. As much as her murder brought me to my despair about the future, the answer to my questions about her death lay only in the future. What I did, how I lived my life as the result of knowing and caring for Darcie would bring meaning to her life and death. Her beauty and love for life, her compassion and light, are carried on in me and all of us who loved her.

That summer, because I was hurting so much, I chose to visit Plum Village, the practice community of my spiritual teacher, Thich Nhat Hanh. Because he had witnessed the worst things humans can do to each other during the Vietnam War, I knew he would understand my suffering. Although he offered me no explanation for why such horrible things happen, I was able, in the presence of my spiritual community, to heal some of my despair. Contrary to my belief that few young people have Darcie's radiance, sensitivity, compassion, and caring, I discovered at Plum Village that many such young people—Darcie's kindred spirits—exist all over the world. It gave me hope. I realized that just as Thich Nhat Hanh dedicated his life to peace and healing as the result of his experiences with human suffering, I too had to begin now to act on the wishes of my deepest self.

Since Darcie's murder, I have come to see that one form the future takes is that of our wholeness calling to us. We can touch the future now in the shape of our aspirations, visions, and longings. It is not simply some place we are striving to arrive—it unfolds from within our lives as we live them, from the events in our lives. And just as our lives are formed by the past, they are formed by the future. Through our spiritual yearnings, it calls to us, beckoning us toward wholeness.

Yet the future has more to do with how we live in the present moment than it does with the plans we make. We can have flashes of clarity about the future—intuitions and premonitions—because we are in direct relationship to it even now. We can practice the choice to go toward our dreams, visions, and aspirations right now—not just wait for them to arrive, but practice creating them in the present.

We do not arrive at peace, love, joy, compassion, stability, and clarity solely by working through our pain. When we live in the world, we are never entirely free of pain. In this life, there are always limitations and challenges, sickness and death, horror as well as beauty. Our relationship with this pain—how we treat it, what resources we bring to it—matters; it creates the quality of our lives. In other words, we have peace, love, joy, compassion, stability, and clarity by practicing peace, love, joy, stability, and clarity.

Darcie's murder has brought me further into the practices in this book. She helped me to recognize the call of the future. Her horrible death forced me to wake up, to choose life. I became aware of how important it is for me to live my life fully, to love deeply those close to me, to express that love by practicing understanding and compassion. In the course of my healing from the pain of this tragedy, I have had to acknowledge my fear and not let it stop me from doing what my spirit needs to do in my lifetime. My despair at Darcie's murder forced me to use my spiritual resources, which in turn have helped me to transform my despair into a bigger commitment to be doing my spirit's work in the world right now. As I write these words, I feel the essence of Darcie's spirit within me; I feel her smile, her values, her inspiration.

I know that I am not alone in this process. There are other people in the world who experience tragedy and transform their despair into a deeper commitment to their spirit. Our intentions and their cultivation make possible the kind of present, and therefore the kind of future, where our wholeness can thrive.

We do not have to wait for the future (until we are enlightened or until we die) to touch The Mystery. We only have to recognize, practice, and cultivate it right now. We open into the future from the present moment, from the choices we make, and the practices we do now.

Practices for Encountering The Mystery and Entering the Unknown

Check In

Throughout the day, when you find yourself in new situations, check in with what it is like for you to be at the edge of the unknown. Or check in throughout the day to your relationship to The Mystery.

Not Knowing

Tell a story about a time when things turned out better than you had hoped.

Name the positive things present in your life that you did not plan for.

Spend a day practicing not knowing. When you find yourself planning, tell yourself, "Let's just wait and see what happens."

Orienting to the Unknown

When you find yourself at the edge of the unknown, tell yourself, "I am at the edge of the unknown." Notice what it is like in your body. What feelings come up for you? What kinds of thoughts do you have?

Describe the differences between your fear and your excitement.

Relationship to Curiosity

Describe your current relationship to your curiosity.

Draw a picture of your curiosity.

What does curiosity feel like in your body?

Write ten rules you learned about curiosity.

List ten things you do with your curiosity.

Unleashing Curiosity

Spend a day being curious about everything you encounter. Notice how this changes your attitude about things. When you find yourself making judgments or jumping to conclusions, return to being simply curious. Good questions for practicing curiosity are "how? and "what?" (rather than "why?"). Respectfully share your curiosity. At the end of the day, take stock of the things you learned.

The Return of Intuition

Make a list of some of the non-rational experiences (inspirations, premonitions, coincidences, signs, surprises) that you have had.

Think about a situation in your life that is difficult for you. Imagine taking a journey to consult a wise person about this situation. What is the place like where this wise person lives? What kind of qualities does this wise person have? You tell the wise person about the difficult situation and he or she gives you a one-sentence answer. What does he or she tell you? Then the wise person gives you a gift to take back with you. What does he or she give you?

Write out a dialog between you and the wise person.

Throughout the day, practice asking questions and listening to the wise person. Make use of the gift the wise person gave you.

Setting Your Intention

Think about your goals for your spiritual transformation. State these goals in the form of an intention.

At the beginning of each day, take a few minutes and listen to your intuition for your intention for that day. Do this at the beginning of each week or each month. On New Year's Day or on your birthday, set an intention for yourself for the whole year.

Throughout the day, practice returning to your intention. When things feel stressful or difficult, simply return to your intention.

Put signs up around your home or office that remind you of your intention.

Allies

Our spiritual allies are those people and things which intentionally and unintentionally aid and inspire us in our spiritual unfolding. Make a list of your spiritual allies.

Spend a day with this attitude: *My spiritual allies are everywhere*. Notice what happens.

At the beginning of the day, call in your spiritual allies. Acknowledge them when they show up.

When you feel lost or stuck during the day, practice calling in your allies.

Encountering The Mystery

The Mystery makes itself available to us in many forms, both spectacular and ordinary. It takes us beyond the realm of our everyday perceptions and allows us to experience awe, aliveness, wonder, peace, wholeness.

Tell a story of a time when you encountered The Mystery.

Draw a picture of your relationship to The Mystery.

Spend a day with this attitude: *The Mystery is everywhere.* Notice what happens.

The Present Moment Revisited (or We Can Never Practice This Too Much)

Once again, spend a day returning to the present moment. Notice what you are doing, feeling, thinking, wanting, needing. Notice what is going on around you. Suspend judgment and look at the people and things around you with the eyes of the present moment, as if those people and things were really new.

As you return to the present moment, practice noticing the nourishing elements that are available here.

As you practice being in the present moment in your daily situations, notice what choice points (places in the day where you have choices about how to be, what to feel and think, and what to do) are there. At the end of the day, write about these choice points.

Change Inventory

Review the changes that are happening in your inner and outer life right now. What things can you do to support these changes? What things can you do to trust the timing that is truly right for you (not pushing too hard or bogging down)? What do you do with your impatience? With your fear? What resources can you bring to your impatience or fear?

Unfolding into the Future

Draw a picture of yourself unfolding toward your future.

Place your future across the room from you. Feel it pulling you toward it. Dance toward it. Take your time. What is your dance like?

Imagine that your future is calling to you. What is it saying? Write a dialogue with it.

Altars

Make an altar:

> to your curiosity
> to your intention
> to your intuition
> to your allies
> to the future
> to The Mystery

Creativity

Invent a practice that helps you become receptive to The Mystery. Spend time doing this practice.

Part 3
The Practice of Wholeness

If my heart could do my thinking
And my head begin to feel
I would look upon the world anew
and know what's truly real.
Van Morrison
I Forgot that Love Existed

Reality is the ground of effective liberation.
Thich Nhat Hanh

Chapter 9
The Cycle of Transformation

In the previous chapters of this book, we explored and practiced the elements that make up our wholeness, and those involved in the transformation process. Now we will look at the stages of transformation. The individual elements of transformation—the door to transformation, getting stuck, integration and alignment, and encountering The Mystery—can occur at every stage of a larger process, the *Cycle of Transformation*.

This particular map for the Cycle of Transformation has its basis in the *Five Elements* or *Five Phases* of Oriental Medicine. Each phase—Water, Wood, Fire, Earth, Metal—has a series of internal correspondences relating to the physical body, emotions, mental constructs, and spiritual capacities; and external correspondences relating to the seasons, climate, color, direction, food, and time of day.*

---

*A discussion of these aspects of the Five Phases can be found in the book *Traditional Acupuncture: The Law of the Five Elements* by Dianne Connelly (see *Resources*).

In my work both as a Western psychotherapist and practitioner of Oriental Medicine, I have, in addition to more traditional uses, used the Five Phases as a process-oriented map for psycho-spiritual transformation. This has proven useful in helping clients understand where they are in the transformation process. In the Cycle of Transformation, Water corresponds to *Entering the Unknown,* Wood to *Assertion,* Fire to *Manifestation,* Earth to *Integration,* and Metal to *Letting Go*.

Entering the Unknown

We begin the process of transformation, consciously or unconsciously, by entering the unknown. As we have seen, our relationship to the unknown—to newness, to The Mystery, to our intuitive mind—is crucial. At this stage in the transformation process, things are not yet realized in full consciousness. This, the *Water Phase* in Oriental Medicine, is the stage of energy before structure; it is potential—the reserve of energy waiting to take form. In the Water Phase, our will arises. Indeed, we navigate the unknown using our will—our determination—and our willingness. Our will begins to form the raw energy from this unconscious state and provide it with direction.

To access this phase of transformation, we must create space and quiet within us to mindfully look and listen. We direct this deep looking and listening to the world inside and around us. It is here that we begin to know what we want or what is necessary. It is here that we set our intention.

Let's say, for example, we are unhappy in our work. Perhaps we have trouble dealing with our boss. We have various options: we can act—find a new job, find a way to get along with our boss, pretend nothing is wrong, let the quality of our work slip, just do the minimum our job requires, malign our boss to our coworkers, work to change our boss; or before blindly taking action, we could do the practice that entering the unknown requires.

This phase of the process requires stillness, rest, and reflection.

It requires quieting our minds and bodies so we can turn inward to find direction for our lives. Many of us skip this stage. We do not like the kind of quiet and stillness it takes. When we are unhappy, we usually don't like to feel our unhappiness and learn more about it. More often we look for something or someone to blame, try to cover up our unhappiness, or find some way to distract ourselves from it. We go from possession to possession, relationship to relationship, project to project without bothering to discover what is truly fulfilling. As a result, because we have not taken the time to know what we really want or need and how to nourish it, we make the same mistakes over and over again.

If we are unhappy in our work and quit our job without taking the time to explore the deeper source of our dissatisfaction, what is to keep us from finding ourselves in a similar situation in a new job? The same is true in relationships. To find the answer, we must look mindfully into the nature of our unhappiness; we must take the time and space to turn our attention toward our unhappiness.

Perhaps our unhappiness at work is partially due to our boss's personality. Yet, if we look mindfully, we may find that his unhappiness simply shines a light on our own. Perhaps we are unhappy because we don't feel fulfilled, our work does not reflect our gifts and talents, or our job does not support our spiritual values. Perhaps we are unhappy at work because we have not taken the time to take care of ourselves—to find elements within our lives that are refreshing and inspiring. The question then becomes this: What inside of us wants to manifest (for example, creativity, spirituality, nourishment, communication) and how should we support its manifestation? Once we answer this question, we can set our intention toward this element—we can intend to take better care of ourselves or to allow our creativity to manifest—and then ask ourselves how to support this intention.

Because this stage of the process involves entering the

unknown, we typically feel our fear here. Our relationship to our fear can help us or hinder us. We can see it as a signal for entering the unknown, The Mystery, newness, the earliest stages of something. We can learn to calm our fear and take the time to go deeply inside. If we know how to quiet ourselves and make space to look and listen deeply, we arrive at direction and intention.

Assertion

In this, the *Wood Phase* of the Cycle of Transformation, energy moves from potential to the beginnings of manifestation. Like seeds germinating in springtime, energy once dormant begins to take root and project itself into the world in the form of plans and decisions. Psycho-spiritually, this stage is indicative of energy moving from the unconscious (given focus and direction by will and intention) to the conscious. Thus, we begin to envision how to best nourish and manifest our intentions.

Going back to the example of being unhappy at work, we have taken the time to understand our unhappiness and have perhaps discovered it arises from not feeling creative. Possibly we have uncovered an inherited belief that work is drudgery and therefore not supposed to be creative. Next, we set our intention to allow creativity into our lives. In this phase, we envision what this might look like and make plans to achieve it. It is here that we begin to assert our intention. We find allies and gain insight into which actions, beliefs, and feelings support our intentions, and which ones hinder them.

To plan something well, we must be able to clearly see the pathways through situations. Many of us suffer from the inability to see ourselves in fulfilling situations, or we don't know how to identify the steps to achieving our goals. So this stage of transformation requires our willingness to look at the mental constructs that tell us what we want is unattainable.

This phase asks that we practice flexibility, even as we begin to make plans, so that we remain open to the allies and resources available along the way. Often when we embark upon a process such as this, the end result is quite different from what we first imagine.

In this phase, we may feel angry and frustrated, signals that some aspect of ourselves is trying to assert itself. Our irritability may be caused by not taking the kinds of actions that best support our deep intentions. The way we respond to and with our anger can also help our intentions or hinder them. It is here that we meet our rigidity, powerlessness, or need to control, as well as our flexibility, spontaneity, and ability to let things unfold.

In our example of bringing more creativity into our lives, it is through assertion that we begin to have insight about our creativity. We explore our feelings and beliefs and make plans to touch the elements in the world that inspire our creativity. We allow our creativity to begin asserting itself, maybe at work, but at first in the most supportive places. Perhaps we take classes, read books, or get together with friends. We find our allies and we talk with and listen to them. We allow our creativity to express itself at home; perhaps we rearrange our bedroom to include elements that inspire creativity so that when we wake up every morning we are immediately reminded of our intention.

The practice here is to envision the pathways to fruition, to begin taking actions that support these pathways, to allow for input and help from allies and resources outside of us, and to be flexible about how we get where we are going. The insight and practice of this phase of the transformation process allow our intentions to move forward into manifestation and fruition.

Manifestation

In the manifestation phase of the Cycle of Transformation, energy, having reached full consciousness, moves into the world in the form of expression. This phase concerns our ability to respond in such a way that our intentions are truly realized.

According to Oriental Medicine, the gift of this phase is propriety, or right action. The archaic definition of propriety is "true nature." In this stage, our spirit or true nature expresses itself. Having followed our practices through the other phases of this cycle, we act or respond in a manner aligned with our intention. It is in this phase that we act, respond, express our will, execute our plans and our decisions, assert our true nature, and make the mark of our individual character on the outside world.

In our example, we have decided to be creative, despite our situation at work. The major obstacles to our creativity have been overcome and we allow our creativity to flower, to manifest in our lives, and to have an effect. Instead of spending time after work feeling tired and complaining about our work, we cultivate our creativity. Once this happens, we notice our creativity has a life of its own, and we respond to the world on the basis of this manifested gift.

Perhaps we produce art, write, dance, complete a project, create a business, solve a problem, or help others. Perhaps our creativity expresses itself more subtly—we adorn our workspace with flowers and inspiring art, wear vibrant colors, or talk to our coworkers about inspiring and uplifting subjects. Our journey into our creativity has taken us to new places and we have met new people or connected more deeply with the people we know. We feel joyful and our joy is visible to others. We are no longer so concerned about our boss' personality because we have addressed our own unhappiness. We have allowed our larger self to emerge, and it has taken our life in a new direction.

The challenge of this phase is learning to expand our capacity to tolerate joy without over-exhausting ourselves. In Oriental Medicine, this is called the *Fire Phase*, the energetic peak of the process. We need to be mindful of how we use our energy so that we don't burn out. This is where the practice of right action comes in handy. If we allow ourselves not to overdo, not to overspend our energy, we will be able to create a home base from which our true self can express itself. We will find ourselves radiating peace and joy, and will be able to reap the benefits of our practice as we enter the next phase of the cycle.

Integration

In this phase of the Cycle of Transformation—the *Earth Phase* in Oriental Medicine—we reap the rewards of our actions. This phase involves integrating what we have learned from the process thus far and taking nourishment from what we have manifested or created. Here, our intentions have been assimilated into our everyday reality; our efforts have matured into tangible benefits. We feel fulfilled and satisfied, or have become aware of what stops us from feeling this way. Integration, like the first phase, Entering the Unknown, is one of settling in. This time we reflect upon and savor the results of our efforts.

At this phase, we encounter our ability, or inability, to feel satisfaction. Here we learn to experience the benefits of our efforts. In our personal journey, this is the time to look at our relationship to satisfaction. Like other times that require sitting with ourselves and our feelings rather than busily doing, this practice is sometimes difficult. We often skip this phase, not taking the time to feel satisfied with the fruits of our efforts. In my experience, we must practice satisfaction to undo the habits of restlessness and dissatisfaction that fill our lives.

This dissatisfaction takes many forms. On the weekend we spend time at the mall purchasing new things, while not taking the time to enjoy what we already have. We have become so focused on the acquisition—of things or relationships—we often don't know what to do with them once we have them. So we blindly go from thing to thing, relationship to relationship. The current focus in some areas of our culture on living simply and enjoying basic low-cost activities, like time in nature or with family and friends, is an attempt to change some of the habits which perpetuate dissatisfaction.

In our example, we have allowed our creativity to flourish. Instead of waiting for the situation at work to change so we can be happier, we have taken our happiness into our own hands and found what we need to cultivate it. This has taken us on a new path. We may have discovered work that is more in line with our intention, or our satisfaction with work may have improved because it no longer seems a hindrance to our creativity. Our creativity has been integrated; it is now a part of our daily life. The old habits and beliefs that hindered its expression are gone, replaced by nourishing habits that engender new beliefs.

The practice of satisfaction is a deep one which leads to gratitude and peace. We become aware of the bounty of available resources, of all the beings and things which have contributed to our efforts. This awareness helps us cultivate generosity and compassion. We become willing to give back, to share our gifts with others.

Letting Go, Giving Away

This phase in the Cycle of Transformation—the *Metal Phase* in Oriental Medicine—is associated with the process of completion. Completion consists of retaining what is necessary, vital, or essential from the process and letting go of what is not useful, necessary, or available to us. We are aware of a great sense of release, of freedom, but we also feel sadness or grief. This bittersweet feeling is often experienced as the "let down" that usually follows a big project.

Sometimes our sadness is about limitation. We see there are things we intend which are not possible. Sometimes this sadness is simply the letting go of old habits, ways of being that are no longer useful. We may mourn the self that was imprisoned by these habits. It is said that every time we learn something new, a part of us goes back through our lives and places the new information in all the circumstances where it didn't formerly exist. This process connects us with our past and gives us the opportunity to bring parts of ourselves frozen in the past up to date.

In this phase, we grieve the loss of behaviors, habits, places, possessions, and people who have meant a lot to us in our journey. A client of mine, Tim, successfully gave up drinking at which point he was able to mourn the loss of his marriage, several years earlier, from his alcoholism. He had made a tremendous transformation in his life, and was feeling a great deal of freedom, clarity, and peace. At the same time, he felt sad about not having been able to offer these qualities to his marriage. He had to take the time to mourn his losses. His practice became using his sadness as a reminder to practice compassion and understanding toward himself.

This phase also involves getting in touch with the limitless source of spiritual energy available to us so that we might give freely of our gifts. Our sense of satisfaction, rooted in the previous phase, allows us to generously give of ourselves. Here we are able to use our talents and resources in service of others, giving back to the world which has nourished and supported us, and which needs our nourishment and support.

In our example of our blossoming creativity, we say good-bye to the habits, attitudes, and beliefs that have hindered our creativity. We mourn the person we were who thought it necessary to neglect our creativity. We mourn for the people who contributed to this neglect because of their own lack of understanding. We understand and feel compassion for the mistakes we and others have made. We give freely of our creativity because we know how to contact it, nourish it, and act from it, knowing it is always available to us—a source of joy for us and others. We reflect upon where we are in our life right now and begin listening again for what wants to emerge.

Back to the Unknown

Our journey has brought us again to the unknown. We have gained experience and wisdom. We know more about what works and what doesn't, about how to focus our intention, how to act in support of it, how to manifest it in the world, how to feel satisfied, how to let go of what is no longer necessary or satisfying, and how to give freely of our gifts. We take time again to be quiet, listen inside, make space for new intention and direction.

Getting Stuck Revisited

We can get stuck at any stage in The Cycle of Transformation—unable to enter the unknown, allow our intention to assert itself, manifest our plans, feel satisfied, or let go. Some phases are easier for us than others. Some people readily discover what they need, but find it difficult to take action. Others find it hard to know what they need, but are quite reactive. Some have a hard time making decisions. Others are decisive, but have a harder time letting go. Most of us have difficulty feeling satisfied with what we have created in our lives.

Getting Stuck in Entering the Unknown

Stuckness at this phase may be due to not being able to slow down enough to feel ourselves, to look at and listen to what we need or want. Or we may know what we want but be unable to set our intention and stay focused on it. Stuckness here can also arise from our fear of the apprehension that naturally comes with entering the unknown—and letting this relationship to fear immobilize us.

Going back to our example of hating our job, let's say we don't take the time to find out that our unhappiness is really due to neglecting our creativity. Instead, we react to our boss' behavior and are convinced he or she is the cause of our unhappiness. We complain to our coworkers who commiserate with us—which leads to more tension. We come home from work irritable, feel too tired to prepare nourishing food, complain to our spouse, and spend the evening sitting in front of the television watching reruns. Since we do not take the time to explore our unhappiness, we are powerless to do anything to change it.

Getting Stuck Around Assertion

We can get stuck in this phase due to lack of insight into what actions would nourish our intention. Or we may make copious plans, yet be unable to decide about the best way to proceed. Or we become fixated on one right way of proceeding rather than remaining open to a variety of possibilities as they arise. Stuckness at this phase has much to do with our relationship to our power—our ability to have an impact, to allow our actions to matter, to be flexible and not tyrannical or dogmatic. Stuckness in this realm often takes the form of "Yes, but..." We come up with plans and ideas and then find all the reasons they won't work.

Back to our example: We are aware that we hate our job because we are not feeling creative, but we don't know what to do about it. We are unable to figure out a way to be more creative at work. We believe we could be more creative if we had a different boss or job. We don't recognize our power to have an impact on our own creativity. People recommend classes, workshops, and other creative outlets but we find fault with all recommendations. We become irritable and depressed and our work performance deteriorates. This makes things worse at work and we lose our job. Our lousy boss has forced us to take some action but we are desperate at this point and get a job that is not much better than the last one. Our creativity continues to suffer.

Getting Stuck During Manifestation

Stuckness in this phase often results from having too many things going on at once—from spreading ourselves so thin that we misuse our resources. Or it can come from not taking the steps necessary to put our plans and intentions into action. We know what we need to do but we are not able to take the appropriate actions. Or we act out—take actions that are rash and damaging—because we feel that we need to do something. We can be stuck in restlessness and ceaseless activity or frozen in anxiety. We may have the energy to begin our projects but not to see them through to fruition, becoming easily discouraged by setbacks.

In our example, we know we need to cultivate our creativity and have many ideas about how to do so, but don't act upon them. We take a few classes but drop out in the middle. We start too many projects at once and don't finish any. We push too hard at work to get our creativity recognized and further alienate our boss. We spread ourselves thin, must always be doing, can't say no, and "burn out."

Getting Stuck in Integration

We get stuck at this phase when we are not able to feel satisfied or accurately assess the results of our actions. We can't recognize, take in, and savor what nourishes us; or we can't recognize and avoid what is toxic to us. In this phase we encounter our attitudes and beliefs about nourishment. This phase also has much to do with our relationship to our own worth. Other types of stuckness here include becoming complacent about where we are, getting into a rut, or becoming greedy or acquisitive.

In our example, we begin acting on our creativity, but we don't know how to feel nourished by our efforts. We don't feel satisfied with the small improvements we make. Our boss has made an effort to change his or her behavior, but we aren't satisfied—we feel it is too little, too late. Or we have created the kind of life we want but never take time to enjoy it. We go from creative act to creative act without feeling the satisfaction we have earned. We receive recognition for our creativity but it doesn't feel like enough. We are always aware of the people who are doing better than we are and constantly compare ourselves to them.

Getting Stuck with Letting Go

Stuckness in this phase results from being unable to complete. Transformation, by nature, means change. Change means letting go of something—circumstances, habits, beliefs, people, places, or things. Letting go is often accompanied by mourning or sadness, so our relationship to our sadness and our ability to mourn are important here.

We can get caught by melancholy, regret, or bitterness about the past. We may become stuck in relationships that have ended. We can get stuck in our habits, in our beliefs about ourselves, in roles we think we must play. We can get stuck in our beliefs about others and in what roles we think they must play.

Another aspect of stuckness in this phase is in letting go of everything, not being able to make deep and lasting connections, feeling "non-attached." Or on the other end of the spectrum, we may not know how to recognize limitation, or when or how to say good-bye. We don't know when to quit, when enough is enough.

Back to our example, we recognize that we will never be able to be creative at our job, but we don't know how to quit. We believe if we leave, the company will go down the drain without us. Instead, we persist in trying to turn our boss into a different person, so he or she will allow for our creativity. At meetings, we take up time insisting on projects our boss will never accept. We work harder and harder thinking he or she will someday notice our true merit. On other days, when we are discouraged, we tell ourselves it doesn't really matter, we are just working for the money. We become stingy with our time, energy, and resources.

When we get stuck at any point in the Cycle of Transformation, it is important to do the practices for stuckness offered in Chapter 6: recognizing that we are stuck, uncovering the mental constructs that contribute to our stuckness, taking care of the feelings that come up, finding the bigger space, calling upon our allies and resources for help, and finding encouragement for doing what is difficult. It also helps to orient ourselves to where we are in the Cycle of Transformation and to do practices that reflect that particular phase.

Using the Cycle

The Cycle of Transformation represents a map for the general flow of the transformation process. It is important to know that the actual process of transformation is not linear. We may be at several places on the cycle at once. We may go back and forth for quite a while between two phases before going on to the next phase. We may be at different phases for different parts of our lives, and whole years of our lives may be devoted to one phase or another.

When working with clients, I try to get an idea of where the client is in the cycle. They find an orientation map helpful: "Oh, I'm working on learning to feel satisfaction." "I need to take time out to listen in inside in order to know what is going on with me." "I'm going into the unknown, it's normal to feel fear." "This involves manifesting; I have to take risks putting myself out there." Once oriented, we look for the ways the elements of our wholeness—body, emotions, mind, and spirit—participate in that phase. We also invoke and study the elements of transformation—the door to transformation, getting stuck, integration and alignment, and encountering The Mystery—and their roles in the cycle. Using this information about where one is and how he or she gets stuck, one can then design specific practices that nourish and enhance the transformation process.

Practices for the Cycle of Transformation

Checking In

For the different parts of your life (e.g., your relationships, your work, your family life, your creativity, your spirituality), where are you in the Cycle of Transformation? Check in with the ways that you may be stuck in any phase of the Cycle.

The Unknown Revisited

Think of your goals for spiritual transformation in your life. Pick one that seems to be important right now. Spend a week with this goal in your consciousness. Set an intention around it. Throughout the day, practice being quiet and listening inside for what your spirit tells you about this goal. Record any dreams that seem relevant. Let yourself wander through a bookstore and notice which books you are drawn to. Open one and see what it says to you. Notice what you are drawn to in nature. Notice if any spiritual allies arrive.

Throughout the day, practice letting yourself be on the edge of the unknown. Bring your curiosity and willingness.

Notice how you get stuck when entering the unknown. Is it hard for you to quiet down and go inside? What do you do with any fear that arises? What kinds of things do you tell yourself?

If you get stuck, call in allies and resources and do other practices for stuckness.

Assertion

Envision a path for moving toward the spiritual goal you picked above.

Make some plans to help you get closer to this goal. Notice what you tell yourself about your plans. List any "Yes, buts..." that you may have.

List the things you feel might be obstacles to this goal. Notice what you tell yourself about these obstacles. Notice any feelings that come up. What do you do with your feelings?

List the ways you procrastinate.

If you get stuck, call in allies and resources and do other practices for stuckness.

Manifestation

From your plans above, pick one action that is easily accomplishable. Do this.

Do one simple thing a day that brings you toward the spiritual goal you have picked. Notice what feelings come up for you.

Notice what you tell yourself about manifesting your goal. What thoughts and images arise for you?

List ten things you do with your impatience.

List the ways you overdo.

List the ways you stop yourself from doing.

What do you do with the energy that manifesting your spiritual goal brings you? Practice letting that energy settle into your body. Relax your body into that energy.

If you get stuck, call in allies and resources and do other practices for stuckness.

Integration and Satisfaction

Find ways to integrate your spiritual goal into your daily life.

List the areas of your life where you feel satisfaction.

When you feel satisfied, what is it like:

in your body?
in your emotions
in your mind?
in your spirit?

List ten things you do with your satisfaction.

List the areas of your life where you feel satisfaction.

When you feel dissatisfied, what is it like:

in your body?
in your emotions
in your mind?
in your spirit?

List ten things you do with your dissatisfaction.

List what stops you from being satisfied in your life right now. What do you say to yourself about these things? How would you find satisfaction if you could not change them?

Spend a day practicing feeling satisfied. Notice what happens. How is this day different from other days?

If you get stuck, call in allies and resources and do other practices for stuckness.

Letting Go, Giving Away

What has your current spiritual goal invited you to let go of?

When you have to let go of something, what is it like:

in your body?
in your emotions?
in your mind?
in your spirit?

What do you do with any sadness that arises?

When you are generous, what is it like:

in your body?
in your emotions?
in your mind?
in your spirit?

List the ways you are generous.

List the ways you are not generous. What stops you from being generous?

Spend a day practicing generosity. This can be generosity of resources, time, energy, or even generosity of thoughts, attitudes, and words. Notice what happens.

If you get stuck, call in allies and resources and do other practices for stuckness.

Altars
Make an altar:

to the unknown
to assertion
to manifestation
to satisfaction
to letting go
to generosity

Creativity
Invent practices that help in the Cycle of Transformation. Spend time doing them.

Chapter 10
Life Beyond the Wall

When we practice allowing ourselves to be who and where we are right now, transformation is possible. Transformation brings us to a life beyond the wall of separateness, limitation, and despair.

Beyond The Wall, we become present for ourselves and our experiences. We come to recognize, tolerate, and then appreciate all parts of ourselves—our bodies, emotions, minds, and spirits. Fear—of ourselves, others, and life—becomes less of a determining factor as we recognize it to be simply a part of entering the unknown.

We become familiar with our limitations—with the learned and inherited patterns of being, thinking, feeling, perceiving, and acting that limit us and keep us from experiencing our inherent wholeness, deepest spiritual aspirations, and wisdom. We become familiar with how we are, the way we change, and our relationship to the Cycle of Transformation. We are able to look at the reality of the moment with a steady gaze and tolerate the feelings that arise in us. We learn to understand how we become stuck and how to bring resources to our despair.

We set our sights beyond the Zone of Admonition, and begin to practice empowering our spirit by connecting with our spiritual allies and resources. We feel light, spacious, awake, capable of taking action, compassionate, and free. We realize we are not alone: We are connected to and supported by the world around us. Our experiences nourish us. We recognize life as a miracle and become involved in creation. We uncover our spiritual gifts and want to share them with the rest of the world. We support the spiritual gifts of others and with others create the kind of world in which spirit can flourish.

Finding The Daily Miracle

The real miracle is not to walk either on water or in thin air but to walk on the earth.

-Thich Nhat Hanh

While traveling in Oaxaca, Mexico, I stopped to rest on the steps of a church. Although the morning was beautiful and warm, I was feeling sad and homesick. As I was sitting there, a young boy around seven years of age approached me. He was dressed in torn clothes and carrying two pails of milk to the nearby market. He sat down beside me, looked up, grinned, and said, *"Cada día tiene un milagro; solamente hay que buscarlo."* (Every day has a miracle; one only has to look for it.) I was dumbfounded. "How do you know this?" I asked. He replied, *"Es obvio, no?"* (It's obvious, isn't it?) I laughed aloud at the unlikelihood of this conversation having taken place at any point in my life up until now. For the rest of the day I was happy: I had found today's miracle, or rather it had found me.

After this encounter, I began looking for the daily miracle. Skeptical at first, I often didn't recognize the miracle until the very end of the day, when it dawned on me and I burst into laughter. Yet it was always there to be found. After a while, I came to expect the miracle and discovered at least one every day—big and small miracles, present as though under a thick layer of dust that only needs wiping away. I had never known to look for them; I had specific expectations about what constituted a miracle and had not let myself feel the part of me that touches such things.

The word "miracle" comes from the Latin *miraculum*, "a wonder, marvel," and *mirari*, "to wonder at." As my practice of looking for the daily miracle deepened, I began to see that the real miracle was every morning having a new day. I was alive on this beautiful earth— there were flowers, animals, people, and a multitude of wonders I could feel and witness. The everyday became marvelous.

While looking for the daily miracle, we are likely to encounter our cynicism. This practice may awaken the wondering, trusting parts of ourselves that have been hurt or humiliated in the past. When we are hurt like this, we set these parts of us aside or bury them alive within us. As I began to experience my sense of wonder, I also felt a habitual, protective skepticism arise. Beneath this skepticism was a fear of being laughed at by my family and friends who already thought I was weird enough. I felt how my cynicism closed me to my experience of the miraculous.

Because cynicism often protects parts of us that have been hurt, our practice when we encounter it is to direct loving attention and tenderness to these hurt parts. When we nourish these parts, our capacity for wonder expands, as does our ability to feel joy.

A sense of the miraculous can astound us by taking us out of our habitual way of seeing the world. Life becomes surprising and new, as our beliefs and prejudices are challenged. On the steps of the church in Oaxaca, I was astonished to hear wise words coming from the mouth of a seven-year-old child. I must have unconsciously believed that boys in rural Mexico were not capable of such wisdom. This prejudice evaporated on those steps as I began to recognize spiritual wisdom everywhere.

I recommend this practice of looking for the daily miracle to clients or students who are feeling despondent, or who are unable to see the ways in which their lives are blessed. Difficult at first, this practice helps them get out of themselves and into the world. It broadens their perspective and makes them aware of spiritual gifts and resources. Often they see that the things they seek are right in front of them. Doing this practice, they encounter many kinds of miracles—all the marvels that make up daily life.

Empowering Our Spiritual Gifts

In my classes, I sometimes have a participant stand in front of the group. The group looks at the person before them and calls out the spiritual qualities they see in him or her. I ask the group to name qualities they actually see at that moment, not things they know or can surmise about the person. Because we have mental constructs about, for example, what patience and grace are, we may not recognize our own patience or grace. But these spiritual qualities are more easily recognized by those who do not have the same mental constructs. Because most of us have spiritual qualities longing for recognition, this process is often quite moving.

Sometimes, when we experience this recognition by others, we are grateful. Other times, we are embarrassed or feel selfish, because we have been taught it is vain to think highly of ourselves. The Latin root of the word "vanity," *vanitas*, means "emptiness, worthlessness," which is not at all the experience that comes from acknowledging our spiritual gifts and allowing a felt sense of our true worth.

The recognition and empowerment of our spiritual gifts take practice. We know this intuitively. People say things like: "I am practicing patience." "I am practicing forgiveness." "I am practicing gratitude." Although we have these gifts within us, we must cultivate them in order for them to fully blossom.

Here is a partial list of spiritual gifts:

abundance
adventure
balance
boundaries
caring
clarity
communication
compassion
connection
courage
creativity
curiosity
dedication
delight
earnestness
empowerment
enthusiasm
equanimity
expansiveness
fairness
faith
fierceness
firmness
flexibility
focus
forgiveness
freedom
friendliness
generosity
gentleness
grace
gratitude
groundedness
happiness
harmony
honesty
hope
humility
humor
insight
inspiration
integration
integrity
joy
justice
kindness
lightness
love
loyalty
luminosity
mindfulness
nurturance
openness
patience
peace
perseverance
playfulness
power
protectiveness
prudence
purity
purpose
radiance
responsibility
satisfaction
sensitivity
simplicity
sincerity
solidity
spaciousness
spontaneity
steadfastness
strength
tenacity
tenderness
tolerance
transformation
trust
truth
understanding
virtue
wholeness
willingness
wisdom

Here is some room for you to add ones I've missed:

These gifts are available both within and around us. The first step is to remember, to acknowledge, that they are there. Then we must invoke them, just as we invoke our spiritual allies. As with the practice of finding what is not wrong, the practice of empowering our spiritual gifts involves allowing them space, letting them have a voice, listening to their wisdom, and giving them power to act in the world. Finally, we must acknowledge the fruits of our practice.

Although I am a patient person with my clients and students, I can be quite impatient with my husband and daughter. Recently, I have made a conscious decision to offer my family members the same patience I offer my clients. I have had to consciously replace the habit of reacting with the practice of patience. First, I had to stop at the point where I would normally react, take a few conscious breaths, then invoke patience. It has become easier as the pathway to patience has become more well-worn. The fruits of this practice have been wonderful. Both my husband and daughter seem happier and have been more loving, kind, and patient with me.

I learned the habit of impatience from my own family experiences as a child, and from living in a culture that wants everything right now. I know I want family members to be patient and gentle with me, and I thrive in the presence of such treatment. I also know I have the gift of patience within me because I use it every day in my work. By giving to my family what I want to receive, I have gotten it in return. By cultivating the gift of patience, I have helped create a fertile ground where patience can grow in family life. I have discovered that we often have within us the gifts we want to receive.

Our spiritual gifts are aspects and expressions of our true self, our spirit, our wholeness. This part of us remains intact despite what has happened to us in our lives. Our wholeness, often buried under pain and neglect, is waiting to be recognized, empowered, and employed. Using our spiritual gifts empowers our wholeness, giving it room to manifest and take action in our lives. As tools of our wholeness, our spiritual gifts are powerful because they transform our lives. They can heal our pain and alleviate the suffering of others. They are their own reward. By empowering these gifts, we are able to live in a world where they are easily accessible, making life extremely satisfying.

Everything Is Useful

Because wholeness connects us to everything, allies and teachers are everywhere. As a result, it becomes possible to connect with spirit even in the most challenging and difficult of situations, to see what Thich Nhat Hanh calls the flowers that grow from the garbage.

When I lived in California years ago, I had an opportunity to work with young women who had been refugees from the Vietnam War. I was amazed by the resiliency of spirit in these women. All of them had lost loved ones, their homes, and their possessions. Some of them made dangerous journeys across a vast ocean in tiny boats crammed with people. They had seen the worst things that people can do to others, yet they came to this new country with hope and a willingness to begin anew, to face the hardships and seize the opportunities available for them here. They made use of their experiences. They taught me about the innate capacity of the human spirit for transformation and gave me much hope.

In the transformation process, we make use of what we have. Just as flowers are fed with compost made from garbage, we can put the raw material of our life experiences to use toward our spiritual transformation. We learn that life contains difficulties. It is not a matter of arranging our life to avoid them, but of learning to bring our resources to face them. When we face our problems, we gain experience, we become experienced, we learn. We become wise, which the dictionary defines as "marked by deep understanding, keen discernment, and a capacity for sound judgment."

Everything in the universe constitutes the unbroken wholeness that is reality. Everything in the universe, both positive and negative, connects us with our wholeness. Everything is useful. As we gain the ability to go more and more deeply into our present experience, we see interrelationships everywhere. When we practice looking at the world in this way, we feel a great sense of support. We learn that we do not have to turn our back on suffering—our own or that of others. We know there are resources available for us, and that we too can become a resource to share with the world.

When we recognize our capacity to be a resource in the world and act from our desire to express this capacity, we become spiritually empowered. As our capacity to tolerate reality grows, so does our freedom. We experience an internal sense of both solidity and spaciousness.

The Process

Many people, when they come to this place beyond The Wall, are shocked they have lived any other way. They often describe feeling as if a burden has been lifted, or as if they had been living their whole lives in an illusion or under a curse.

At first, we may mistrust these new feelings. We feel vulnerable, open, new. We wonder why others around us don't feel the way we do. We may become critical of others, at first, or self-righteous as we struggle to protect our new-found feelings. We become angry, impatient. We fall back on our old habits. We forget. All these things are normal landmarks on the road to wholeness. The key to transformation is to not get off the bus at any of these landmarks, but to continue journeying. This means to continue practicing.

As we continue to practice, we mature. We are able to look deeply at ourselves and the world around us to cultivate true understanding. We become capable of more and more compassion—toward ourselves and toward others. We recognize that seeking wholeness is not the same as seeking perfection. We become able to see the world as it is—both its beauty and its horror. We do not turn our backs on suffering, nor do we turn our backs on wonder. We are able to more easily acknowledge and empower our spiritual gifts. We become more and more able to offer our gifts to the world, in genuine desire to alleviate suffering.

Practices for Life Beyond the Wall

Finding the Daily Miracle

Every day for a week, look for the miracle of the day. It may be big or subtle; just let yourself be open to it. At the end of each day write down what you found.

Empowering Your Spiritual Gifts

Make a list of your spiritual gifts. What do you tell yourself about your gifts?

Have a friend make a list of the spiritual gifts he or she sees in you. Or if you can, stand in front of your friend and have him or her tell you what spiritual gifts he or she sees in you. Notice what this is like for you. Try to avoid diminishing what your friend is saying, or notice the way you diminish it. After your friend is done, simply thank him or her. Or you can do the same for your friend, if he or she is willing.

Pick one of your spiritual gifts from your list (or your friend's list) and draw a picture of your relationship to it.

Pick one of your spiritual gifts from your list (or your friend's list) and give it a voice. Have it speak to you (or write to you) about its role in your life and your relationship to it. Let it tell you anything it wants from you.

Have a dialog with one of your spiritual gifts.

Pick a spiritual gift for the day and act from it. For example, spend a day acting from your patience. Notice what happens.

When you act from your spiritual gifts, what is it like:

in your body?
in your emotions?
in your mind?
in your spirit?

List what stops you from acting from your spiritual gifts.

Everything is Useful
Spend the day with this attitude: *Everything is useful.* Notice what happens.

The Process
Take time to contemplate your spiritual process, whatever that means to you. What is your spiritual process like? How is it different now than it was when you were younger? Last year? Last month? Since beginning this book?

Draw a picture of your spiritual process.

List the things that discourage you on your spiritual journey. What do you do when you are discouraged? Practice calling in allies and resources when you feel discouraged.

List ten things you do with your perfectionism.

List the ways you are critical of or feel superior toward others.

List the ways you offer your spiritual gifts to the world.

List the ways you are available to the gifts the world offers you.

List the ways you have matured.

Altar
Make an altar to one of the spiritual gifts you are cultivating.

Creativity
Invent practices to help you empower your spiritual gifts and journey beyond The Wall.

Chapter 11 Connection

Much of this book has been dedicated to cultivating our connection with our true selves. We have learned to recognize and make space for all parts of ourselves, and to understand the process of spiritual transformation that leads us to our true selves, selves which are part of the unbroken wholeness that is reality. At this important point in our practice, we become conscious of our connection to the world outside of ourselves—to others, to community, and to the universe—and we recognize our desire to understand and practice this connection.

When we are born, we spend the first months of our lives in undifferentiated fusion with everything. During early childhood, we learn to have a self and to connect with others as that self. Much of what we know about connection—our attitudes, beliefs, and feelings about relationships—we learned as children, from our families, cultures, and personal experiences.

In wholeness, everything is connected; this is a basic truth.

Nonetheless, connection must also be recognized and practiced. What we have learned about connection from our past experiences can be limited, based on wrong thinking and hurt. In fact, most of the psychological and spiritual pain I see has been caused by abuse and neglect in relationships. Abuse and neglect occur when we are cut off from our true selves, our wholeness, our connection to others and to all things. The separation from our wholeness and our spiritual gifts causes us to act from ignorance in ways that create suffering in others, and ultimately in ourselves. We create a Zone of Admonition and don't go beyond it to seek true happiness. We live in the tiny box of the familiar because we are afraid of the unknown, and we miss the wonder that is connection.

This sets up a vicious cycle, where patterns of abuse and neglect are passed on from relationship to relationship, and from generation to generation. This happens until we consciously make the effort to heal this hurt and practice another kind of connection. The ways we have been hurt by and hurt others are so deep and subtle, we typically can't see them until we are in active relationships. In order to heal these wounds, we must consciously practice connection.

We practice connection, a deep practice, to strengthen it, bring understanding to it, and allow our wholeness to express its true nature. Our wholeness can heal us because, by its nature, it *is* connection. Wholeness allows us to tolerate and then have compassion for all parts of ourselves and others, to bring our spiritual gifts into our relationships, and to help others bring forth their spiritual gifts

Kinds of Connection

There are many kinds of connection, but I will discuss four: connection with self *(intrapersonal)*; connection with another *(interpersonal)*; connection with community; and universal connection. Each type forms a basis for the others.

Connection with Self

The practices in this book have focused on cultivating our relationship to self, so I will only say a few words about this type of connection here. I believe our connection with self is important (important enough to write an entire book on it!) because the quality of this relationship affects all aspects of our lives, including all of our other relationships. The more able we are to know ourselves, to be compassionate with ourselves, to allow ourselves to be ourselves, the more we will have these skills available in our relationships with others. The deeper this connection is, the deeper our relationships with others can be.

But connection with self is not enough. I went through a period in my life when I lived alone with my infant daughter and dedicated much of my time to my spiritual learning and practice. I got to know myself very well, and had achieved a solid and satisfying peace with myself. I was truly happy being with myself. But at the same time, I knew I wanted an intimate, committed, day-to-day relationship with another adult. My time alone allowed me to discover what I wanted in a relationship and to decide to have one that contained these elements: honesty, commitment, humor, joy, love, gentleness, strength, willingness—rather than settle for one lacking these just because I was sometimes lonely.

When I found myself in a relationship, I was amazed by how my peace and equanimity were tested! Those years of practice came in handy, helping me to hang in there, because I knew the worst that could happen was I could go back to being alone, something I enjoyed. Yet, because there are things we learn from a connection with another that we can't learn on our own, I wanted to persevere.

Part of the practice of being in relationship to ourselves is becoming conscious of our feelings and mental constructs about relationship itself. These feelings are formed from the role models for relationships we have seen around us. We may believe no one will ever love us, there are no good men or women out there, commitment is stifling, or we can't trust anyone. Yet, if we have these beliefs, what kinds of relationships will we have? Indeed, because of our beliefs, when we try to relate to another we may not be able to see clearly the person who is really before us.

So we use the practice of relating to ourselves to clarify what we truly want from a relationship, to learn to see ourselves as we really are, and to get in touch with and empower the spiritual gifts that we bring to relationship. Then, when we are in a relationship with another, these gifts will be accessible.

If we want commitment from another, we can practice making a commitment to ourselves. We can commit to being with ourselves, not abandoning ourselves when we are confused or hurt, and sticking with ourselves through thick and thin. We can make a commitment to our relationship vision, and take care of the hurt parts of ourselves that don't believe this vision is possible. Practicing commitment to ourselves will allow us to recognize what commitment looks and feels like when it is being offered by another. We will be able to bring our true selves to relationships.

Connection with Another

Connection with another is a second kind of connection, and of course, it is more complicated. This connection can take place with any kind of being—for example, my connection with the owl that lives in the tree by my house—but I will mostly focus here on connections with other people, because these tend to be the most challenging.

Our first connection is with our mother in the womb. We are literally attached to her by the umbilical cord. We share her blood. Her nourishment is our nourishment. We are swimming in a sea of her—her body, her feelings, her energy. We do not yet know we have a self. We just experience what is.

Our next connections are with our caretakers—family

members or others, depending on our circumstances. Our siblings offer another kind of connection, as do our early playmates and friends. Some of us connect at an early age with our spiritual allies, the beings—people, animals, plants, and minerals—that help nourish us by giving us the kinds of relationships we need in order to grow spiritually. As we get older, we learn about other ways to connect, such as intimacy with lovers. Most of this learning takes place unconsciously, yet has a profound effect on us.

All of us have interpersonal relationships that take many forms—casual interactions, acquaintances, friendships, intimate relationships, and relationships which take place entirely inside our minds. How we are in these relationships—how we relate to and treat others—affects the quality of our lives, as well as the quality of many lives. Our interaction at the complaint desk of a department store can affect our lunch date with our lover. Our interactions at work affect our relationships at home. Many people come to therapy seeking to improve their interpersonal relationships. They feel they can't get what they want, they can't communicate well, or they believe the other person is keeping them from something they need.

I have found that a good relationship with another is based on the presence of four conditions: the ability to let ourselves be ourselves, the ability to let others be themselves, the willingness to change for another, and the willingness to let another change. All the relationship problems I see come from not being able to do one or more of these.

The practice of letting ourselves be ourselves

The practice of letting ourselves be ourselves is described in all the chapters of this book. Contrary to what we may believe or have experienced, we do not have to give up our true selves to be in relationships. In fact, our true selves are crucial to good relationships.

Many of my clients with "relationship issues" deny or suppress important parts of themselves for the sake of their relationships. Some of us, in the deepest part of ourselves, want a committed relationship. Yet because we are afraid to be alone, we settle for casual ones. We tell ourselves this is satisfying; we even invent philosophies that denigrate commitment. This sets up a battle between the part of us that wants commitment and the part that is afraid to be alone. Our casual relationships may be full of conflicts because we are not truly satisfied.

Or we may be in a long-term relationship that doesn't allow us space to cultivate the things important to us. We look for the other person to provide these things, but he or she doesn't. We constantly defer our needs to the other person because we don't know how to ask for what we want. We blame him or her for our not letting us be ourselves, for not nourishing us, for not giving us what we need.

The more we can be aware of ourselves and our needs, respect those needs, let ourselves be ourselves, and be true to ourselves, the easier it is to be in a relationship. When we let ourselves be ourselves, we feel empowered, we trust ourselves, and we find it easier to ask for what we want. We create room for ourselves in relationships. We know our limitations and don't blame them on others. We know which relationships are good for us, and which are not.

The more in touch we are with our true selves and the more we empower ourselves, the more resources we have available for us in relationships. We can freely offer our gifts to relationships, without bitterness. We aren't afraid to say "I'm sorry" when we have done something to hurt another. And when we give ourselves room to be ourselves, we can more easily practice allowing others to be themselves.

The practice of letting others be themselves

My greatest teacher of letting others be themselves has been my daughter, Lisa. Watching her become herself has been a delight to me over the years. I have approached each stage of her development, even the difficult ones, with curiosity. When I have faltered in this, she has always let me know. Even in our conflicts, I have seldom assigned devious, undeserved motives to her behavior. My deep love for her has allowed me to practice letting her be herself more easily than with anyone else.

Somehow, I had different expectations for a partner. When I entered into my relationship with my partner, John, I discovered I had to practice letting him be himself. I was pretty good at letting myself be myself; I had practiced that for years. But I was inept at letting John be himself, despite the fact that I knew how to let others be themselves through my experiences with my clients and students. I knew I had it in me, yet seemed to have difficulty practicing this with John.

Early in our relationship, we had terrible fights because I felt that he was not in touch with his feelings, or not dealing with something I thought important. Instead of letting him know what I needed, I became angry with him for doing things differently than I did.

Over time, I learned that he is sincere in his commitment to our relationship, but that he is not like me. His way of dealing with things is different; his timing is different; his methods are different. For example, when I brooded over some difficulty between us, he often asked me to take a walk. I discovered that if, instead of accusing him of not dealing with the problem, I went with him, I felt much better afterward and was more able to clearly see what was bothering me. I now trust John's values and realize him to be a good person. I know he wants many of the same important things I do from life. I know we are in this together.

Our ability to be true to ourselves and different from someone else while still remaining connected creates a paradox, one that generates great freedom. Many of us believe that to have connection with someone else we have to be the same. This attitude limits us in relationships, because each person is unique: We are not the same as anyone else.

Many relationship fights are about the struggle for each member of the couple to be themselves. In these struggles, we often look at the other person as the enemy. Many of the worst struggles take place when we have similar longings but different methods. In my own relationship, I have had to learn to give John the space to experience his feelings; while many of mine are immediately available, his take time to percolate up through his consciousness. I have learned to observe his steadfastness and solidity. He has learned to not be so overwhelmed by my reactivity—which had helped me calm down, and call on other resources. John has learned to appreciate my passion, and I have learned to love his patience.

When we first meet someone we like, or when we fall in love, we are willing and able to let the other person be themselves. We are curious about the other person and we want to get to know him or her. We may see some limitations but are willing to overlook them, because we see the appealing characteristics.

Later in the relationship, we may become more critical of the other person's limitations. We see these flaws as harmful to us. While some characteristics really are harmful, here I refer to how we surrender ourselves to the other person's limitations, blaming our unhappiness on him or her. This creates conflict because we expect the other person to change to make us happy. Because he or she can't or won't change, especially without our compassion, we make the other person the enemy.

When we see the limitations of others, we can then offer them our compassion instead of our fury. When we see another person clearly, we are more able to decide what kind of relationship to have with him or her, and make better relationship choices. Had I known how to let others be themselves in the past, I could have saved myself from some heartbreaking relationships. My partners were telling me, through their actions, that they could not give me what I wanted. Yet, I did not believe them because I was fixated on my relationship dream rather than on the person who was actually before me. If I had been able to see them clearly as themselves, I would never have asked them to give me what they could not.

When our habit is to make the other person the enemy during conflicts, we miss what is really going on; we miss the gifts of our differences. If we practice letting others be themselves, we can see them as they truly are—with their gifts and limitations. The practice of letting others be themselves while being true to ourselves helps us expand into compassion and true love.

The practice of being willing to change for another

When I introduce this practice in classes or lectures, someone invariably challenges me. "Isn't that co-dependency? Isn't that submissiveness?" they ask. We have been so indoctrinated into the idea of not giving ourselves away to others that we are afraid of this practice. In order to practice changing for others correctly, we must be grounded in the first practice: the practice of letting ourselves be ourselves. If we can really do this, then we can let ourselves change for another.

This practice has to do with the willingness to offer a person what he or she needs because we care for that person and see his or her need, even if it is not natural for us to meet it. It may mean opening up to parts of ourselves we don't normally experience, because the other person needs those parts to be available. Currently in my own relationship, this practice is my willingness to be patient with John when I'm more inclined to be reactive, because I know he needs my patience and it will benefit him.

Again, my daughter has been my greatest teacher in this practice. Time and again, I have changed my beliefs, feelings, and behavior because it is in her best interest. When I was pregnant, I gave up alcohol and caffeine. I avoided violent movies and other things that would upset me in order to create a peaceful mother for my child. After she was born, I rearranged my work schedule, practiced patience, learned tolerance, and activated my curiosity, all because I saw her benefit from these things.

While it has been easier to change myself for my daughter than for my partner, I now see that the willingness to change for each other has been an important element of my relationship with John over the years. And, my willingness to change for him has contributed to my own development. Doing this has helped me cultivate aspects of my true self.

The practice of being willing to change for another challenges us, for it puts us right up against our limitations. Had my client, Tim, been willing to change for his wife he would still be married to her. His wife wanted him to stop drinking because she saw it as harmful. Indeed it was, but he interpreted her wanting him to stop drinking as an affront to his freedom. Eventually he had to choose between drinking and his relationship, and he chose his drinking, acting out in more and more destructive ways. Because his wife knew she could not change him, and that his behavior was harmful to himself, her, and their children, she left him.

Tim knows now that his wife's leaving was the consequence of his actions. At the time, he used it as an excuse to drink more, until he lost connection with his family and friends. Now that he's not drinking, he has regrets. Tim loved his wife, but he was not willing to change for her. Yet, he's learning to let himself be himself, understand his gifts and limitations, see the reality and consequences of his choices, and acknowledge that he can change. It is his hope—and mine—that some day he will be strong enough in himself to be able to change for another.

The practice of changing for another comes from our strength and solidity. It is not a form of submissiveness. It is not a deal in which we give up our self in order to earn someone's love. We change for the other person because we love and value him or her, and we want to do what we can to support his or her happiness and well-being. It is not an easy practice, because in order to do it we must be in touch with our own power. But as we practice it, it gets easier and our power becomes more available to us.

The practice of being willing to let another change

I have a friend who for several years has been complaining about her husband. He's not sensitive enough; he's not in touch with himself; he doesn't communicate what he's feeling; he's a workaholic. I know my friend's husband, and I agree that these things are true about him, although I also know he is a wonderful person, a good father, a good provider, and dedicated in his own way to his family. My friend simply put up with her husband's faults, until recently, when a series of stresses pushed her to consider divorce. She and her husband agreed these problems were serious enough to go into couple's therapy. In the course of therapy, my friend's husband saw that his wife was right, and decided to change. But instead of being thrilled that she was finally getting what she wanted, my friend became furious.

We had a long talk about this and she realized she'd been angry for a long time, but hadn't been true to this feeling, because she thought it would destroy her marriage. She had felt it her job to keep the marriage going, even if she wasn't happy. Now that things were better she had space to feel her anger, and she saw her feelings were deeper than that—she was afraid. Now that she was getting what she wanted—a husband who was more sensitive to her, attentive, and in touch with his own feelings—she knew that she had to change, too. She saw she was responsible for her own happiness. She feared she couldn't do what it takes to have a healthy relationship.

Often we don't let others change because we have some investment in them being how they are: We get to feel righteous or superior, we get to get by on our not-so-best behavior, we get to blame them for our unhappiness. When we let someone change, we have to change, too.

Letting someone change means updating the mental constructs we have of them. This is especially relevant in long-term relationships. People change over time, many times for the better. They mellow with age, they realize the folly of their past ways, they connect with their deeper gifts. Acknowledging the capacity for this type of change brings hope and heals despair. When others change in this way, we need to recognize this and update our relationships to include a new view of them. This allows them to blossom.

If we practice these four things in relationship—allowing ourselves to be ourselves, allowing others to be themselves, willingness to change for another, and willingness to let another change—our capacity for connection and intimacy will deepen and flourish. These practices are challenging because we learn about relationships by being in them, not just by thinking about them. Being in a relationship with another means learning how to be open to that person. It means learning when to deepen the connection, when to provide distance, how to have conflict, and how to allow for resolution and forgiveness.

Empowering the Spiritual Gifts of Another

Another connection practice involves empowering the spiritual gifts of another. When we focus all the time on what is wrong in our relationship or with the other person, we practice neglect. We are neglecting to acknowledge the spiritual gifts and resources of that person, which are expressions of their innate wholeness. In my own relationship, when instead of obsessing about what I'm not getting, I practice focusing on all that I receive from my partner—his generosity, wisdom, patience, lightness, humor, and love—I have more resources available to deal with the difficult times. If I remember that he is not a monster, but a good person, with limitations *and* gifts, it makes it easier to find resolution when we are in conflict. If I take the time to help him find and empower his spiritual gifts, things get even better, and I benefit from the fruits of these gifts in my life.

Intimacy

My vision of intimacy is a series of concentric circles, going inward toward our deepest heart, our true selves, and then outward again into the world. Each circle represents a deeper stage in the relationship. At each circle is a gate. In deep, long-term relationships, there are times we find ourselves standing with our beloved in front of one of these gates. We know we are at a gate because the gates are marked—often by conflict, turbulence, stress, hard times, or periods of estrangement.

When we find ourselves at a gate, we must renew our commitment to our relationship, and to each other. We must say to our beloved, "We are at a gate to deeper intimacy. Are you coming through this gate with me?" Then we must wait for their answer. Sometimes our beloved gets to the gate first and waits for us. While we are waiting, a good thing to do is to invoke spirit, so that we can wait with all our gifts and resources, ready for our beloved and for our relationship.

Connection with Community

Just as there are many types of interpersonal connections, there are many types community connections. We have the community we live in: our neighborhood, city or town, state or country. We have work communities, school communities, church communities, communities of friends, and intentional communities. More and more, because of media and technology, we are becoming aware of the global community in which we live.

Yet, in spite of our increasing awareness of community, people commonly report a loss of the sense of community in their lives. Many of us don't know our neighbors. We may be part of many communities, but we don't know how to connect. We are in communication all over the globe, but we live in isolation.

Sometimes I am asked to work with organizations. These are usually social service organizations that call me in to help them work with various issues that arise in their work community: conflict, empowerment, team building, communication, leadership, burn out. What I have learned is that most of us don't know how to work as a community. We have never learned. Our models for being together as a group reflect roles we learned in our families, with parents and siblings. Needless to say, this creates difficulties.

Nonetheless, because of our increasing global awareness—because of our awareness of diversity and the rights of each person or group to be themselves—we are being called to create a container expansive enough for us all. This container can be a family, an office, a neighborhood, a town, a country, or the world.

There are various ideas about group dynamics, team building, and creating community, but these ideas are only as good as the intentions, consciousness, and actions of the people practicing them. At the core of group interaction is our connection with ourselves, and our own level of interpersonal connection. The more grounded we are in these two types of connection, the more resources we can bring to group interaction.

Community also has an energy of its own. It takes more time—it is not as immediate as intrapersonal or interpersonal relationship. In order for community connection to work, we have to practice different kinds of thinking, perceiving, and interacting from the ones we use in individual interactions. Community relationships are complicated because multiple dynamics are operational—especially those of power and cooperation. Indeed, we need to understand our relationship to power when practicing this level of connection.

When we get together in a group, right away we are aware of our differences. Frequently, these differences are seen as polarities—right wing and left wing, women and men, young and old, haves and have-nots, gay and straight, and so on. Conflict occurs when we perceive these polarities as mutually exclusive and opposed to one another. We then lose focus on our common characteristics and goals. As with couples, sometimes these differences are simply a matter of method rather than values. Our habit of considering differences "bad" prevents us from seeing the resources available in our community. Because we are not used to thinking with a "community mind," our view of community is limited. We take a personal view when a larger view is needed.

One of my colleagues recently related her experiences in this regard. The clinic where she works was being restructured and she was engaged in a power struggle with her supervisor over unclear roles. My colleague was clear about what role she wanted, but because the group was in transition, there was a great deal of confusion. She saw this as a personality problem between her and her boss, feeling as though she always had to prove herself to her boss. I saw it more as a group dynamic. Often when groups are undergoing transition, there are periods of destabilization where roles become confused. This creates stress on the individual members, and people react in habitual ways, which may not benefit the group goals. Taking it personally makes it worse.

Seeing this larger perspective enabled my colleague to come up with ideas to help the group stabilize during this transition. She came to see her clarity as a strength in the group. Once she stopped taking the process personally, she stopped feeling resentful and became willing to offer her gift to the group. I see this dynamic happen over and over in groups—we take it personally when our differences aren't automatically respected because we don't understand how groups work. We don't see that "suspicion" is a stage in the group process. When we are personally hurt, we feel resentful. We neglect to offer our talents and skills because we don't feel appreciated.

Communities are a microcosm of the whole. Each member of a group represents part of the whole. Each role an individual member plays is important to the whole. Some roles people play include: leader, peacemaker, authority, mediator, witness, caretaker, rebel, rabble-rouser, visionary, doer, speaker, and elder.

In groups, we can come to understand our role and decide if it's one we want to be playing. If it is, we can empower this in ourselves. We cannot wait to be appreciated by others for our role before we offer our resources. In one organization I worked with, a participant complained it was her job to be the caretaker for the group. She was the one who remembered birthdays, asked people how they were doing after they had been sick, checked on staff morale, made snacks for her coworkers, and otherwise made sure the work environment was pleasant and comfortable. This was not an assigned role in her job description; she had taken it on herself because she cared about these things. I asked her why this bothered her. She was angry because she felt no one appreciated her efforts. She seemed to be the only one who cared. I told her, "But this is an aspect of your power—you like creating an environment where such things are present." She was shocked. She had never understood this as an element of her power.

For a while she was silent, but then she reported that I was right. Her caring was a talent she had and enjoyed. She just wanted to know she was appreciated for making her work environment a pleasant, more connected place. At this point, most people in the group acknowledged her talent and expressed their appreciation for what she did for their community.

Community connection is essential. Everything in our lives exists as a network of interconnections. Community is wholeness. Learning how to cope with, tolerate, benefit from, and contribute to it enhances our personal wholeness. Connection with community is also unavoidable. Acknowledging community connection allows us to learn about it and work with it, to respect our connections rather than damage them.

Connection to community is also important because it is a resource. My spiritual teacher believes that without spiritual community, spiritual practice is difficult. Practicing alone, we lose energy and enthusiasm after a few weeks or months. Community can give us energy and support us—this is especially the case in communities united around a goal or set of values.

We have had glimpses throughout history of the power of community—of the combined energy of a large group set on a common goal—but we have only begun to tap into the power of this type of connection. More and more focus is being placed on the knowledge and practice of group and community dynamics. We need to learn how to tolerate and use the energy of community. Most of the problems that face us on our planet today, by their nature, cannot be solved by one or two people. They require community cooperation.

Universal Connection

Yesterday, while having lunch with me, my friend Denise told me about a ritual she did on the land around our houses. We were lamenting the rapid over-development of our community, a delicate high desert ecosystem replete with wildlife—coyotes, hawks, bobcats, mountain lions, snakes, lizards, rabbits, birds—beautiful desert plants, limited water, and a growing population of humans. Denise had gone out to meditate with the intention of connecting with the beings that shared her environment and to open herself up to their wisdom.

I agreed with Denise that the meditation on connection with all beings was a wonderful practice. We talked about the changes happening in our community, and how fortunate we were to live in such a beautiful place, how linked we felt to the environment around us. We wondered what we could do to protect the animals, plants, and minerals in our community. We had already tried letters of protest, community meetings, government meetings, talking with attorneys, writing articles in the local paper, and decided that we would continue to express ourselves in these ways. But we also felt a need to keep alive our connection with the elements we loved in our community, so we would not grow bitter. We felt a need to draw upon the strength and wisdom of the other beings so we would not feel alone.

The dictionary defines "universe" as "the totality of all things that exist, creation, the cosmos." Universal connection manifests itself in many ways and there are practices that can help us get in touch with this level of connection, where we become aware that we are part of a greater whole. For example, we can become conscious of our sharing life at this moment with all other beings on the planet. Their life is our life. The quality of life of all other beings affects our quality of life and vice versa. If people are suffering in another part of the world, this affects us.

As I write this, fires are raging in southern Mexico and Central America. Here in New Mexico, thousands of miles away, the air is filled with haze from the smoke, so thick that the mountains a few miles from my house are not visible. The state of Texas to the south of us is on a health alert. The health of our air, our oceans, and of all the beings on our planet affects us, and vice versa. When we cultivate a deep relationship with our planet and the beings on it, we begin to find ways to live that honor these connections.

When we practice universal connection, we see our relationships are not made up of "us" and "them." In my own rage, I can see the young man who murdered my friend Darcie. In my own greed, I can see the crack dealer who sells out his own community. In my own neglect, I see evils created by neglect all over the planet. And in my caring, I understand my connection to all the others who care, all over the planet.

We can also become conscious of our existence in the stream of time. At this moment we are connected to all people who came before us, our ancestors, and to all people who will come after us, our descendants. When I work with clients, I am very aware of this dimension of universal connection. When someone is trying to transform a deep mental construct, for example, I can feel the energy of that person's ancestors in them. Some of what we believe, we have believed for generations. When we make a deep spiritual transformation, it transforms—frees—not only us, but our ancestors and descendants as well. As much as we may like to deny it, we are connected to our ancestors. We are the continuation of them. They are us; they live inside our cells. Similarly, our choices today have a direct effect upon those who will live after us.

When we practice getting in touch with these connections, across space and time, we realize we are bigger than we think. Our body is the whole earth. Our consciousness is the consciousness of every being on it. We can practice holding this connection in our consciousness and tolerating the sensations of it in our body; we can root this awareness in our whole being.

In addition to our connection with all beings across space and time on this planet, we are connected with the unbroken wholeness throughout the universe. This is The Mystery, for we know little about our actual place in this wholeness. But we can practice feeling this connection and the awe it inspires in us. We can feel the whole cosmos in our body; that our body is part of the cosmos.

Many people also experience this universal connection in their relationship with what they call God, the Supreme Being, the Higher Power, Christ, Buddha, Yahweh, Allah, Jehovah, the Creator, the Great Spirit, the divine, angels, bodhisattvas, and so on. Regardless of the mental constructs we carry concerning any of these particular words, we can cultivate a direct experience of the divine in our lives.

Universal connection puts us in touch with unbroken wholeness. Like all kinds of connection, we must practice and cultivate it. When we do, we learn how to tolerate the experience of our vastness. We can let it inform us and affect how we live our lives. If we do, we become compassionate and wise, and our fear of limitation and death diminishes.

Connection and Impermanence

My friend Denise said that when she was meditating to connect with all beings, she learned about impermanence from a flower. She saw that the flower, like most non-human beings on the planet, does not live in fear of change or death. A flower's life is very short but it offers its beauty and gifts freely, without fear of impermanence. Impermanence is part of life—and as humans we are conscious of it. Yet, we do not know how to relate to it. So many of us avoid, ignore, and live in unconscious fear of it.

Connection and impermanence are very close to each other. Each connection we make in our lives reminds us of impermanence. Thich Nhat Hanh says that we do not suffer because things are impermanent; we suffer because things are impermanent and we pretend that they are permanent. I know that someday, perhaps, my beautiful rural community will be gone, transformed into another type of community. This makes me sad, but it also makes me want to be awake—fully present for, paying attention to, appreciating, and understanding what is here before me now. This is also true of my loved ones—my partner, my daughter, my family, my friends. Knowing about impermanence enriches connection.

In the reality of unbroken wholeness, connection is a mystery. My partner John exists in my life because of a combination of elements, many of which I had no control over. Many circumstances led to our meeting, some of them chance, some happening before we were born. We met at a certain place and time, and we each wanted the same thing from a relationship. What made it work was us both admitting we wanted a partner. We liked each other, and our intention at the beginning of our relationship was to learn how to cultivate partnership with each other. We saved a lot of energy that many couples use when they are together simply deciding whether or not they are going to be together. We used this energy instead to create the kind of relationship we wanted.

In the years that we have been together, my relationship with John has grown and deepened and taken me beyond many of my mental constructs concerning relationship. I know no matter how long we are together, eventually we will come up against impermanence. This makes me want to connect with him even more, love him with my best love, see him clearly, and understand him deeply.

Practicing connection brings us up against impermanence. Practicing the understanding of impermanence connects us back to The Mystery of unbroken wholeness. When we die, our bodies are transformed. They become part of the earth, dissolving into the elements that make them up. We do not know for sure what happens to our spirits. Most spiritual thinking concurs that we are not limited to this body or to this life span, that after we die, our spirits are also transformed. But the reality of what happens to us after death is a mystery.

I do know that my friend Darcie, who died violently at a young age, lives on in me and in all the people who love her. As does the person who murdered her. Darcie is a part of me, as are all my relations. I know my blood ancestors and my spiritual ancestors live on through me. I feel them inside me. My life is an affirmation of them.

The realm of unbroken wholeness exists both in and beyond our daily lives. If we use our understanding of impermanence to empower our spiritual gifts, we touch our wholeness. The deep practice of connection—to ourselves, others, community, and the universe—is the ground, the base, for our practice of wholeness.

Practicing Connection

Checking In

Throughout the day, check in to your level of connection in your life (to yourself, to others, to community, to the universe).

Relationship to Connection

When you are connected (to yourself, to others, to community, to the universe), what is it like:

in your body?
in your emotions?
in your mind?
in your spirit?

List ten things you do when you feel connected.

When you are disconnected (from yourself, from others, from community, from the universe), what is it like:

in your body?
in your emotions?
in your mind?
in your spirit?

List ten things you do when you feel disconnected.

Write ten rules you learned, overtly or by example, about connection (to yourself, to others, to community, to the universe).

List the ways other people hurt you.

List the ways you hurt others.

List the beliefs you have about relationships.

Commitment to Yourself

Make a relationship commitment to yourself. Let it include all parts of yourself. Practice this commitment. Write it down and post it where you can see it.

Draw a picture of your commitment to yourself. In this picture, what are you: Doing? Saying? Wanting? Needing? Giving yourself?

Relationship Vision

Create a relationship vision (for a relationship with another) for your life. What are the qualities of this relationship? How do you treat each other when things are difficult? Describe an ordinary week in this relationship. How do you feel about this vision? What do you tell yourself about it? Write your relationship vision down and post it where you can see it.

Draw a picture of your relationship vision. In this picture, what are you: Doing? Saying? Wanting? Needing? Giving?

Are your current relationships aligned with your vision? How or how not? If not, how can you bring them into alignment?

Do one simple thing a day to bring one of your relationships closer to your vision.

Create a relationship vision together with a friend, partner, or lover. Discuss things you can do together to bring your relationship closer to your vision. Do these things.

The Practice of Letting Ourselves Be Ourselves

Describe the ways you abandon yourself when you are in a relationship. What parts of you get left behind? Find ways to allow these parts into the relationship.

The Practice of Letting Others Be Themselves

For a day or a week, practice letting others be themselves. Say to yourself: *This person is not me. He or she may feel, think, and act differently from how I do. His or her thoughts, feelings, and behaviors are about him or her, not about me.* At the end of the day, write down the ways this changes your relationships.

Think of a significant relationship in your life. List the ways this person is different from you. List the other person's gifts. List his or her limitations.

List the ways you let this person be him or herself. List the ways you don't.

List the ways you make this person "the enemy."

Practice offering your compassion and understanding to this person, especially when he or she does something that annoys you.

If your relationship really is damaging to you, get help.

The Practice of Being Willing to Change for Another
Think of a significant relationship in your life. Think about one small thing you would be willing to do that you don't do now to bring the other person more happiness or peace. Practice offering this to him or her. What comes up for you as you practice this?

The Practice of Being Willing to Let Another Change
Think of a significant relationship in your life. Think about this person's limitations. List the thoughts, attitudes, and beliefs you have about this person's limitations. Next to each, write how you act toward the other person when you have that thought, attitude, or belief.

Spend a day with this attitude: *This other person is on his or her own spiritual journey. This person is changing and growing at his or her own pace.* Notice what happens.

Think of a significant long-term relationship in your life. List the ways that person has changed for the better over time.

Empowering the Spiritual Gifts of Another
Think of a significant relationship in your life. List that person's

spiritual gifts. Find ways to acknowledge and appreciate those gifts.

Connection with Community

Describe the various kinds of communities in your life and your relationships to them. List the roles you play in these communities. What are some of the roles other people play?

Pick a community you are in that is important to you. Make a list of the things you can do to be more connected to that community.

What gifts do you have available to give that community?

Make a list of the things that prevent you from being more connected or offering your gifts. Next to each item on your list, write a thought, feeling, or attitude you have about that item.

Draw a picture of your vision for community. What do you tell yourself about this vision?

When you eat, practice acknowledging all the people that made your food possible. See yourself as a link in this chain of people. Say a blessing over this food, thanking all these people and wishing them well.

Practice recognizing all the people who have made the place where you live possible. Practice feeling yourself part of all these lives.

Universal Connection

When you are outside, practice acknowledging the people, animals, plants, and minerals that share your world with you. Acknowledge the stars and planets and worlds beyond our own. Practice feeling yourself part of all these things, woven in, in unbroken wholeness. Notice what this kind of connection is like for you.

Connection Meditations

Stand or sit comfortably in front of a mirror. Allow your eyes to focus softly on your reflection, and bring to your consciousness the people who have made up your life: your family, friends, acquaintances, teachers, ancestors, lovers, enemies. All these people are part of the wholeness that is you. Let yourself see their gifts and limitations. Acknowledge what they have given you. Offer them all a blessing of well-being.

Sit comfortably or lie down with the front of your body against the earth. Place yourself in the stream of your family lineage. Know that you are a continuation of your ancestors, that you have inherited gifts and limitations from them. Allow the pains and limitations that you inherited from your family to dissolve from you into the large vessel that is unbroken wholeness. Imagine their pain and limitations also dissolving from them. Know that the work you do for spiritual transformation transforms everyone in your lineage. Offer all your family members a blessing of well-being.

Do the same for your spiritual lineage.

Do the same for a specific person who has caused you pain.

Use your consciousness to place yourself everywhere on the planet at once—in places where there is joy and in places where there is suffering. Know the joy and suffering of all beings on the planet is also your joy and suffering. Connect yourself with the victims as well as the perpetrators of suffering. Ask to see how the abuse and neglect that exists on the planet is connected to the abuse and neglect that exists within you. Offer a blessing of well-being for all beings on the planet. Know that the work you do for spiritual transformation, and the behavioral and lifestyle changes that result, are for the well-being of all.

Connection and Impermanence
When you are aware of impermanence, what is it like:

in your body?
in your emotions?
in your mind?
in your spirit?

Throughout the day, use your awareness of impermanence to allow you to be fully present for the people around you.

When you are angry at someone, imagine both of you 200 years from now.

If someone you love has died, continue to have a relationship to him or her. Keep this relationship alive, by connecting with that person in your thoughts and in your actions. Update your relationship as time goes on.

Altars
Make an altar:

to connection with yourself
to connection with another
to connection with community
to universal connection
to impermanence

Creativity
Invent practices that help you feel more connected. Do them.

Chapter 12
Practicing Wholeness

We do not know why we are here, or how we got here. We all know someday we will die, but we don't really know what it means to die. We have many theories, ideas, notions, beliefs, and feelings about life and death, but life and death are, in reality, a mystery. Life unfolds as we go along, not a moment sooner. People can tell us what something will be like, but until we live it for ourselves, these are just ideas. The ideas in this book are just ideas, until you live them, practice them, for yourself.

The practice of wholeness is the practice of how we live our daily lives. We understand from this practice that we have choices. We can fill our lives with suffering, or we can fill our lives with the gifts of spirit. We can live as if life is meaningless, or we can live as if life is an opportunity to manifest our true selves. Living our lives as a means to manifest our wholeness brings us a certain kind of life. When we live our daily lives connected to wholeness, we have many resources available for ourselves and for others.

Thich Nhat Hanh says, "There is no way to enlightenment. Enlightenment is the way." It is the same with wholeness. We are not practicing in order to one day be whole. We are practicing wholeness itself so we can learn to tolerate, embody, and employ it more and more in our everyday lives.

When we practice, we are rewarded with the fruits of our practice. We get to enjoy our spiritual gifts, share them with others, and share in the spiritual gifts of others. We get to live in a world where these gifts are manifested, where they are working the magic of transformation. In the words of my friend, Sally Crocker:

When I experience wholeness, I am not afraid. I am not distracted. I am not stuck. In those moments, I feel like I am filling out my whole body—it feels light and substantial at the same time. When I am moving and feeling and speaking from this place of wholeness, I don't feel divided in any way (like between inner thoughts and outer communication, body and mind, motives and actions, feeling and appearances, etc.). In those moments, I am aware that I am somehow big enough to include all of this—and more.

The "more" sometimes includes the space around me or deep connection with others or maybe a strong sense of being part of a whole that includes much more than just "me" as I know me. Different people have different words to talk about this sense, but whatever beliefs there are about it, the experience *of it is very profound—ultimately comforting and illuminating, a great "Yes!" and a knowing that is so big and deep and rich—heaven and earth all together.*

Practicing wholeness takes us beyond duality—beyond the realm of whole and not whole, more and less, us and them, birth and death. The practice of wholeness is the practice of connection with everyone and everything in the universe. Our practice allows us to develop a felt sense of this connection—which at first we can barely tolerate, but then grows and deepens throughout our lives.

One of the most direct fruits of the practice of wholeness is joy. We feel and radiate joy—not a giddy, transitory happiness—but a solid joy. It lies beneath all our experiences, even our suffering. This joy allows us the capacity for deep wisdom, because it gives us the ability to be present in the moment—to bring our true selves to what is right before us. Our capacity to be present with joy and wisdom permits us to meet challenges and adversity with resources from both within and around us. This allows us to feel solid and free. We feel our love and share it with the world.

We do not have to leave the world to live spiritual lives. We still work, go shopping, drive cars, do laundry, have relationships, get sick, have good days and bad days—but when we practice wholeness, our daily lives take place in a larger context. We stay close to our expansive self, to our wholeness. We feel, see, and hear its voice inside and around us. Our wholeness informs us and has a say in how we move through the world, in our interactions with ourselves and others. When we lose our connection with this wholeness—after minutes, hours, days, or weeks—we notice something is not right and we stop and reconnect.

Wholeness is always right here for us. As we return and return and return to our practice, our connection to wholeness deepens and expands, illuminating the wonder and mystery of the universe, and the sacredness of life itself.

Enjoy the fruits of your practice!

Resources

We are fortunate to live in a time when a great many resources for psycho-spiritual transformation are available. Here are some which have been especially valuable to me:

Thich Nhat Hanh

Vietnamese Buddhist monk, poet, author, peacemaker.

Books

Thich Nhat Hanh is the author of over 35 books in English, including:

The Miracle of Mindfulness
Being Peace
Touching Peace
Peace is Every Step
The Heart of the Buddha's Teaching
Living Buddha, Living Christ
Coming Home: The Buddha and Christ as Brothers

Tapes, Public Lectures, Retreats, and Practice Centers

Tapes of talks by Thich Nhat Hanh are also available, as well as a publication, *The Mindfulness Bell*, with information on retreats and public lectures by Thich Nhat Hanh and his students, and on mindfulness practice communities throughout the world.

Contact:

Parallax Press
PO Box 7355
Berkeley, California
www.parallax.org

or

www.plumvillage.org

Yvonne Agazarian/ Systems Centered Therapy

Yvonne Agazarian is the originator of Systems Centered Therapy, an innovative method for individual and group psychotherapy, couples and family therapy, and organizational change.

Books

Systems-Centered Therapy for Groups
by Yvonne M. Agazarian
The Visible and Invisible Group
by Yvonne Agazarian and Richard Peters
Autobiography of a Theory
by Yvonne M. Agazarian and Susan P. Gantt
A Picture Book of the Theory of Living Human Systems
by Yvonne M. Agazarian

Workshops and Trainings in Systems Centered Therapy

Contact:

www.sct_institute.org

Gabrielle Roth

Movement, theatre, and recording artist and teacher of five universal rhythms for awareness and transformation.

Books

Sweat Your Prayers
Maps to Ecstacy

Tapes, CDs, Videos, Workshops, and Trainings

Contact:

The Moving Center
PO Box 2034
Red Bank, NJ 07701
(973) 642-1979
ravenrec@panix.com
www.ravenrecording.com

Hakomi Experiential Psychology

A system of psychotherapy which uses mindfulness to explore the body, psyche, and spirit.

Books

Body-Centered Psychotherapy: The Hakomi Method
by Ron Kurtz
Grace Unfolding: Psychotherapy in the Spirit of the Tao-Te Ching
by Greg Johanson and Ron Kurtz

Workshops and Trainings in the Hakomi Method

Contact:

The Hakomi Institute
PO Box 1873
Boulder, CO 80306
(888) 421-6699.
HakomiHQ@aol.com
www.hakomi.com

Oriental Medicine

Books

The Web that Has No Weaver: Understanding Chinese Medicine
by Ted Kaptchuk

Between Heaven and Earth: A Guide to Chinese Medicine
by Harriet Beinfield and Efrem Korngold

Traditional Acupuncture: The Law of the Five Elements
by Dianne Connelly

For information about practitioners of Oriental Medicine contact:

American Association of Oriental Medicine
433 Front Street
Catasauqua, Pennsylvania 18032
(610) 266-1433
www.aaom.org

About the Author

Lorena Monda is a Doctor of Oriental Medicine, psychotherapist, and student of Zen Master Thich Nhat Hanh. The co-founder of The Mindfulness and Healing Institute, she teaches The Practice of Wholeness to healers and lay people. She lives with her husband and daughter in Placitas, New Mexico.

For information on workshops in The Practice of Wholeness,
or to contact Lorena directly, please write:

The Mindfulness and Healing Institute
PO Box 865
Plactias, New Mexico 87043